Lecture Notes in Artificial Intelligence 4898

Edited by J. G. Carbonell and J. Siekmann

Subseries of Lecture Notes in Computer Science

T0223163

Manuel Kolp   Brian Henderson-Sellers
Haralambos Mouratidis   Alessandro Garcia
Aditya Ghose   Paolo Bresciani (Eds.)

Agent-Oriented Information Systems IV

8th International Bi-Conference Workshop, AOIS 2006
Hakodate, Japan, May 9, 2006
and Luxembourg, Luxembourg, June 6, 2006
Revised Selected Papers

 Springer

Series Editors

Jaime G. Carbonell, Carnegie Mellon University, Pittsburgh, PA, USA
Jörg Siekmann, University of Saarland, Saarbrücken, Germany

Volume Editors

Manuel Kolp
Université catholique de Louvain, IAG/ISYS, Louvain-la-Neuve, Belgium
E-mail: kolp@isys.ucl.ac.be

Brian Henderson-Sellers
University of Technology, Fac. of Information Technology, Sydney, Australia
E-mail: brian@it.uts.edu.au

Haralambos Mouratidis
University of East London, Sch. of Computing and Technology, Dagenham, England
E-mail: h.mouratidis@uel.ac.uk

Alessandro Garcia
Computing Department, InfoLab 21, Lancaster University, UK
E-mail: garciaa@comp.lancs.ac.uk

Aditya Ghose
University of Wollongong, Sch. of IT and Computer Science, Wollongong, Australia
E-mail: aditya@uow.edu.au

Paolo Bresciani
European Commission, DG Information Society and Media, Brussels, Belgium
E-mail: paolo.bresciani@ec.europa.eu

Library of Congress Control Number: 2008920060

CR Subject Classification (1998): I.2.11, H.4, H.3, H.5.2-3, C.2.4, I.2

LNCS Sublibrary: SL 7 – Artificial Intelligence

ISSN   0302-9743
ISBN-10   3-540-77989-2 Springer Berlin Heidelberg New York
ISBN-13   978-3-540-77989-6 Springer Berlin Heidelberg New York

Springer is a part of Springer Science+Business Media

springer.com

© Springer-Verlag Berlin Heidelberg 2008
Printed in Germany

Typesetting: Camera-ready by author, data conversion by Scientific Publishing Services, Chennai, India
Printed on acid-free paper   SPIN: 12226788   06/3180   5 4 3 2 1 0

Preface

This is the eighth year that the Agent-Oriented Information Systems (AOIS) workshops have been held. Papers submitted to AOIS show an increase in quality and maturity as agent technology is being increasingly seen as a viable alternative for software and systems development. In AOIS, we focus on the application of agent technology in information systems development and explore the potential for facilitating the increased usage of agent technology in the creation of information systems in the widest sense.

This year's workshops were held in conjunction with two major, international computing research conferences: the first, in May 2006, was affiliated with the AAMAS conference in Hakadote, Japan and chaired by Garcia, Ghose and Kolp. The second was held in conjunction with the international CAiSE conference held in Luxembourg (June 2006) and chaired by Bresciani, Henderson-Sellers and Mouratidis. (Details of all preceding workshops are to be found at http:// www. aois. org.)

The best papers from both these meetings were identified and authors invited to revise and extend their papers in light of the reviewers' comments and feedback at the workshop. Following submission to this compendium volume, another round of reviews was undertaken resulting in what you can read here. These re-reviews were undertaken by three members of the Programme Committee – we wish to thank both the authors for undertaking the necessary revisions and the reviewers for this extra call on their precious time.

We have grouped these papers loosely under four headings: Modelling; Methodologies; Agent-Oriented Software Engineering; and Applications. These categories represent fairly the breadth of current AOIS research as well as encompassing the papers presented at the two AOIS workshops. We trust you will find the content of these selected and revised papers to be of interest and utility.

October 2007

Manuel Kolp
Brian Henderson-Sellers
Haralambos Mouratidis
Alessandro Garcia
Aditya Ghose
Paolo Bresciani

Organization

Workshop Co-chairs

Manuel Kolp (Université catholique de Louvain, Belgium)
Brian Henderson-Sellers (University of Technology, Sydney, Australia)
Haralambos Mouratidis (University of East London, UK)
Alessandro Garcia (Lancaster University, UK)
Aditya Ghose (University of Wollongong, Australia)
Paolo Bresciani (European Commission, DG Information Society and Media,
    Brussels, Belgium)

Steering Committee

Yves Lesperance (York University, Canada)
Gerd Wagner (Eindhoven University of Technology, The Netherlands)
Eric Yu (University of Toronto, Canada)
Paolo Giorgini (University of Trento, Italy)

Program Committee

Carole Bernon (University Paul Sabatier, Toulouse, France)
Brian Blake (Georgetown University Washington, DC, USA)
Paolo Bresciani (European Commission, Belgium)
Jaelson Castro (Federal University of Pernambuco, Brazil)
Luca Cernuzzi (Universitat Católica Nuestra Señora de la Asunción, Paraguay)
Massimo Cossentino (ICAR-CNR, Palermo, Italy)
Luiz Cysneiros (York University, Toronto)
John Debenham (University of Technology, Sydney)
Scott DeLoach (Kansas State University, USA)
Frank Dignum (University of Utrecht, The Netherlands)
Paolo Donzelli (University of Maryland, College Park, USA)
Bernard Espinasse (Domaine Universitaire de Saint-Jérôme, France)
Stéphane Faulkner (University of Namur, Belgium)
Behrouz Homayoun Far (University of Calgary, Canada)
Innes Ferguson (B2B Machines, USA)
Alessandro Garcia (Lancaster University, UK)
Chiara Ghidini (ITC-IRST, Italy)
Aditya Ghose (University of Wollongong, Australia)
Marie-Paule Gleizes (University Paul Sabatier, Toulouse, France)
Cesar Gonzalez-Perez (University of Technology, Sydney, Australia)
Giancarlo Guizzardi (University of Twente, The Netherlands)

Table of Contents

Applications

Modeling MAS Properties with MAS-ML Dynamic Diagrams

Viviane Torres da Silva[1], Ricardo Choren[2], and Carlos J.P. de Lucena[3]

[1] Dept Sist Informáticos - UCM, C/ Prof J.G. Santesmases s/n, Madrid 28040, Spain
viviane@fdi.ucm.es
[2] Computer Engineering Dept - IME, Pça Gen Tibúrcio 80, RJ 22290-270, Brazil
choren@ime.eb.br
[3] Computer Science Dept - PUC-Rio, Rua M. de S. Vicente 225, RJ 22453-900, Brazil
lucena@inf.puc-rio.br

Abstract. A crucial part of a multi-agent system (MAS) design is the specification of agency properties. Traditional approaches to agent systems modeling use diagrams that focus on defining the set of structural and interactive elements such as agents, organizations, actions and messages. Such approaches do not exhibit a proper notation to show agent behavioral properties such as adaptation, mobility and concurrency. The MAS-ML approach to designing agent systems proposed an extension to UML 2.0 to provide a proper notation to model structural and dynamic characteristics of a MAS. In this paper we enhance MAS-ML dynamic diagrams, the extended sequence and activity diagrams, to describe the basic guidelines to model behavioral properties and we show some examples of how these diagrams support the behavioral properties specification, allowing a flexible and easier modeling of agency characteristics.

1 Introduction

Agents are goal-oriented entities that have beliefs, plans, actions and interactions. To specify a MAS, a designer must elicit and describe these entities. However, agents can have intrinsic properties such as adaptation, mobility and concurrency. These properties are usually introduced later in the application development, e.g. in the detailed design or in the implementation phases. There is little support to describe these properties while modeling the application.

Currently, there has been an increasing effort to use UML to specify MAS (e.g. [1,3,4,6,7,8]). Nevertheless, these efforts focus on the structural and interactive aspects of the system. To overcome these limitations, we proposed the MAS-ML [12] modeling language, which extended the UML metamodel to introduce new notation elements and diagrams to model agent-specific features.

In two previous papers [13,14] we introduced the MAS-ML dynamic diagrams, which are extensions to the UML 2.0 sequence and activity diagrams. This extension proposes the basic definitions of agent-oriented behavioral concepts, including the creation of proper notation elements. These diagrams were discussed and we showed the modeling language potential by examining some case studies.

M. Kolp et al. (Eds.): AOIS 2006, LNAI 4898, pp. 1–18, 2008.
© Springer-Verlag Berlin Heidelberg 2008

In this paper, we use these basic definitions to consider the problem of how to clearly model some of the agents' properties that may appear on a MAS (goal-orientation, interaction, adaptation, distribution, mobility and concurrent execution). Our goal is to show how the modeling language can be used to model these properties on dynamic diagrams. We believe that providing a consistent way to describe agent properties while modeling the system actions and protocols shall support an effective communication between stakeholders, increase traceability and ease the design.

This paper is structured as follows. Sections 2 and 3 describe the MAS-ML extended dynamic diagrams. Section 4 presents some sample scenarios that will be used to show how MAS-ML dynamic diagrams support agent properties modeling. Section 5 discusses how each property should be modeled using MAS-ML. Section 6 describes the related work, and Section 7 concludes and presents some ongoing work.

2   MAS-ML Extended Sequence Diagram

A sequence diagram shows how cooperating objects interact with each other by emphasizing the time ordering of messages being sent and received [10]. This diagram is used to identify objects, their interactions (objects calling methods) and their internal execution (objects executing the methods). MAS-ML extends the UML sequence diagram [13] to be possible to also model the following multi-agent entities: agents, organizations, sub-organizations and environments. Below we briefly present the MAS-ML extended sequence diagram.

2.1   Entity Representation

A MAS entity (e.g. an agent or an organization) is immersed in an environment [5] and is able to play several roles in different organizations [9]. Thus the MAS-ML sequence diagram provides notation to model the entity itself, its roles, the organizations these roles are being played, and the environment it executes. Table 1 shows a summary of the entity identification in MAS-ML sequence diagram. For example, in order to completely identify an agent it is necessary to identify the environment where the agent is immersed in, the organization where the agent in playing, and the role being played by the agent. Organizations, environments and roles are instances of organization classes, environment classes and role classes, respectively.

2.2   Interaction Representation

Interaction between agents and organizations is characterized by sending and receiving messages and not by calling methods. Therefore, a speech act message type (different from a method call) to indicate the message semantics and contents was defined [13]. Figure 1 illustrates two agents interacting by sending a Proposal message. Agent Ag1 playing role R1 in organization O1 and inhabiting environment E1 sends a proposal message to agent Ag2 playing R2 that is in the same organization and environment.

Table 1. Entity pathnames

Entity	Pathname
Environment	envInst : EnvClass
Organization	orgInst/envInst : OrgClass/EnvClass
Sub-organization	subOrgInst/roleInst/orgInst/envInst:
	subOrgClass/RoleClass/OrgClass/EnvClass
Agent	agentInst/roleInst/orgInst/envInst:
	agentClass/RoleClass/OrgClass/EnvClass
Object	objectInst/envInst : Class/EnvClass

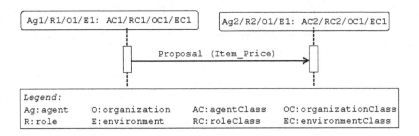

Fig. 1. New message type: speech act message between agents

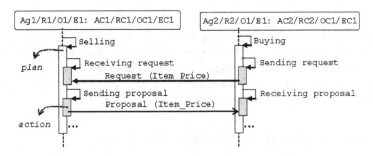

Fig. 2. Agents executing plans and their actions

2.3   Internal Execution Representation

The internal execution of agents and organizations is represented by the execution of plans and actions. While executing their plans and actions, agents and organizations may interact with other entities. Figure 2 illustrates two agents executing their plans (Selling and Buying) and associated actions (receiving request, sending proposal, sending request and receiving proposal).

In MAS-ML, it is possible to represent agents committing to, changing and canceling roles. The diagram was extended with a set of stereotypes to show the dynamic behavior related to roles (Table 2).

Table 2. Role stereotypes

role_committment	Commit to a new role
role_cancel	Cancel one of its roles
role_change	Change from one role to another
role_deactivate	Deactivate one of its roles
role_activate	Activate an inactive role

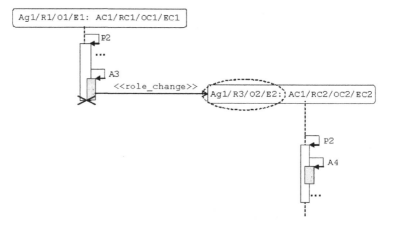

Fig. 3. Sequence diagram showing an agent changing its role

Figure 3 illustrates the use of the stereotype *role_change*. Agent Ag1 playing R1 in O1 and inhabiting E1 changes its role to play R3 in O2 that is in E2. Besides illustrating the agent changing its roles (from R1 to R3), Figure 3 also shows the agent moving from an organization to another (from O1 to O2) and moving from an environment to another (from E1 to E2).

3   MAS-ML Extended Activity Diagram

Activity diagrams illustrate the dynamic nature of a system by modeling the flow of control from activity to activity. These diagrams are flow diagrams that are used to model the business workflow and the algorithmic workflow that represents the execution of an operation.

MAS-ML proposed an extension [14] to the UML 2.0 activity diagram to represent the execution of plans and actions using activities and actions, respectively. Agents execute plans to achieve their goals, thus a stereotype was defined to relate goals with plans. Since a goal can be achieved by several plans, the designer can create several activity models to model all plans that achieve the same goal. Figure 4 illustrates the use of an activity diagram to represent a plan P, its actions (A1 and A2) and the goal (G1) the agent intends to achieve by executing the plan. Similarly to sequence diagrams, activity diagrams were

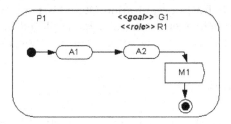

Fig. 4. Activity diagram describing plan P1

extended to represent agent messages. In figure 4, the agent sends the message M1 after executing action A2 in plan P1.

The extended activity diagram includes information to represent roles played by agents while executing plans. Roles can be represented in two different ways: (a) the role is identified in the context of a plan if it is possible to guarantee that an agent will always play the same role during the plan execution, and; (b) the role is associated with an action if an agent commits to, changes, cancels, deactivates or activates a role while executing a plan. For instance, figure 4 shows the role R1 related to the plan P1, which means the agent will always be playing R1 while executing P1.

To relate actions to different roles, MAS-ML proposes the use of partitions or action annotations to identify the roles. Figure 5 illustrates the use of partitions. The agent is playing role R1 while executing action A3 and playing role R3 while executing action A4. To represent the dynamic behavior related to roles (commitment, activation, deactivation, changing and cancellation), the same set of stereotypes used in the sequence diagrams can be used in the activity diagrams. Figure 5 shows an agent changing its roles while executing the action A3.

Partitions are also used to model the organizations in which the agents are playing roles and the environments in which they inhabit. Figure 5 depicts an agent changing its roles by stopping playing role R1 in organization O1 and

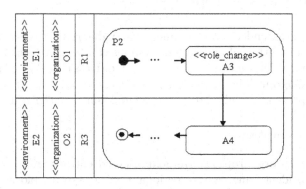

Fig. 5. Activity diagram describing an agent changing its role

beginning playing role R3 in organization O2. This figure also shows that the roles are played in different environments. R1 is played in E1 and R3 in E2. Figure 5 illustrates exactly the same agent behavior shown in Figure 3.

4   Sample Scenarios

In order to illustrate how the agent properties are modeled using MAS-ML sequence and activity diagrams, four scenarios were defined.

Scenario I. Agent Bob wants to buy a new laser printer. After entering a marketplace of brand new goods, Bob negotiates with a seller. Laser printers are expensive items, so Bob bargains for a discount. The seller asks his manager for the available discount and informs Bob. If Bob accepts the final price, Bob pays for the printer.

Scenario II. Suppose Bob accepts the final price of the new printer and decides to sell its old one. Bob does not need to finish the negotiation in which he is buying the new printer in order to sell its old one. Immediately after deciding to buy the new printer, Bob can announce its old one in a market of second-hand goods.

Scenario III. After buying the new printer, Bob decides to buy a toner. Although, Bob usually bargains when negotiating an item, in such situation it uses a different strategy since, historically, toners do not have discounts.

Scenario IV. Suppose Bob receives a buying proposal for its old printer while negotiating the toner and, in order to negotiate its printer, Bob needs to move to the market of second-hand goods. Bob has two alternatives: finish the toner negotiation or move immediately to the market of second-hand goods. In this example, we will suppose that finding a buyer for an old printer is a difficult task, so Bob decides to stop negotiating the toner and to move to the other market to negotiate the printer.

5   Modeling MAS Properties

By analyzing the extended sequence and activity diagrams it is possible to verify that the main properties of multi-agent systems can be successfully modeled. In this paper we focus on some of MAS properties to stress how they can be modeled by using each diagram. The properties presented here are: goal orientation, social behavior, adaptation, mobility, distribution and concurrent execution.

5.1   Goal Orientation

Agents as well as organizations are goal-oriented entities [15]. Goals are used as the basis for identifying agent functionalities, i.e. specific blocks of behavior. These blocks of behavior are implemented as action plans. Thus, a plan is designed to achieve a goal. We have extended the UML activity diagram to model plans, and the goals achieved while executing the plan. We enhanced this diagram with a goal stereotype that semantically means that a plan is designed in the context of a goal and reaching one of its final states means that the goal may have been achieved. It is important to mention that an activity diagram may have several final states, and some of those states may not achieve the goal. Final states related to the achievement of the goal should be highlighted by the goal stereotype.

Figure 6 shows an activity diagram that models the plan executed by sellers in *scenario I*. The Selling plan is executed by sellers to achieve the *To have an item sold goal*. Note that only one final state indicates that the goal has been achieved.

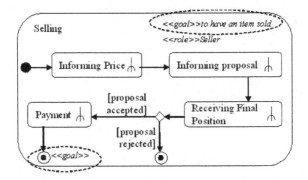

Fig. 6. Activity diagram modeling the goal achieved by a plan

5.2 Interaction

The interaction between the entities can be modeled in both sequence and activity diagrams because both diagrams can model messages being sent and received. Sequence diagrams focus on the time order of the messages exchanged between entities, on the other hand, activity diagrams focus on an agent plan workflow. The sequence diagram allows tracking a message and finding out how such message influences the execution of the agent that receives it. An activity diagram focuses on modeling the messages sent and received by a single agent in the context of the plan being modeled. It is not possible to model the how a message sent by an agent will affect the execution of the agent that receives it.

Therefore, if it is important to focus on modeling numerous agents interacting, sequence diagrams should be used. However, if it is important to picture the messages sent and received by one agent without concerning about the execution of other agents, activity diagrams should be used. Figure 7 illustrates *scenario I* by using a sequence diagram. Such diagram models the interaction between agent Bob that wants to buy a printer, agent John that is selling it and agent Mary that is the manager of the marketplace. The sequence diagram was chosen since it is important to see all the messages being sent and received by all the agents involved in the interactions in order to understand such complex scenario.

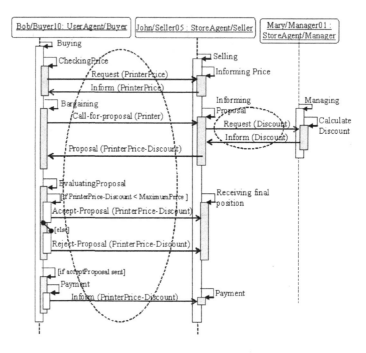

Fig. 7. Sequence diagram modeling an interaction (buyer and seller)

5.3   Social Behavior

While specifying a system as a set of autonomous agents, the designer needs a way to specify the agents' expected behavior without exactly knowing which agents enact that behavior. Roles solve this problem and they are used to design social structures in multi-agent systems.

In sequence diagrams, roles and organizations are associated with the pathname of the entity (table 1). In activity diagrams, agent roles are illustrated in two different occasions. The plans modeled in these diagrams can be associated with the roles played while executing the plan. Figure 6 identifies the role that will be played by the agent while executing the plan.

As mentioned before, roles can be associated not only be with a plan as a whole, but also with specific actions. To associate a role with an action, partitions and action annotation can be used. Figure 8 shows the use of partitions and stereotypes in the activity diagram of *scenario II*. The role_commitment stereotype pictures an agent committing to a new role. The *Preparing to sell* action is decorated with the role_commitment stereotype to indicate that the agent playing the *buyer* role is committing to the *seller* role. After accepting the proposal, the buyer sells its old printer while paying for the new one.

Such scenario can also be modeled in a sequence diagram. Figure 9 illustrates the slice of the buying plan that shows a user agent, playing the *buyer* role, committing to the *seller* role after accepting the proposal sent by a store agent.

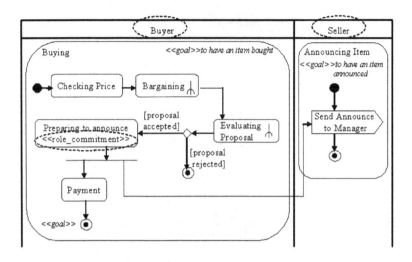

Fig. 8. Activity diagram modeling an agent committing to another role

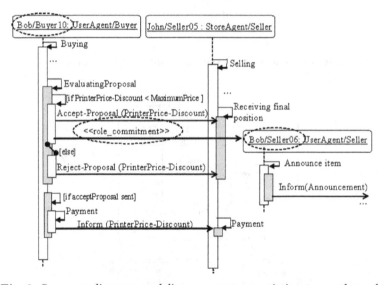

Fig. 9. Sequence diagram modeling an agent committing to another role

5.4   Adaptation

Agents typically operate in dynamic environments. If the context (e.g. the social environment) of an agent changes to the extent that an agent is unable to cope with its current goal, the agent needs to adapt. In this paper, adaptation refers to the ability of an agent to abandon a previous goal or plan and adopt a new goal or plan that better fits its current situation.

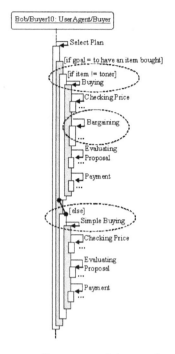

Fig. 10. Sequence diagram modeling a plan adaptation

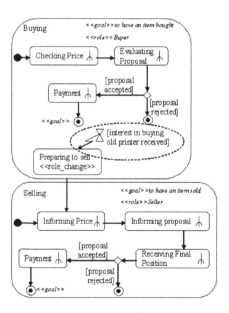

Fig. 11. Activity diagram modeling a goal adaptation

Models that specify adaptation should express preference relations among goals or plans. The designer must have a deep knowledge in the application domain to guide the adaptation process, both in deciding which goals to pursue or how to indicate the change of plans. In an adaptation process, either the goal an agent was trying to achieve is no long the highest priority goal to pursue in the given context (goal adaptation) or the plan an agent was executing is no long the best fit to achieve its current goal (plan adaptation). In both cases, neither the goal nor the plan is changed; in the adaptation context, they are replaced by another goal or plan respectively.

Scenario III describes a situation in which agent Bob presents a *plan adaptation*. Usually, its strategy is to bargain for an item. Yet, while buying toners, Bob knows that it should not spend its time bargaining for toners that never have discounts. This is an illustration of an agent executing a behavior (not bargain) that is different from its usual (bargain). This behavior adaptation only takes place in this particular context. This scenario is modeled in Figure 10, using a sequence diagram. The *Buying* plan that presupposes the agent will bargain is not select if the item to buy is a toner.

Scenario IV gives an example of *goal adaptation*. In this scenario Bob dynamically changes its goal priorities. In the beginning, the goal that has the highest priority is the *To have an item bought* (the toner) goal. However, when Bob receives a proposal of an agent that wants to buy the old printer, the priorities of the goals change. The goal with the highest priority becomes *To have an item sold* (the old printer). After achieving the *To have an item sold* goal, the agent may resume the *To have an item bought* goal, if the developer indicates so. Figure 11 illustrates *scenario IV* by using an activity diagram.

The diagram element *Interruptible Activity Region* proposed in the UML 2.0 meta-model is used to indicate an interruption in the execution of the *Buying* plan. If the condition identified in the diagram element holds, i.e. if the agent is informed that another one is interested in buying the old printer, the agent stops the execution of the *Buying* plan and starts the execution of the *Selling* plan. This notation serves the purpose of modeling that the priority of the To have an item bought goal decreases and the priority of the *To have an item sold* goal increases.

Although we have used a sequence diagram to model plan adaptation, an activity diagram could also be used. In this case, both diagrams perfectly represent the same situation. On the other hand, the goals adaptation is not easily represented in sequence diagrams. The goals' adaptation interrupts the sequence of the actions being executed at any time. Such interruption cannot be easily represented in sequence diagram. However, the diagram element *Interruptible Activity Region*, used in activity diagrams, entirely represents such situation.

5.5   Distribution

UML 2.0 sequence and activity diagrams do not provide explicit support for modeling distribution. Sequence diagrams could be used to model the interaction

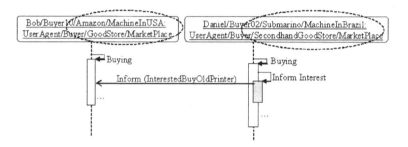

Fig. 12. Sequence diagram modeling agents inhabiting different environments

between objects that inhabit in different environments, but it provides no graphical notation to explicitly indicate this situation. MAS-ML extended sequence diagram identifies the environments that the entities inhabit. So, it is possible to explicitly model two entities interacting and inhabiting different environments. For instance, figure 12 illustrates *scenario IV* where Bob receives a messages from an agent that is executing in another marketplace.

Agent Daniel, which is executing in a market of second-hand goods, informs that wants to buy Bob's old printer. The activity diagram was also extended to represent environments where the agents execute. While modeling the plan of an agent, it is possible to indicate the environment that the agent will inhabit while executing the plan. As stated before, we propose the use of partitions to illustrate environments.

5.6   Mobility

Both diagrams were extended to model agents moving. In the extended sequence diagram, we propose the use of the *role_change* stereotype to model a mobility process. Mobility refers to a two-step process: leaving the current environment and entering a new one. To leave an environment, the agent must quit all its roles, which means that the agent is stopping all its plans. To execute in a new environment, the agent must start playing a role. Thus even if the roles (the old and the new ones) are the same, there is a change of roles. Mobility is modeled through the entity pathname which indicates that the new role is played in another environment.

In *scenario IV* agent Bob moves from an environment to another when he is informed that Daniel is interested in buying its old printer. Figure 13 illustrates Bob receiving a message from Daniel saying the he is interested in the printer. Then, Bob moves to the market of second-hand goods that is localized in a machine in Brazil to negotiate with Daniel.

The same mobility process can be modeled using the extended activity diagram. The *role_change* stereotype is used to show the leave/enter process and partitions are used to show that the environments are different. Figure 14 depicts the same scenario illustrated in figure 13 by using an activity diagram.

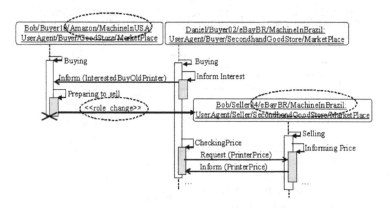

Fig. 13. Sequence diagram modeling agents moving to another environment

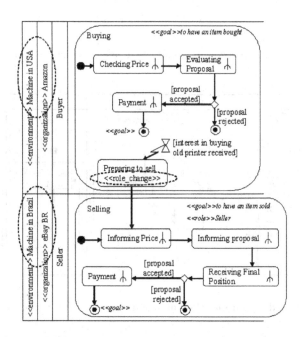

Fig. 14. Activity diagram modeling agents moving to another environment

5.7 Concurrent Execution

The UML 2.0 sequence diagram provides support for annotating messages with a parallel symbol (//) to indicate that they will be executed concurrently. We extended this diagram to model different MAS entities executing concurrently and the same agent concurrently executing different roles. Figure 15 illustrates three agents executing concurrently, Bob, John and Mary.

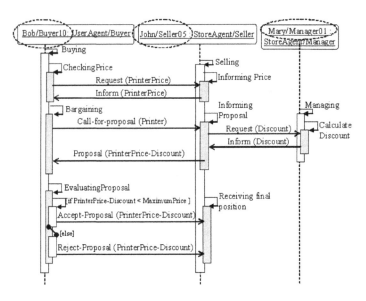

Fig. 15. Sequence diagram modeling three agents executing concurrently

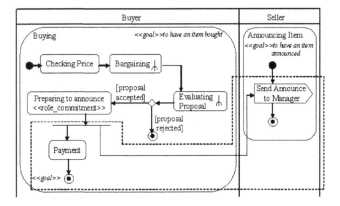

Fig. 16. Activity diagram modeling an agent executing two actions concurrently

The UML 2.0 activity diagram provides support for modeling actions executing concurrently by using graphic symbols that represent forks and joins. Therefore, by using the extended activity diagram and these available symbols it is possible to model an agent executing several concurrent actions while executing the same plan. The extended activity diagram also provides support for modeling the same agent executing different plans concurrently. Figure 16 illustrates an agent executing concurrently the *Payment* action of *Buying* plan and *Send announce to manager* action of *Announcing item* plan.

6   Related Work

In this section, we will compare MAS-ML to several works that use UML sequence and activity diagrams to model MAS properties ([1,2,3,4,6,7,8,9,11]).

Goal-orientation: Only one approach [7] relates the plan being modeled to a goal. However, it simply treats goals as events that trigger plans. In the MAS-ML activity diagram a plan can always be associated with the goal it pursues.

Goal Orientation

[1,2,3,4,6,8,9,11]	not present
[7]	goal is event that triggers plan
MAS-ML	direct association in activity diagram

Interaction: No other approach represents the environment where agents are executing in sequence and activity diagrams. Therefore, the main difference between our approach and those ones it that by using MAS-ML sequence and activity diagrams it is possible to model agents from different environments interacting.

Interaction

[1,2,9,11]	agents/roles interacting
[3]	not present
[4]	distinct roles in distinct organizations interacting
[6]	ACL and signals to represent messages
[7]	agents interaction
[8]	send and receive stereotypes in activity diagram
MAS-ML	notation on both diagrams

Social behavior: Most analyzed approaches model the relationship between agents, roles and organizations that characterize the social behavior of agents.

Social behavior

[1]	roles in sequence diagrams
[2]	roles in action annotations
[3,6,7]	not present
[4]	roles and organizations on sequence diagrams
[8]	swimlanes for roles
[9]	stereotypes for dynamic aspects of roles
[11]	organizations on both diagrams
MAS-ML	notation on both diagrams (also using partitions)

Adaptation: None of the proposed approaches demonstrates the adaptation of goals and plans illustrated by using the MAS-ML sequence and activity diagrams.

Adaptation

[1,2,3,4,6,7,8,9,11]	not present
MAS-ML	notation on both diagrams

Mobility: No approach satisfactorily represents agents moving from an environment to another. In [6] it is possible to indicate which agents may move and when the movements may occur but it is not possible to indicate the environments. In [3] it is possible to model the environments and the actions that will move the agents but it is not clear which agents are being modeled. Although in [1] it is possible to indicate the agents that can move to another environment, we cannot model when such movement may occur by using deployment diagrams. By using MAS-ML sequence diagrams it can be clearly modeled (i) the agents that may move, (ii) when the agents may move and (iii) what are the environments involved.

Mobility

[1,3]	stereotype to identify the moving agent
[2,4,7,8,9,11]	not present
[6]	stereotyped host
MAS-ML	notation on both diagrams

Distribution: One approach [3] identifies environments only in activity diagrams. Our proposal also uses swimlanes to identify environments but also represents environments in sequence diagrams.

Distribution

[1,3,4,6,7,8,9,11]	not present
[2]	swimlanes and stereotypes
MAS-ML	notation on both diagrams

Concurrency: Several approaches model different agents executing concurrently and the same agent executing different roles in parallel. Yet, they do not model agents from different environments executing concurrently. In [3] it is possible to model different agents in different environments executing in parallel, but it is not possible to identify the roles that they are playing. In MAS-ML it is possible to model agents playing different roles in different environments executing concurrently.

Concurrency

[1]	concurrent agents in sequence diagrams and concurrent roles in activity diagrams
[2,4]	concurrent roles in activity diagrams
[3]	swimlanes for locations
[6,7]	not present
[8]	concurrent agents in activity diagrams
[9]	agents executing concurrent roles
[11]	concurrency only in different organizations
MAS-ML	notation for agent and role concurrency on both diagrams

7 Conclusion

In this paper we propose the use of MAS-ML sequence and activity diagrams to model agent properties. We provide guidelines to help agent designers to model goal orientation, interaction, adaptation, distribution, mobility and concurrent execution in the application agents.

We are in the way of analyzing how other properties, such as learning and autonomy, can be modeled using MAS-ML dynamic diagrams. These properties are more horizontal and affect (and possibly change) more than one plan and one interaction protocol at once. The notation should provide the means to clearly show the trace of these effects on the diagrams.

Acknowledgments. This work has been partially supported by CNPq (ESSMA Project 552068/2002-0), by the Juan de la Cierva Program (PROMESSAS S-0505/TIC-407) and by the Ministério de Educación y Ciencia (MIDAS TIC2003-01000).

References

1. Bauer, B., Müller, J., Odell, J.: Agent UML: a formalism for specifying multiagent interaction. Software Engineering and Knowledge Engineering 11(13), 203–207 (2001)
2. Bauer, B., Odell, J.: UML 2.0 and agents: how to build agent-based systems with the new UML standard. Engineering Applications of Artificial Intelligence 18(2), 141–157 (2005)
3. Baumeister, N., Kosiuczenko, P., Wirsing, M.: Extending activity diagrams to model mobile systems. In: Aksit, M., Mezini, M., Unland, R. (eds.) NODe 2002. LNCS, vol. 2591, pp. 278–293. Springer, Heidelberg (2003)
4. Ferber, J., Gutknecht, O., Michel, F.: From agents to organizations: an organizational view of multi-agent systems. In: Giorgini, P., Müller, J.P., Odell, J.J. (eds.) Agent-Oriented Software Engineering IV. LNCS, vol. 2935, pp. 214–230. Springer, Heidelberg (2004)
5. d'Inverno, M., Luck, M.: Understanding agent systems. Springer, New York (2001)
6. Kang, K., Taguchi, K.: Modelling mobile agent applications by extended UML activity diagram. In: Enterprise Information Systems (ICEIS) Conference Proceedings, pp. 519–522 (2004)
7. Kinny, D., Georgeff, M.: Modeling and design of multi-agent systems. In: Jennings, N.R., Wooldridge, M.J., Müller, J.P. (eds.) Intelligent Agents III. Agent Theories, Architectures, and Languages. LNCS, vol. 1193, pp. 1–20. Springer, Heidelberg (1997)
8. Lind, J.: Specifying agent interaction protocols with standard UML. In: Wooldridge, M.J., Weiß, G., Ciancarini, P. (eds.) AOSE 2001. LNCS, vol. 2222, pp. 136–147. Springer, Heidelberg (2002)
9. Odell, J., Parunak, H., Fleisher, M.: The role of roles in designing effective agent organizations. In: Garcia, A.F., de Lucena, C.J.P., Zambonelli, F., Omicini, A., Castro, J. (eds.) Software Engineering for Large-Scale Multi-Agent Systems. LNCS, vol. 2603, pp. 27–38. Springer, Heidelberg (2003)
10. OMG: UML Specification, v.2 (2007), http://www.uml.org

11. Parunak, H., Odell, J.: Representing social structures in UML. In: Wooldridge, M.J., Weiß, G., Ciancarini, P. (eds.) AOSE 2001. LNCS, vol. 2222, pp. 1–16. Springer, Heidelberg (2002)
12. Silva, V.T., Lucena, C.: From a conceptual framework for agents and objects to a multi-agent system modeling language. Autonomous Agents and Multi-Agent Systems 9(1-2), 145–189 (2004)
13. Silva, V.T., Choren, R., Lucena, C.: A UML based approach for modeling and implementing multi-agent systems. In: Kudenko, D., Kazakov, D., Alonso, E. (eds.) Adaptive Agents and Multi-Agent Systems II. LNCS (LNAI), vol. 3394, pp. 914–921. Springer, Heidelberg (2005)
14. Silva, V.T., Choren, R., Lucena, C.: Using the UML 2.0 activity diagram to model agent plans and actions. In: Autonomous Agents and Multi-Agent Systems (AAMAS) Conference Proceedings, pp. 594–600 (2005)
15. Shoham, Y.: Agent-oriented programming. Artificial Intelligence 60, 51–92 (1993)

Providing Contextual Norm Information in Open Multi-Agent Systems

Carolina Felicíssimo[1,3], Ricardo Choren[2], Jean-Pierre Briot[1,3], Carlos J.P. de Lucena[1], Caroline Chopinaud [3], and Amal El Fallah Seghrouchni [3]

[1] DI, PUC-Rio: Rua M. de São Vicente, 225, Gávea Rio de Janeiro, RJ, 22453-900, Brasil
{cfelicissimo,lucena}@inf.puc-rio.br
[2] SE-8, IME: Pca General Tiburcio 80, 22290-270, Rio de Janeiro RJ, Brazil
choren@de9.ime.eb.br
[3] LIP6, Paris VI: 104 Avenue Kennedy, 75016, Paris, France
{jean-pierre.briot,caroline.chopinaud,amal.elfallah}@lip6.fr

Abstract. Agents can freely migrate among open MASs in order to obtain resources or services not found locally. In this scenario, agent actions should be guided for avoiding unexpected behaviour. However, open MASs are extremely dynamic and, thus, a solution for guiding agent actions is non-trivial. This work details DynaCROM, our solution for continuously supporting agents in open MASs with updated norm information. The main asset of DynaCROM is that it decreases the complexity of norm representation by using contexts. DynaCROM proposes (i) a top-down modelling of contextual norms, (ii) an ontology to explicitly represent norm semantics and (iii) a rule inference engine to customize different compositions of contextual norms. Thus, DynaCROM offers a solution for both developers to enhance their open MASs with norm information and agents to be continuously supported with precise norm information.

1 Introduction

Multi-agent systems (MASs) have emerged as a promising approach to develop information systems that clearly require several goal-oriented problem-solving entities [21]. Following this direction, we believe that in the near future information systems will be implemented as open MASs, which will be composed of many sets of heterogeneous self-interested agents. These agents will be mobile agents, i.e. they will have the capability to freely migrate among MASs for obtaining resources or services not found locally. An MAS can be considered an open system when it presents the following characteristics [13]:

Heterogeneity: agents are possibly developed by different parties, in different programming languages, with different purposes and preferences.

Accountability: agent actions must be monitored to detect the execution of behaviours that may not be according to the overall expected functioning of the system.

Social change: agent societies are not static; they may evolve over time by updating their information. So, future changes should be easily accommodated.

M. Kolp et al. (Eds.): AOIS 2006, LNAI 4898, pp. 19–36, 2008.
© Springer-Verlag Berlin Heidelberg 2008

In open MASs, agents may be heterogeneous, but they all must know how to assimilate information provided to them for effective execution. In this sense, information should be expressed in a meaningful way for agents, avoiding misunderstandings. Moreover, the intrinsic dynamics of open MASs should be supported by a flexible mechanism that easily permits data updates. Regarding these points, we have developed a solution for continuously providing contextual norm information to agents in open MASs. In our opinion, open MASs should be enhanced with norm information for guiding agent actions. Our solution, called DynaCROM (meaning *dynamic contextual regulation information provision in open MASs*) [8-11], proposes (i) a top-down modelling of contextual norms, (ii) an ontology to explicitly represent norm semantics and (iii) a rule inference engine to customize different compositions of contextual norms.

DynaCROM allows for accountability since MASs and their agents continuously have information about which norms they should follow. DynaCROM also allows for social changes since information is defined in a central resource (an ontology) that can easily have its data composed (thanks to rule support) and updated.

It is important to stress here that, in this work, we make no assumptions about whether agents decide or not to be compliant with norms. DynaCROM allows the modelling and representation of customized compositions of contextual norms, offering precise norm information for agents to consider in a given context. Thus, DynaCROM provides the way for agents to reason about norm compliance and for developers to implement normative MASs. Norm-aware agents are more likely to perform correctly and, consequently, to achieve their goals faster.

The remainder of this paper is organized as follows. Section 2 details DynaCROM, including its top-down modelling, use of ontology and rules, and implementation. Section 3 describes a case study. Section 4 briefly presents how DynaCROM answers (contextual norm information) can be used. Section 5 compares DynaCROM with two related works. Finally, Section 6 concludes the paper and outlines future work.

2 Contextual Norm Information Provision in Open MASs

MASs are generally made up of environments, organizations and agents [20]. Environments [36] are discrete computational locations (similar to places in the physical world) that provide conditions for agents to inhabit. Environments can have refinement levels, such as a specialization relationship (e.g. country, state), but there cannot be overlaps (e.g. there cannot be two countries in the same place). An environment also can have many organizations. Organizations [12] are social locations inside which groups of agents play roles. Furthermore, an organization can have many sub-organizations, but each organization belongs to only one environment [28]. An agent can be in different organizations; and agents with the mobility characteristic can migrate among environments or organizations. Roles [32] are abstractions that define a set of related tasks for agents achieving their designed goals. Agents interact with other agents from the same or different environments, organizations and roles. Environments, organizations, roles and agent interactions suggest different contexts (*implicit situational information* [7]) found in open MASs.

2.1 Modelling Contextual Norms

Research in context-aware applications suggests top-down architectures for modelling contextual information [22,18]. Thus, DynaCROM defines that norms of MASs should be modelled according to the following four levels of abstractions: *Environment, Organization, Role* and *Interaction* contexts. We call these contexts *regulatory contexts* and they are differentiated by the boundaries of their data (norms). *Environment Norms* are applied to all agents in a regulated environment; *Organization Norms* are applied to all agents in a regulated organization; *Role Norms* are applied to all agents playing a regulated role; *Interaction Norms* are applied to all agents involved in a regulated interaction.

Fig. 1 illustrates the boundaries of environment, organization, role and interaction norms. There, agents are regulated by compositions of contextual norms. For instance, the agents on the left side of the figure are regulated by compositions of common environment and interaction norms and by compositions of different organization and role norms; the agents on the right side of the figure are regulated by compositions of common environment, organization and interaction norms and by compositions of different role norms; the two agents interacting, from the different environments, are regulated by compositions of different environment, organization, role and interaction norms.

We believe that the four DynaCROM regulatory contexts are not targeted to a particular application domain, but rather they represent a minimum set for a general contextual norm information provision in open MASs. For more complex MASs, this set should be improved with additions and refinements of regulatory contexts for representing particular domain norms.

Norms define which actions are *permitted, obliged* and *prohibited* to be executed by agents in an open MAS. A *permitted norm* defines that an act is allowed to be performed; an *obliged norm* defines that an act must be performed; a *prohibited norm* defines that an act must not be performed. These three types of norms described represent the three fundamental deontic statuses of an act [1] from Deontic Logic [37]. Deontic Logic makes it possible to address the issue of explicitly and formally defining norms and dealing with the possibility of violation. In normative (i.e., regulated) open MASs, agents need to be norm-aware entities for taking into account the existence of social norms in their decisions (either to follow them or to violate them) and to react to norm violations by other agents [5].

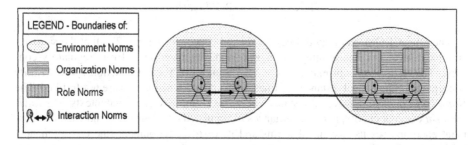

Fig. 1. The boundaries of Environment, Organization, Role and Interaction Norms

2.2 Representing Contextual Norms

Norms should have their semantics explicitly expressed in a meaningful way for heterogeneous agents to process their contents. Regarding this, DynaCROM uses ontologies for representing its regulatory contexts and data. For the DynaCROM ontology,
the following definitions are valid: an *ontology* is a conceptual model that embodies
shared conceptualizations of a given domain [17]; a *contextual ontology* is an ontology that represents contextual information [3]; and a *contextual normative ontology* is
an ontology that represents contextual norm information, having the norm concept as
a central asset. The DynaCROM contextual normative ontology, or simply the DynaCROM ontology, is illustrated in Fig. 2.

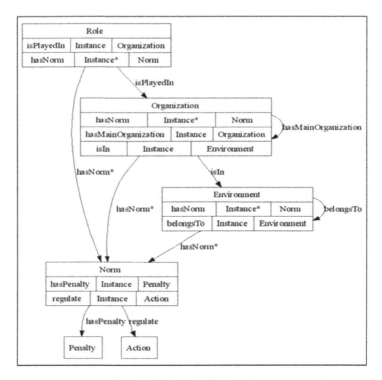

Fig. 2. The DynaCROM ontology

The DynaCROM ontology defines six related concepts (see Fig. 2), all at the same hierarchical level, for representing its environment, organization and role regulatory contexts. The *Action* concept encompasses all instances of regulated actions. The *Penalty*
concept encompasses all instances of fines to be applied when norms are not fulfilled. The
Norm concept encompasses all instances of norms from all regulatory contexts. The *Environment* concept encompasses all instances of regulated environments; and each environment encompasses its associated norms and its owner environment (the environment it
belongs to). The *Organization* concept encompasses all instances of regulated organizations; and each organization encompasses its associated norms, main organization (the

organization to which it is associated) and environment. The *Role* concept encompasses all instances of regulated roles; and each role encompasses its associated norms and organization. The Norm and Penalty concepts are specialized into sub-concepts according to the permitted, obliged and prohibited statuses of an act from Deontic Logic.

In order to effectively be used in an open MASs, the DynaCROM ontology should be instantiated and it probably should be extended with both particular domain concepts and interaction norms. In the DynaCROM ontology, the interaction regulatory context should be implemented by following the representation pattern [26] from a Semantic Web Best Practices document. This pattern defines that the relation object itself must be represented by a created concept that links the other concepts from the relation (i.e. reification of relationship). Thus, in the DynaCROM ontology, an interaction norm should be represented by a new *Norm* sub-concept linking two *Role* concepts. For instance, suppose that a supplier deals with a customer and the interaction between them is regulated by a norm describing the obligation to pay when a deal is done. The interaction norm in the DynaCROM ontology is represented by a new obligation concept, called for example *"ObligationToPay"*, linking the supplier and customer *Role* sub-concepts.

2.3 Composing Contextual Norms

After manually classifying and organizing user defined norms, according to a top-down modelling, and explicitly representing these norms into an ontology instance, DynaCROM uses rules to automatically compose contextual norms. This process is simple and can be summarized as follows: DynaCROM reads an ontology instance for getting data and the information about how concepts are structured; then, it reads a rule file for getting the information about how concepts have to be composed according to activated rules; and, finally, it infers a new ontology instance based on the previous readings. Fig. 3 illustrates an overview of the DynaCROM process.

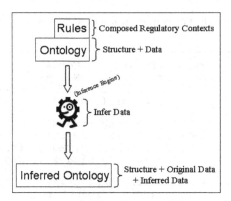

Fig. 3. The DynaCROM process

DynaCROM rules are *ontology-driven* rules, i.e. they are created according to the ontology structure and they are limited according to the number of related concepts to which each concept is linked. DynaCROM has four pre-defined rules for creating a hierarchy from its regulatory contexts (e.g. every role has its norms composed with the norms of its organization). These rules, presented in Table 1, receive as input parameters instances of the *Environment*, *Organization* and *Role* concepts from a DynaCROM ontology.

Rule1 (lines 1 – 4) states that a given environment will have its norms composed with the norms of its owner environment (the environment it is linked to by the "*belongsTo*" relationship). More precisely, the following process is executed: in (4), the owner environment ("?OEnv") of the given environment ("?Env") is discovered; in (3), the norms of the owner environment ("?OEnvNorms") are discovered; finally, in (2), the norms of the owner environment are composed with the norms of the given environment.

Rule2 (lines 5 – 8) states that a given organization will have its norms composed with the norms of its main organization (the organization it is linked to by the "*hasMainOrganization*" relationship). More precisely, the following process is executed: in (8), the main organization ("?MOrg") of the given organization ("?Org") is discovered; in (7), the norms of the main organization ("?MOrgNorms") are discovered; finally, in (6), the norms of the main organization are composed with the norms of the given organization.

Rule3 (lines 9 – 12) states that a given organization will have its norms composed with the norms of its environment (the environment it is linked to by the "*isIn*" relationship). More precisely, the following process is executed: in (12), the environment ("?OrgEnv") of the given organization ("?Org") is discovered; in (11), the norms of the environment ("?OrgEnvNorms") are discovered; finally, in (10), the norms of the environment are composed with the norms of the given organization.

Rule4 (lines 13 – 16) states that a given role will have its norms composed with the norms of its organization (the organization it is linked to by the "*isPlayedIn*" relationship). More precisely, the following process is executed: in (16), it is discovered the organization ("?Org") of the given role ("?Role"); in (15), the norms of the organization ("?OrgNorms") are discovered; finally, in (14), the norms of the organization are composed with the norms of the given role.

Table 1. Rules for creating a hierarchy from the DynaCROM regulatory contexts by composing their norms

```
(1)   Rule1- [ruleForEnvWithOEnvNorms:
(2)           hasNorm(?Env,?OEnvNorms)
(3)              <- hasNorm(?OEnv,?OEnvNorms),
(4)                 belongsTo(?Env,?OEnv)]

(5)   Rule2- [ruleForOrgWithMOrgNorms:
(6)           hasNorm(?Org,?MOrgNorms)
(7)              <- hasNorm(?MOrg,?MOrgNorms),
(8)                 hasMainOrganization(?Org,?MOrg)]

(9)   Rule3- [ruleForOrgWithEnvNorms:
(10)          hasNorm(?Org,?OrgEnvNorms)
(11)             <- hasNorm(?OrgEnv,?OrgEnvNorms),
(12)                isIn(?Org,?OrgEnv)]

(13)  Rule4- [ruleForRoleWithOrgNorms:
(14)          hasNorm(?Role,?OrgNorms)
(15)             <- hasNorm(?Org,?OrgNorms),
(16)                isPlayedIn(?Role,?Org)]
```

Rules can compose data (e.g. norms) of concepts from the same type (e.g. `Rule1`) or from different types (e.g. `Rule3`), and they also can compose data of concepts directly related (hierarchical form) or indirectly related (non-hierarchical form). Table 2 presents `Rule5`, which is an example of rule for composing the norms of concepts indirectly related (the *Role* and *Environment* concepts from the DynaCROM ontology).

Table 2. A rule for composing the norms of two concepts indirectly related

```
(17)  Rule5- [ruleForRoleWithOrgEnvNorms:
(18)          hasNorm(?Role,?OrgEnvNorms)
(19)          <- hasNorm(?OrgEnv,?OrgEnvNorms),
(20)             isIn(?Org,?OrgEnv),
(21)             isPlayedIn(?Role,?Org)]
```

2.4 The DynaCROM Implementation

In open systems, no centralized control is feasible. Their key characteristics are: agent heterogeneity, conflicting individual goals and limited trust [1]. Heterogeneity and autonomy rule out any assumption concerning the way agents are implemented and behave. Thus, a mechanism not hard coded inside agents' original codes and whose data (e.g. norms) can be dynamically updated is the only viable solution for regulations in open MASs [16]. Regarding this, the DynaCROM execution process (see Fig. 3) was implemented as a self-contained JAVA [15] solution and encapsulated as a JADE [33] behaviour. Thus, DynaCROM is a general solution that can be used in many application domains without the need for extra implementations. It is only necessary to instantiate the DynaCROM ontology and, probably, to extend it with domain concepts. Domain rules can also be joined with DynaCROM rules.

Table 3. The core of the DynaCROM implementation

```
(1)  Model m = ModelFactory.createDefaultModel();
(2)  Resource configuration = m.createResource();
(3)  configuration.addProperty ( ReasonerVocabulary.PROPruleSet,
(4)                     ontologyDir.concat ("rulesToComposeNorms.rules") );

(5)  Reasoner reasoner =
(6)          GenericRuleReasonerFactory.theInstance().create(configuration);
(7)  InfModel inferredModel = ModelFactory.createInfModel(reasoner, this.getOntModel());
```

Table 3 presents the core of the DynaCROM implementation. The process starts when the "*getOntModel()*" method (see line 7) retrieves a DynaCROM ontology instance. This ontology instance represents the regulatory contexts (by the ontology structure) and user defined norms (by the ontology data) from an application domain. The customized compositions of contextual norms are specified by the rules defined in the "*rulesToComposeNorms.rules*" file (called in line 4). The "*reasoner*" variable (see line 5) represents the rule-based inference engine which, based on the retrieved ontology instance and active rules, automatically deduces the customized compositions of contextual norms. This result is kept in the "*inferredModel*" variable (see line 7), which will be continuously read by DynaCROM for keep informing agents about their updated contextual norms.

3 Case Study

The domain of multinational organizations is used for presenting our case study. This domain was chosen because it well illustrates important implicit contextual information found in open MASs. Fig. 4 illustrates our world, created as follows: USA is an environment that belongs to North America; Cuba is an environment that belongs to Central America; Brazil is an environment that belongs to South America. PUCie-Rio and Dellie Brazil are organizations located in Brazil; Dellie Cuba is an organization located in Cuba; Dellie Brazil and Dellie Cuba are branches of the Dellie headquarters, which is located in USA. All Dellie organizations define the supplier and customer roles; PUCie-Rio defines only the customer role. Dellie organizations sell computers; PUCie-Rio is a university.

Environment Organization	Organization Role

North America
USA
  Dellie
	Dellie
	  Dellie supplier
	  Dellie customer

Central America
Cuba
  Dellie Cuba
	Dellie Cuba
	  Dellie Cuba supplier
	  Dellie Cuba customer

South America
Brazil
  Dellie Brazil
  PUCie-Rio
	Dellie Brazil
	  Dellie Brazil supplier
	  Dellie Brazil customer
	
	PUCie-Rio
	  PUCie-Rio customer

Fig. 4. The environments, organizations and roles created for our case study

3.1 Examples of Environment, Organization, Role and Interaction Norms

Usually, organizations do not make their norms public because they are of strategic importance to their businesses. Because of this, we created the following environment, organization, role and interaction norms based on the available information collected from several corporate Web sites.

3.1.1 Examples of Environment Norms

a. In Central America, if the delivery address is outside one of its environments, every shipped order is obliged to have its price increased by 15% as taxes.

b. In Cuba, all negotiations are obliged to be paid in Cuban pesos (CUP), its national currency. Negotiations outside Cuba are obliged to have their values converted from CUP to the national currency of the country in which the seller is located.

c. In Brazil, all negotiations are obliged to be paid in Reais (R$), its national curency. Negotiations outside Brazil are obliged to have their values converted from R$ to the national currency of the country in which the seller is located.

d. In USA, all negotiations are obliged to be paid in American dollars (USD), its national currency. Negotiations outside USA are obliged to have their values converted from USD to the national currency of the country in which the seller is located.

3.1.2 Example of Organization Norms

a. Dellie organizations are obliged to ask Dellie headquarters the prices of its products for every large order placed (more than 100 items).

b. Dellie organizations are prohibited from delivering orders during holidays in their final destinations.

3.1.3 Example of Role Norms

a. In Dellie Brazil, sellers are obliged to ship complete orders on their due dates.

b. In Dellie Cuba, sellers are prohibited to offer more than 8% as discounts.

3.1.4 Example of an Interaction Norm

a. In Dellie Cuba, customers are obliged to make a down payment of 10% for every order placed to a seller.

3.2 Representing Our Created World

The DynaCROM ontology was extended and instantiated, by using the Protégé Editor [31], for representing the world of our case study. As an example, the *Environment (DynaCROM)* concept was extended with the *"Continent"* and *"Country" (domain)* sub-concepts. Thus, *"NorthAmerica"*, *"CentralAmerica"*, and *"SouthAmerica"* were created as instances of the *"Continent"* concept; and *"USA"*, *"Cuba"* and *"Brazil"* were created as instances of the *"Country"* concept.

For explaining how domain contextual norms are represented, we will use the organization norm 3.1.2.b as motivation. For this norm, precise information about holidays is important data. Environments can have both *federal holidays*, which are applied to all cities from a country, and *city holidays*, which are only applied for a city. Yet, these holidays can be in the same dates, as Christmas Day (December, 25) and New Year's Day (January, 01), or on different dates, as Independence Day (e.g. September, 07 in Brazil and July, 04 in USA) and Labor Day (e.g. May, 05 in Brazil and in the first Monday of September in USA). For representing the information about holidays, the *"Holiday"* concept with its *"FederalHoliday"* and *"CityHoliday"* sub-concepts were created in a DynaCROM domain ontology. Then, these concepts were instantiated for supporting the organization norm 3.1.2.b. For instance, Fig. 5 illustrates the *city* and *federal holidays* created for a city called *"RioDeJaneiro"* located in *"Brazil"*.

As previously mentioned, domain rules can be freely created and joined with Dy-naCROM rules. Table 4 illustrates a domain rule (Rule6), which states that a given city will have its holidays composed with the holidays of its country. More precisely, the following process is executed: in (25), the country (?Country) of the given city (?City) is discovered; in (24), the holidays of the country (?FederalHolidays) are discovered; finally, in (23), the holidays from the country are composed with the holidays of the given city.

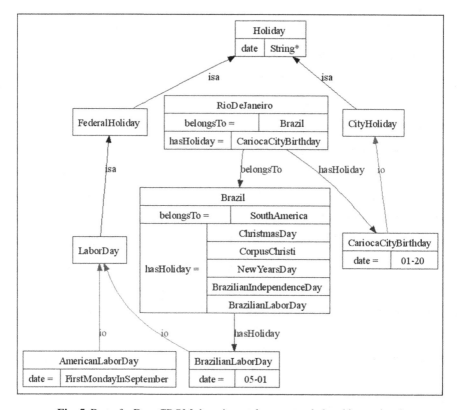

Fig. 5. Part of a DynaCROM domain ontology, extended and instantiated

As previously mentioned, domain rules can be freely created and joined with Dy-naCROM rules. Table 4 illustrates a domain rule (Rule6), which states that a given city will have its holidays composed with the holidays of its country. More precisely, the following process is executed: in (25), the country (?Country) of the given city (?City) is discovered; in (24), the holidays of the country (?FederalHolidays) are discovered; finally, in (23), the holidays from the country are composed with the holidays of the given city.

For instance, regarding the organization norm 3.1.2.b and that PUCie-Rio is an or-ganization in a city called "*RioDeJaneiro*" (located in "*Brazil*"), Rule6 provides the information that Dellie suppliers are prohibited to deliver PUCie-Rio orders during the following holidays: "*CariocaCityBirthday*", "*ChristmasDay*", "*CorpusChristi*", "*NewYearsDay*", "*BrazilianIndependenceDay*" and "*BrazilianLaborDay*" (see these instances in Fig. 5).

Table 4. A rule for composing *city* and *federal holidays*

```
(22)  Rule6- [ruleForCityWithFederalHolidays:
(23)          hasHoliday(?City,?FederalHolidays)
(24)          <- hasHoliday(?Country,?FederalHolidays),
(25)          belongsTo(?City,?Country)]
```

3.3 Implementation

Our case study was implemented in JAVA, using JADE and the JENA API [19]. *JADE containers* were used for representing the abstractions of environments and organizations. Agents were implemented extending the *JADE Agent class* with both an attribute for agents' locations and two specific behaviours. One behaviour is called *Migratory* and it makes agents move randomly from one location to another. The other behaviour is called *Normative* and it continuously informs agents about their current contextual norms, representing the DynaCROM core. Once an agent migrates, its location attribute is updated and, consequently, the answers from its *Normative* behaviour change for informing its new contextual norms. Moreover, because DynaCROM is implemented as an active *JADE behaviour*, it always executes the process illustrated in Fig. 3. Thus, if any norm is updated in a DynaCROM ontology instance or if any new composition of contextual norms is done in a DynaCROM rule file, agents concerned with these changes will automatically receive different answers.

Fig. 6 illustrates the *JADE containers* created for representing the USA, Cuba and Brazil environments and for representing the Dellie, Dellie Cuba and Dellie Brazil organizations. These containers offer possible locations for mobile agents to move to. For instance, an agent called "******MobileAgent*", which has the *Migratory* and *Normative* behaviours, is in Cuba. There, DynaCROM informs the agent about

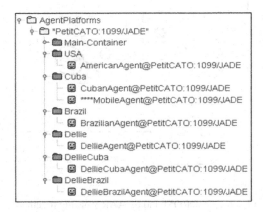

Fig. 6. *JADE containers* for representing our environments and organizations

environment norms 3.1.1.a and 3.1.1.b. If the agent migrates to Dellie Brazil, then, DynaCROM informs the agent about environment norms 3.1.1.c and 3.1.1.d, organization norms 3.1.2.a and 3.1.2.b, and role norm 3.1.3.a. All informed norms are in compliance with the norms of our case study, DynaCROM hierarchical form and agent contexts.

4 Using Contextual Norm Information

In the current version of DynaCROM, norms are not enforced. DynaCROM keeps relaying information about them to agents, who are free to decide if they will or not use the information. However, DynaCROM can have its output (agents' updated contextual norms) used as a precise input for norm enforcement solutions and, in turn, it can make use of the outputs from these solutions (e.g. information about agents' violated norms).

4.1 Using DynaCROM Output as an Input for a Norm Enforcement Solution

We are currently studying both how DynaCROM output can be used as a precise input for a norm enforcement framework and what DynaCROM can have back from this framework. The chosen framework is called SCAAR (meaning *Self-Controlled Autonomous Agents geneRator*) [6] and it enhances agents with a self-monitoring capability for avoiding norm violation. Because the current version of SCAAR is implemented in SICStus Prolog [29], we still could not use it as a fully norm enforcement mechanism for DynaCROM (implemented in JAVA). However, we are already being able to use SCAAR for informing DynaCROM about norm violations.

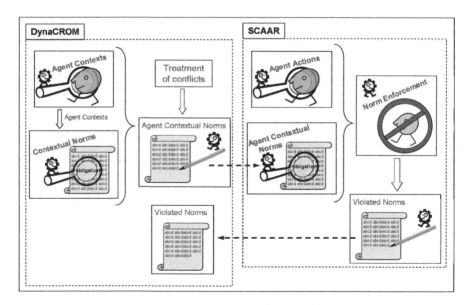

Fig. 7. DynaCROM and SCAAR working together

Fig. 7 illustrates how DynaCROM and SCAAR work together. DynaCROM is responsible for continuously informing SCAAR about the norms of agents, according to their current contexts. SCAAR uses this information as a precise updated input instead of using general and pre-defined *(outdated)* information. SCAAR keeps verifying norm compliance and, if a norm is violated, SCAAR sends that information to DynaCROM.

4.2 Using a Norm Enforcement Solution for Detecting Norm Violation

For exemplifying how DynaCROM and SCAAR can represent a powerful complementary solution while detecting norm violation in open MASs, a simple (not completed) scenario is proposed. The scenario is created according to the world and norms from Section 3 and it can be summarized by the following steps:

a. A Dellie Brazil supplier receives a large order (1500 computers) from PUCie-Rio.

b. Dellie Brazil does not have all the CPUs necessary to build the computers ordered. So, 500 more CPUs will need to be bought.

c. The Dellie Brazil supplier decides to buy the missing 500 CPUs from Dellie Cuba.

d. The Dellie Brazil supplier asks Dellie the price of each CPU.

e. Dellie answers to the Dellie Brazil supplier the price of US$100 for each CPU.

f. The Dellie Brazil supplier multiplies the value (in US$) of each CPU by 500 and converts the value to CUP (Cuban Pesos), the Cuban national currency. The final price for the order is: US$100 * 500 = US$5000 * CUP1 = CUP5000.

g. The Dellie Brazil supplier (being a Dellie Cuba customer) sends the order to a Dellie Cuba supplier with the value of CUP500 as a down payment for the placed order.

h. The Dellie Cuba supplier informs the Dellie Brazil supplier that the value for the down payment is wrong because it is necessary to increase the final price by 15% as taxes. The correct value for the down payment is: (CUP5000 +15%) *0.1 = (CUP5750) *0.1 = CUP575.

After step 4.2.c from the scenario above, all the following steps have contextual norms associated to them. These norms are re-written by DynaCROM according to both SCAAR syntax and current agent contexts and sent, in a sequence order one by one, from DynaCROM to SCAAR as different inputs (see Fig. 7).

Table 5 presents the SCAAR contextual norms written for the proposed scenario. SCAARNorm1 (lines 1 – 4) represents the DynaCROM organization norm 3.1.2.a for regulating step 4.2.d. SCAARNorm2 (lines 5 – 9) represents the DynaCROM environment norm 3.1.1.0 for regulating step 4.2.e. SCAARNorm3 (lines 10 – 13) represents the DynaCROM environment norm 3.1.1.b for regulating step 4.2.f. SCAARNorm4 (lines 14 – 18) represents the DynaCROM interaction norm 3.1.4.a for regulating step 4.2.g. SCAARNorm5 (lines 19 – 24) represents the DynaCROM environment norm 3.1.1.a for regulating step 4.2.h.

SCAAR makes use of DynaCROM inputs (contextual norms) for regulating agent actions. These actions (e.g., *"askPrice"*, *"informPrice"*, *"giveDownPayment"*, *"sendOrder"*, *"addTaxes"* from Table 5) are known *a priori* by SCAAR. Then,

Table 5. SCAAR contextual norms

```
(1)  SCAARNorm1-
(2)  [(agt: aDellieSupplier)
(3)    OBLIGED (agt do askPrice with receiver = Dellie)
(4)    BEFORE  (agt do informPrice with quantity > 100)]

(5)  SCAARNorm2-
(6)  [(agt: aSupplier)
(7)    FORBIDDEN (agt do givePrice with
(8)                currency # usDollars)
(9)    IF (agt be location with country = USA)]

(10) SCAARNorm3-
(11) [(agt: aSupplier)
(12)   FORBIDDEN (agt do givePrice with currency # CUP)
(13)   IF (agt be location with country = Cuba)]

(14) SCAARNorm4-
(15) [(agt: aDellieCubaCustomer)
(16)   OBLIGED (agt do downPayment with percent = 10)
(17)   BEFORE  (agt do sendOrder with
(18)              shipperOrganization = DellieCuba)]

(19) SCAARNorm5-
(20) [(agt: aDellieCubaCustomer)
(21)   OBLIGED (agt do addTaxes with percent = 15)
(22)   BEFORE  (agt do sendOrder with shipperCountry # C)
(23)   IF (agt be location with
(24)         situated = Central America and country = C)]
```

Table 6. The SCAAR algorithm for norm enforcement

```
(1)   Let I be information about the agent behaviour.
(2)   Let {t1,...,tn} be the set of transitions associated with I.
(3)   Let {P1,...,Pm} be the set of Petri nets associated with the agent.
(4)   Let {Pact1,...,Pactp} be the set of activated Petri nets (i.e. associated with the
      norms to be manage)
(5)   Let tij be the transition i of the net j.
(6)   for all Pk in {P1,...,Pm} with t1k in {t1,...,tn}}
(7)       Pact(p+1)<- create an instance of Pk
(8)       add Pact(p+1) in {Pact1,...,Pactp}
(9)   end for
(10)  Let {Pact1,...,Pactl} be the set of the activated Petri nets including a tij in
      {t1,...,tn}, j in {1,...,l}
(11)  for all Pactj in {Pact1,...,Pactl}
(12)      inform Pactj of the information associated with tij
(13)  end for
```

SCAAR adds in agent codes both control hooks and an enforcement core. These additions are completely transparent to agents. While an agent is executing, its control hooks *(automatically)* keep informing the enforcement core about the execution of regulated actions. Table 6 presents this algorithm. Then, the enforcement core *(automatically)* keeps verifying if each action is executing according to its norms. If not, it stops the execution of the action and informs the violation to DynaCROM.

Verification of norm compliance is done by using Petri nets [25] for representing norms and by following the algorithm presented in Table 7.

Table 7. The SCAAR algorithm for verifying norm compliance

(1) Let $\{t1,..,tn\}$ be the set of transitions of the Petri net.
(2) Let I be the sent information.
(3) Let tI be the transition associated with the information I in $\{t1,...,tn\}$
(4) A transition ti is *activated* if a token stands in all the previous places of ti (in SCAAR Petri net, arcs are one-valued).
(5) **if** tI is activated **then**
(6)   **if** tI is fireable **then**
(7)   fire the transition tI
(8) **else** throw exception

Returning to our example, SCAAR detects the norm violation that occurred in step 4.2.h by using the algorithms presented in Table 6 and Table 7 as follows: the control hook for the action "*sendOrder*" of the Dellie Cuba supplier sends to the agent enforcement core notification that the action is being performed. Thus, the agent enforcement core creates instances of Petri nets for representing the norms of the action (SCAARNorm3, SCAARNorm4 and SCAARNorm5 from Table 5). For instance, P1 (see below) is the Petri net created for representing the norm SCAARNorm5.

P1: <P, T, Pre, Post>: $((p_1,p_2,p_3,p_4), (t_{location}, t_{sendOrder}, t_{addTaxes}), (Pre(p_1, t_{location}), Pre(p_2, t_{addTaxes}), Pre^*(p_2, t_{sendOrder})), (Post(p_2, t_{location}), Post(p_3, t_{addTaxes}), Post(p_4, t_{sendOrder})))$

*: it means an inhibitor arc between the transition and the previous place. A transition with an inhibitor arc can be fired when the previous place is empty.

The enforcement core of the Dellie Cuba supplier retains the information about $I_{location}$, $I_{addTaxes}$ and $I_{sendOder}$ from the associated control hooks of the agent. When the agent arrives in Cuba, the enforcement core receives the information about $I_{location}$. Thus, the Petri net P1 is activated and the transition is fired by putting the Petri net token in the next place (p_2). When the Dellie Brazil supplier tries to perform the action "*sendOrder*", its enforcement core blocks the execution of the action, because the transition $t_{addTaxes}$ was not yet executed (the Petri net token didn't pass through p_2 before being in p_3), and throws an exception.

5   Related Work

García-Camino *et al.* [14] propose a distributed architecture to endow MASs with a social layer, in which normative positions are explicitly represented and managed via rules. Every external agent from the architecture has a *dedicated governor agent* connected to it, enforcing the norms of executed events. DynaCROM also uses rules to manage normative agent positions, although its focus is on executed actions instead of executed events. Norm enforcement in DynaCROM can be done with a few *dedicated governor agents* responsible for monitoring only executed actions. For instance, an open MASs from the traffic domain enhanced with DynaCROM can have only *dedicated governor agents* (e.g. playing the police officer role) for monitoring the speed of the cars that pass through regulated crossroads. Thus, it is not necessary to duplicate the number of agents for having the norm enforcement. Moreover, DynaCROM provides a more precise mechanism for norm representation while using contexts.

Vázquez-Salceda *et al.* [34] propose the OMNI framework (*Organizational Model for Normative Institutions*) for modelling agent organizations. Comparing DynaCROM with OMNI, we find that both define a meta-ontology with a taxonomy for norm representation. One difference between the works is that, in OMNI, enforcement is carried out by any internal agent from an MAS; in DynaCROM, enforcement is carried out only by specific trusted agents or by the own regulated agents. A second difference between the works, and the most important, is that, in OMNI, the idea of different levels of abstractions for norms is not explicit, especially for the environment and role levels. On the other hand, DynaCROM is entirely based on different levels of abstractions for norms (its regulatory contexts) for simplifying the tasks of norm management and evolution. For instance, the social structure of an organization in OMNI describes, at the same level of abstraction, norms for roles and groups of roles. A group of roles is used to specify norms that hold for all roles in the group. DynaCROM uses the organization regulatory context to specify organization norms, which hold for all roles from an organization, and it uses the role regulatory context to specify role norms, both regulatory contexts from different levels of abstractions.

6 Conclusion

In this paper, we detail DynaCROM – our ongoing work for providing contextual norm information in open MASs. For agents, DynaCROM retaining updated norm information according to their contexts. Norm-aware agents can use the provided norm information for correct performance and, thus, for achieving their goals faster. For developers, DynaCROM decreases the complexity of norm management in two different cases. The first case is when norms need to be added, updated or deleted. For this case, simply updating the ontology instance concludes the evolution. The second case is when new compositions of contextual norms are desired. For this case, simply activating or deactivating existing rules or creating new ones concludes the evolution. The dynamics for manually customizing several compositions of contextual norms is given by different activations and deactivations of rules, which can be modified at system run-time.

DynaCROM has been used in three different application domains. For the domain of ubiquitous computing [18,30], DynaCROM has been used in the implementation of context-aware pervasive mobile applications [35]. Instead of using *JADE containers* for simulating environments and organizations, we are using MoCA (Mobile Collaboration Architecture) [27] for delivering updated real location information of mobile devices. MoCA infers mobile devices' locations based on the intensity of their signals to 802.11 network access points. DynaCROM uses MoCA answers (device locations) to continuously apply contextual norms in the agents from the mobile devices. For the domain of next-generation wireless communications [2], DynaCROM has been used to automatically change prices and other parameter values (based on pre-defined rules) according to overloads in regulated networks. The idea is to keep balancing the use of network bandwidths by distributing clients in particular networks. Clients will be guided to always use a non-overloaded network by following pricing discounts. Thus, clients can be better distributed in regulated networks by only changing domain rules and data. For the domain of the Brazilian navy [4], DynaCROM has been used for dynamically determining better routes for ships based on climate and other pre-defined conditions.

The current version of DynaCROM has three main points that need improvement. The first improvement is that DynaCROM should deal with conflicts; the second improvement is that DynaCROM should detect norm violations; and the third improvement is that DynaCROM should enforce norms for avoiding their violation. DynaCROM is not currently addressing the issue (general and difficult) of conflicts, but its modularization of norms helps to make this information more manageable. For the second and third improvements, the SCAAR solution for norm enforcement is being studied. We chose SCAAR instead of LGI (a well-known solution for norm enforcement) [23-24], mainly because SCAAR permits the enforcement of norms that are not related only to agent interactions. Thus, SCAAR will make it possible to enforce DynaCROM environment, organization and role norms independently of the enforcement of interaction norms. For future work, we are planning to implement SCAAR in JAVA in order to fully integrate it with DynaCROM. We believe that DynaCROM and SCAAR can represent together a unique and powerful contextual norm enforcement solution for open MASs.

Acknowledgments

This work was partially funded by the ESSMA (CNPq 552068/2002-0) and EMACA (CAPES/COFECUB 482/05 PP 016/04) projects, and by CNPq individual grants.

References

1. Artikis, A., Pitt, J., Sergot, M.: Animated specifications of computational societies. In: AAMAS 2002, Part III, pp. 1053–1061 (2002)
2. Berezdivin, R., Breinig, R., Topp, R.: Next-generation wireless communications concepts and technologies. In the IEEE Communications Magazine 40, 108–116 (2002)
3. Bouquet, P., Giunchiglia, F., Harmelen, F.v., Serafini, L.: C-OWL: Contextualizing Ontologies. In: Fensel, D., Sycara, K.P., Mylopoulos, J. (eds.) ISWC 2003. LNCS, vol. 2870, pp. 164–179. Springer, Heidelberg (2003)
4. Brazilian navy (2006), https://www.mar.mil.br/
5. Castelfranchi, C., Dignum, F., Jonker, C.M., Treur, J.: Deliberative Normative Agents: Principles and Architecture. In: Procs. of the ATAL 1999 (1999)
6. Chopinaud, C., Seghrouchini, A.E.F., Taillibert, P.: Prevention of harmful behaviors within cognitive and autonomous agents. In: Procs. of the ECAI 2006, pp. 205–209 (2006)
7. Dey, A.: Understanding and using context. Personal and Ubiquitous Computing 5(1), 4–7 (2001)
8. Felicíssimo, C.H.: Dynamic Contextual Regulations in Open Multi-agent Systems. In: Cruz, I., Decker, S., Allemang, D., Preist, C., Schwabe, D., Mika, P., Uschold, M., Aroyo, L. (eds.) ISWC 2006. LNCS, vol. 4273, pp. 974–975. Springer, Heidelberg (2006)
9. Felicíssimo, C.H., de Lucena, C.J.P., Briot, J.-P., Choren, R.: Regulating Open Multi-Agent Systems with DynaCROM. In: Procs. of the SEAS (2006)
10. Felicíssimo, C.H., de Lucena, C.J.P., Briot, J.-P., Choren, R.: An Approach for Contextual Regulations in Open MAS. In: Procs. of the AOIS (2006)

11. Felicíssimo, C.H., de Lucena, C., Carvalho, G., Paes, R.: Normative Ontologies to Define Regulations over Roles in Open Multi-Agent Systems. In Procs. of the AAAI Fall Symposium TR FS-05-08. (2005). ISBN 978-1-57735-254-9
12. Ferber, J., Gutknecht, O., Michael, F.: From Agents to Organizations: an Organization View of Multi-Agent Systems. In: Procs. of the AOSE (2003)
13. Garcia-Camino, A., Noriega, P., Rodríguez-Aguillar, J.A.: Implementing Norms in Electronic Institutions. In: Procs. of the AAMAS, vol. 2, pp. 667–673 (2005)
14. García-Camino, A., Rodrígurez-Aguilar, J.A., Sierra, C., Vasconcelos, W.: A Distributed Architecture for Norm-Aware Agent Societies. In Procs. of the DALT 2005. (2005)
15. Gosling, J., Joy, B., Junior, G.L.S., Bracha, G.: The Java Language Specification. ISBN 0-201-31008-2 (2006), http://java.sun.com/
16. Grizard, A., Vercouter, L., Stratulat, T., Muller, G.: A peer-to-peer normative system to achieve social order. In: Procs. of the COIN@AAMAS (2006)
17. Gruber, T.R.: A translation approach to portable ontology specifications. Knowledge Acquisition 5(2), 199–220 (1993)
18. Henricksen, K., Indulska, J.: Developing context-aware pervasive computing applications: models and approach. Pervasive and Mobile Computing. Elsevier, Amsterdam (2005)
19. Jena (2006), http://jena.sourceforge.net/
20. Jennings, N.R.: On Agent-Based Software Engineering. AI 117(2), 277–296 (2000)
21. Jennings, N., Sycara, K., Wooldridge, M.: A Roadmap of Agent Research and Development. The Journal of Agents and Multi-Agent Systems 1, 7–38 (1998)
22. Khedr, M., Karmouch, A.: ACAI: Agent-Based Context-aware Infrastructure for Spontaneous Applications. Journal of Network & Computer Applications 28(1), 19–44 (1995)
23. Minsky, N.H.: The imposition of protocols over open distributed systems. IEEE Transactions on Software Engineering (1991)
24. Minsky, N.H.: LGI (2006), http://www.moses.rutgers.edu/
25. Murata, T.: Petri nets: Properties, analysis and applications. IEEE 77(4), 541–580 (1989)
26. Noy, N.: Rector, A. (eds.): Defining N-ary Relations on the Semantic Web: Use with Individuals (2006), http://www.w3.org/TR/swbp-n-aryRelations/
27. Rubinsztejn, H.K., Endler, M., Sacramento, V., Gonçalves, K., Nascimento, F.N.: Support for context-aware collaboration. Procs. of the MATA 5(10), 34–47 (2004)
28. Silva da, V.T.: From a conceptual framework for agents and objects to a multi-agent system modeling language. Ph.D. Thesis. Port. p. 252 PUC-Rio (2004)
29. SICStus Prolog (2006), http://www.sics.se/isl/sicstuswww/site/
30. Soldatos, J., Pandis, I., Stamatis, K., Polymenakos, L., Crowley, J.L.: Agent based middleware infrastructure for autonomous context-aware ubiquitous computing services. The Journal of Computer Communications (2006)
31. Stanford University School of Medicine: Protégé (2006), http://protege.stanford.edu/
32. Thomas, G., Williams, A.B.: Roles in the Context of Multiagent Task Relationships. In: Procs. of the AAAI Fall Symposium TR FS 2005-2008 (2005) ISBN 978-1-57735-254-9
33. Tilab Co. JADE - Java Agent DEvelopment Framework (2006), http://jade.tilab.com
34. Vázquez-Salceda, J., Dignum, V., Dignum, F.: Organizing Multiagent Systems. The Journal of Autonomous Agents and Multi-Agent Systems 11(3), 307–360 (2005)
35. Viterbo, J., Felicissimo, C., Briot, J.-P., Endler, M., Lucena, C.: Applying Regulation to Ubiquitous Computing Environments. In: Procs. of the SEAS (2006)
36. Weyns, D., Parunak, H.V.D., Michel, F., Holvoet, T., Ferber, J.: Environments for Multiagent Systems State-of-the-Art and Research Challenges. In: Weyns, D., Parunak, H.V.D., Michel, F. (eds.) E4MAS 2004. LNCS (LNAI), vol. 3374, pp. 1–47. Springer, Heidelberg (2005)
37. Wright, G.H.v: Deontic Logic. Mind, New Series 60(237), 1–15 (1951)

A Reputation Model Based on Testimonies

José de S.P. Guedes[1], Viviane Torres da Silva[2,*], and Carlos J. P. de Lucena[1]

[1] Computer Science Dept (PUC-Rio) Rua M. de S. Vicente 225, RJ 22453-900, Brazil
{jguedes,lucena}@inf.puc-rio.br
[2] Depart. of Sist. Inf. y Comp. (UCM) C/ Prof. J.G. Santesmases, s/n, Madrid 28040, Spain
viviane@fdi.ucm.es

Abstract. Reputation mechanisms are used to increase reliability and performance in virtual societies. Different decentralized reputation models have been proposed based on interactions among agents. Each system agent evaluates and stores the reputation of the agents with whom they have interacted and can give testimony to other agents about these reputations. The main disadvantages of these approaches when applied to open large-scale multi-agent systems are the difficulty of establishing strong links between the agents and the sometimes infeasible witness search process. In this paper we propose a hybrid reputation system with centralized and decentralized characteristics to overcome these problems. Reputations are provided by the system agents themselves but also by centralized subsystems that can be easily reached by any agent and can supply reliable reputations of any agent based on testimonies about undesired agent behaviour. Such behaviour is characterized by the violation of system norms.

1 Introduction

Reputation systems collect, distribute, and aggregate feedback about participants' past behaviour. These systems help agents to decide whom to trust and also help agents to discourage participation by those who are dishonest [8]. In centralized reputation models, such as ebay [4], Amazon Auctions [2], and Sporas [15], a reputation system receives feedback about the interactions among the agents. Each agent evaluates the behaviour of the agents with which they interact and reports to the reputation system. The reputation system puts together all evaluations and stores the reputation of the agents. The reputation of each agent is, therefore, a single global value.

An advantage of these approaches is that the reputations of the agents are always available in the centralized reputation system. However, an important drawback of this approach is that the agents are not able to store the reputations with which they have interacted and must therefore use the information stored in the centralized systems.

In contrast, an agent in a decentralized reputation system evaluates and stores the reputations of the agents with which it has interacted. There is no central reputation system with this responsibility. The most important disadvantage of such an approach

* Research supported by the Juan de la Cierva programa, Comunidad de Madrid (PROMESSAS S-0505/TIC-407) and Ministério de Educación y Ciencia (DESAFIOS TIN2006-15660-C02-01).

M. Kolp et al. (Eds.): AOIS 2006, LNAI 4898, pp. 37–52, 2008.

takes place when agents need to know the reputation of other agents with which they have not yet interacted. Since there is no central reputation system with this information, approaches such as [1], FIRE [6], Regret [9,10] and [13,14] propose the use of testimonies provided by agents that have interacted with the desired ones. These agents can provide information about their previous interactions with the desired agents.

However, when considering open large-scale multi-agent systems three problems arise. First of all, agents must meet frequently in order for it to be possible to establish strong links among them and to pass along consistent reputations. This is often not possible when dealing with open systems where agents frequently enter and leave the systems. Secondly, the process of searching for agents that have interacted with the desired agents may take a long time. It may be very difficult or take too much time to discover which agents have interacted with the desired ones in a large-scale system. Finally, reputations are influenced by the agents' point of view. Two agents may evaluate the same behaviour in different ways. The violation of the same norm can be interpreted differently by different agents.

In order to overcome these problems, FIRE proposes to use certified reputations that are references provided by other agents about the agent's behaviour. Each agent has numerous certified reputations (or references) provided by the agents with whom they have interacted with and therefore can offer those references to agents that wish to interact with that agent. Other reputation models such as Policy-Maker [5] and Trust-Serv [12] also use this approach. The main benefit of this approach is the high availability of the reputations since any agent can easily learn the reputation of any other. But the most significant weakness of this approach is that certified information probably overestimates an agent's expected behaviour. Since agents are self-interested entities they will only offer their best ratings. In addition, certified reputations are influenced by the point of view of the agents who provided them.

In this paper we propose a reputation model that combines the features of the centralized and decentralized approaches described above in order to overcome these problems. In our approach, as well as in FIRE and Regret, agents are able to evaluate the past behaviour of other agents and store the reputation of each agent with whom they have interacted (the decentralized part). In addition, our approach also provides individual organizations with the ability to evaluate and store the reputations of agents (the centralized part). We assume that large-scale multi-agent systems are composed of (a hierarchy of) organizations (or groups) where agents are playing roles. The organizations evaluate the reputation of an agent based on testimonies provided by other agents about the past behaviour of this agent.

Different from other systems that deal with testimonies, the organizations do not receive the reputations evaluated by the agents. On the contrary, they receive testimonies about agent's bad behaviour, i.e., about system norms (or laws) violated by the agents. The organizations evaluate the reputation of the agents according to the norms that they have violated. Norm violations characterize undesirable agent behaviour and negatively affect the reputation of agents that commit the violations.

Since our approach combines the features of centralized and decentralized approaches, the problems we have identified are solved:

(i)   Agents did not need frequent meetings in order to be consistent in ranking the reputations of other agents. They can consult organizations that store reputations that have been evaluated based on several interactions with agents;

(ii)   To find out someone that can provide the reputation of an agent is not time expensive. The organizations where the agent is playing roles can be consulted;

(iii)   The reputations provided by organizations are not over estimated unlike the case of certified reputations. Organizations are reliable / certifiable systems that do not make distinctions between agents;

(iv)   The reputations provided by organizations are not biased by the opinions of others. The reputations are evaluated according to the characteristics of the norms that are violated. The specification of each norm describes how its violation influences the reputation of the agent;

(v)   Agents do not need to use the reputations provided by organizations if they do not wish. They are capable of evaluating and storing the reputation of other agents.

In this paper we present the reputation model used by organizations to evaluate the reputation of their agents. The specification of the mechanisms used by the agents to evaluate and store the reputations is beyond the scope of this paper since any available decentralized mechanism, such as FIRE or Regret, can be used.

The paper is organized as follows. Section 2 briefly describes the subsystem that evaluates the testimonies provided by the agents. Section 3 describes the reputation model being proposed in this paper. In Section 4 a case study is used to illustrate our approach. Section 5 examines some related work and Section 6 presents conclusions and some proposals for future research.

2   Evaluating the Testimonies

When an agent violates a system norm, and this is perceived by another agent, the agent can testify to the reputation subsystem about the violation. The agents that testify are those motivated to do so, i.e., they benefit when other agents act according to the norms or they are harmed when those agents violate the norms.

Note that agents can also give false testimony in order to harm other agents or benefit themselves. In an open system, agents are independently implemented and the application cannot assume that agents were properly designed. Therefore, there is a need to verify and establish the truth of the testimonies.

In [11] we propose a judgement subsystem that is responsible for receiving the testimonies and providing a decision (or verdict) verifying whether, in fact, an agent violated a norm. While judging a testimony, the subsystem may use different strategies to determine the violation of the norms specified by the application. These strategies may use the agents' reputation provided by the reputation subsystem to help in making the decision. Both the judgement and the reputation subsystems should be implemented by the organizations where the agents are playing roles.

Moreover, since it may be difficult to find out if a testimony is true or false and, therefore, to provide a correct decision, the judgement subsystem can overcome this problem by using uncertainty. The judgement subsystem may assign blame within an appropriate margin of error.

In this paper we assume that the judgement subsystem uses uncertainty and that it will inform the reputation subsystem about the percentage of blame an agent has for violating a norm. On the one hand, if the verdict provided by the judgement subsystem states the agent has more than 50% of chance of having violated a norm, the agent is condemned and his reputation will be diminished according to the norm violated. On the other hand, if the verdict indicates that the agent has a less than (or equal to) 50% chance of being guilty, the agent is absolved and the witness is condemned for having provided false testimony. Note that it is beyond the scope of this paper to detail the judgement subsystem already presented in [11]. This paper focuses on the presentation of the reputation mechanism that receives the verdicts provided by the judgement subsystem and updates the reputation of the agents.

3   The Reputation Model

The hybrid reputation model proposed in this paper combines the decentralized and centralized approaches as illustrated in Figure 1. In our model, each system agent is capable of evaluating the reputation of the agents with whom it interacts and then stores the reputation of those agents. In this way, the reputation model can be characterized as a decentralized one. To implement the decentralized reputation part any published decentralized reputation model such as [1], FIRE, and Regret can be used.

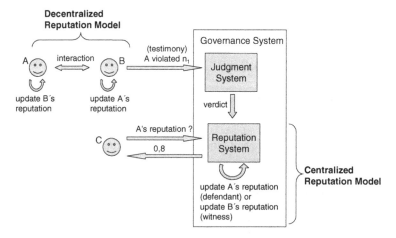

Fig. 1. Hybrid Reputation Model

In addition, we propose a centralized reputation system that evaluates the reputation of the agents based on violated norms. Besides being able to evaluate and store other agents' reputations, agents would also be able to interact with the centralized system in order to provide information about norm violations. Any time an agent perceives a norm violation, it can advise the governance system.

The (centralized) governance system will evaluate the information and, then, evaluate and store the reputations. Not only the reputation of the agent accused of violating a norm (defendant agent) can be updated but also the reputation of the agent that is providing the testimony (witness agent) can be modified.

The governance system is able to provide information about its evaluations of agents' reputations. This information can be particularly useful in two different situations. First, it can be used by agents that want to know the reputation of agents with whom they have never interacted. This is important since we are considering open multi-agent systems where agents enter and leave frequently. Second, such centralized evaluation can also be used to help agents evaluating the reputation of others. Agents that have not been interacting with other agents for a certain period of time store old reputation values of their partners. These reputations may or may not correspond to their current behaviour. Since the centralized reputation system stores up-to-date agents' reputation, this information can be used to update the old reputation values.

3.1 Evaluating Defendants' Reputation

The reputation subsystem evaluates agents reputations based on the verdicts provided by the judgement subsystem. The judgement subsystem informs the reputation subsystems of the verdicts and the testimonies by indicating the witnesses, the defendants and the norm violations. When the defendants are condemned by the judgement subsystem, their reputations are updated according to the norms that they have violated. The more important the norm, the greater the influence it will exert on the agent's reputation. Each norm must stipulate how the reputation of the agent should be modified if it is violated by the agent. This information is called the *power of the norm*. The *power of a norm* can vary from 0, for norms that do not influence the agent's reputation, to 1 for norms that strongly influence the agent's reputation when violated.

Since we assume that the judgement subsystem deals with uncertainty, the reputation subsystem must also consider this when evaluating the reputation of the agents. The reputations of two agents considered guilty of violating the same norm cannot be evaluated in the same way if the judgement subsystem is more certain of the guilt of one agent than another. The same norm cannot influence the reputation of two agents in the same way when one is considered 90% guilty and the other 51% guilty of violating the norm. Therefore, the reputation subsystem applies the *percentage of blame* informed by the judgement subsystem to the *power of the norms*. On one hand, when the judgement subsystem is quite sure that the agent is guilty its reputation is strongly influenced by the *power of the violated norm*. On the other hand, when the judgement subsystem is not so sure about the violation of the norm the agent's reputation is not so strongly influenced by the *power of the norm*. Expression (1) evaluates the influence of the violated norm n_i on the reputation of agent a_j by considering the *power of the norm* and the *percentage of blame*.

$$defRepInf(a_j,n_i) = normPower(n_i) * blamePercentage(a_j, n_i) \qquad (1)$$

The influence of a violated norm on an agent's reputation may change over the agent lifecycle. Frequently, recently violated norms have greater influence on the reputation of an agent than norms violated in the past. In order to overcome this issue, we propose to take into account the time during which a norm will influence the agent reputation. The information about the time during which the norm will influence the agent's reputation must be part of the norm specification. This information is used to estimate the remaining days during which the norm violation will influence the reputation. Thus, recently violated norms will strongly influence the reputations of agents, and norms violated in the past will have less influence the reputations or will not influence the reputation at all, if the time has expired. Expression (2) evaluates the influence of norm n_i on the reputation of agent a_j by considering the *power of the norm*, the *percentage of blame* and the *number of days of impact or influence remaining*. Expression (2) shows that the agent's reputation will automatically improve over time as the *remainingDays* attribute declines.

$$defRepInf(a_j,n_i)=normPower(n_i)*blamePercentage(a_j, n_i)*remainingDays(a_j,n_i) \quad (2)$$

$$where\ remainingDays(a_j,n_i) = \frac{totalTime(n_i) - passedDays(a_j,n_i)}{totalTime\ (n_i)}$$

Although a norm violation may no longer be influencing the reputation of an agent, the information about the violation can still be stored by the reputation subsystem. This is important when considering repeat behaviour, i.e., relapses. The influence of a norm violation on the reputation of an agent may increase in case of relapses. The relapse factor varies from 1 (representing no relapse at all) to a value near zero (representing many relapses) according to the importance of the norm for the system. Note that the result value must not exceed the maximum value of the *norm power* that is 1.

$$normPower^r(n_i) = normPower(n_i) * (1/relapse(n_i)) \quad (3)$$

$$but\ 0 <= normPower^r(n_i) <= 1$$

The influence of a norm violation on the reputation of an agent may decrease in case of *confession*. If the agent confesses, the power of the norm is decreased. Equation (4) modifies the power of the norm by considering *confession*. This factor may vary according to the importance of the norm. The more important is the norm, the less influence this factor will have on the reputation of the agent.

$$normPower^{rc}(n_i) = normPower^r(n_i) * confession(n_i) \quad (4)$$

To evaluate the reputation of a defendant agent it is necessary to consider all the norms that the agent has violated. Its reputation is evaluated by putting together all the partial influences provided by each violation, as stated in equation (5). Equation (6) provides the defendant reputation by combining all of the partial influences. It shows the reputation of a defendant agent a_j by considering that it has violated k norms. Note that it may be the case that the defendant's reputation is equal to zero if the sum of its partial influences is equal to (or greater than) one. It may also be the case that the defendant's reputation is equal to 1 if its reputation is no longer being influenced by past violations. Thus, the reputation values vary from 1 to 0 and we consider reputations greater than 0.5 good and less than (or equal to) 0.5 bad reputations.

$$defRepInf(a_{j,} n_i) = normPower^{rc}(n_i) *blamePercentage(a_j,n_i) *remainingDays(a_j,n_i) \quad (5)$$

$$defendantRep(a_j) = 1 - \begin{cases} \sum_{0<i<=k}[defRepInf(a_j,n_i)], & \text{if } \sum_{0<i<=k}[defRepInf(a_j,n_i)] <= 1 \\ 1 & \text{, if } \sum_{0<i<=k}[defRepInf(a_j,n_i)] > 1 \end{cases} \quad (6)$$

3.2 Evaluating Witnesses' Reputation

In case the defendant agents are absolved by the judgement subsystem, the reputation of the defendant agent is not modified. It is the reputation of the witness agent that should diminished, since it has made an unfounded accusation. The witness' reputation is also evaluated using the *power of the norm*. However, the norm violation itself is usually considered more dangerous than accusing another of a violation. Therefore, we have defined a factor for adapting the power of the norm for witnesses that make false statements. This factor, called the witness factor, must be less than 1 but greater than (or equal to) 0 in order to diminish the power of the norm. Equation (7) modifies the power of the norm by taking into account agent relapses and untruthful witnesses.

$$normPower^{rw}(n_i) = normPower^r(n_i) * witnessFactor(n_i)$$
$$\text{but } 0 <= normPower^{rw}(n_i) <= 1 \quad (7)$$

Equation (9) evaluates the reputation of the witness agent a_j by considering that it has made false statements about k norm violations. It combines the partial influences of inaccurate information it has told that are evaluated according to equation (8).

$$witRepInf(a_{j,} n_i) = normPower^{rw}(n_i) *blamePercentage(a_j,n_i) *remainingDays(a_j,n_i) \quad (8)$$

$$witnessRep(a_j) = 1 - \begin{cases} \sum_{0<i<=k}[witRepInf(a_j,n_i)], & \text{if } \sum_{0<i<=k}[witRepInf(a_j,n_i)] <= 1 \\ 1 & \text{, if } \sum_{0<i<=k}[witRepInf(a_j,n_i)] > 1 \end{cases} \quad (9)$$

3.3 Analyzing the Equations for Evaluating Reputations

The equations used by the reputation subsystem to evaluate the agents' reputation are based on the practices in Brazilian criminal law. The terms used in those equations are related to some of the variables considered by Brazilian criminal code in judging a crime. Note that our goal is not to fully represent Brazilian criminal law in our model. Our intentions are to show that some of the variables used in Brazilian law can be helpful in evaluating agents' reputations.

In Brazilian criminal law, the minimum and maximum penalties that a defendant can receive are determined by the kind of crime being judged. Serious crimes have substantial penalties and simple crimes have small penalties. In the case of the reputation subsystem, each norm states how important the norm is and how much a violation of the norm will influence the reputation of the agent. This influence is defined by the term *normPower*. Important norms have higher *normPower* than simple norms (equation 1). In addition, the norm also states how long the agent's reputation would be influenced by the norm. This information is represented by the term *totalTime* (equation 2).

Since the crimes determine a wide range of penalties, the penalties are fixed according to criteria such as the defendant's culpability. Culpability represents the degree to which the defendant is responsible - blame. In our model, the culpability of the agent is represented by the *blamePercentage* (equation 1). This percentage is provided by the judgement system after judging the violation. It states the degree to which the defendant agent is culpable of violating the norm.

After establishing the penalty, the judge can also apply aggravating and extenuating circumstances to increase or decrease the penalty. In the case of a relapse, the penalty can be increased and in the case of confession the penalty can be decreased. As in criminal law, the reputation subsystem also uses information about *relapse* (equation 3) and *confession* to influence the agent reputation (equation 4). Table 1 states the 5 terms used in the equations and the relationship between them and the variables used in the criminal law.

Table 1. Terms of the equations

Criminal Law	Reputation System	Contribution to the Agent Reputation
minimum and maximum penalties	normPower	decrease
	totalTime	decrease
culpability	blamePercentage	decrease
relapse	relapse	decrease
confession	confession	increase

The five mentioned terms are the ones used to evaluate the reputation of a dependent agent. In order to group these terms, we have defined equation 5. Since we are dealing with terms whose values can vary from 0 to 1, like percentages, the simplest operator used to group those terms is multiplicity. Equation 5 should be used for each violated norm. This equation states how each violation will influence the agent reputation. Equation 6 is used to combine all the violations by simply summing them and subtracting from 1, which is the maximum value for an agent's reputation.

To evaluate the reputation of a witness agent that provided false testimony, we have defined the term *witnessFactor* (also defined by the norm) that reduces the influence a norm has in the reputation of the agent. From our perspective, the violation of a norm should be more severely punished than false testimony. Equations 8 and 9 are similar to 5 and 6, respectively.

3.4 Reputation Types

Trust and reputation are context dependent [9]. If we trust a person when he is driving a car this does not mean that we trust him to pilot an airplane. In addition, if we trust a taxi driver when driving in New York it does not mean that we will trust him when he gives information about a New York address.

In order to take into account the context while evaluating the reputation of agents, we consider the context from two perspectives: the role played by the agent, and the service being provided. A person may have a good reputation as a taxi driver but a terrible reputation as a pilot. Moreover, although a person has a very good reputation driving his taxi, he may have such a good one when giving information about addresses.

To deal with the distinct contexts, we defined three different kinds of reputations: *local reputation*, *role reputation* and *norm reputation*. The *local reputation* of an agent, equation (10), is the one indicated by the average of the results provided by (6) and (9). An agent's *local* reputation takes into account all norm violations and all false testimonies in a given organization Org_n.

$$localRep_{Orgn}(a_j) = [defendantRep_{Orgn}(a_j) + witnessRep_{Orgn}(a_j)] / 2 \qquad (10)$$

Role reputations only consider norms that were violated while playing a specified role or false testimonies that were made while playing this role. Our proposed reputation model is capable of identifying social structures and evaluating the reputation of the agents according to those structures. For each role played, the agent has an associated role reputation. The equation used to evaluate a role reputation is similar to the one used for local reputations, but here we consider only the norms violated while the agent is playing a given role r, as depicted in equation (11). By using the information provided by role reputations it is possible to discover if the agent can be trusted to play a role. For instance, it is possible to know if the reputation of an agent is good while considering to pilot airplanes.

$$roleRep(a_j^r) = [defendantRep(a_j^r) + witnessRep(a_j^r)] / 2 \qquad (11)$$

Norm reputations focus on the violation of a norm and on the false testimonies provided while considering a norm. Norm reputations are independent of the role being played. For each system norm, agents have one norm reputation that is evaluated by the average of equations (5) and (8) as illustrated in equation (12). N_i is the norm being considered. By using the information provided by norm reputations it is possible to know if the agent can be trusted to provide a service. It is possible to know it a taxi driver can be trusted while providing information about the New York addresses.

$$normRep(a_j, n_i) = [defRepInf(a_j,n_i) + witRepInf(a_j,n_i)] / 2 \qquad (12)$$

3.5 Combining Agent Reputations

As stated above, we assume that large-scale multi-agent systems are composed of sets of organizations grouped in a hierarchy structure. In such systems, an organization can define several sub-organizations but a sub-organization can only be part of one super-organization. Each organization defines its own norms that must be obeyed by agents playing roles in it and also by agents playing roles in any of its sub-organizations. Norms defined in organizations are also valid in their sub-organizations. Moreover, a norm defined in a sub-organization cannot contradict a norm defined in its super-organization. Norms of sub-organizations can only be more restrictive than norms of their super-organizations.

Figure 1 illustrates norms defined at different levels of an organization hierarchy. Norms 1, 2, 3 and 4 are defined in the first level of the hierarchy represented by organization Org 1. These four norms must be obeyed not only by agents playing roles in Org 1 but also by agents playing roles in all its sub-organizations, i.e., Org 1.1, Org1.2 and Org 1.2.1. Norm 5 illustrates that sub-organizations can define their own norms. Norms 6, 7, 8 and 9 exemplifies that sub-organizations can refine norms defined in their super-organizations. As a consequence, agents playing roles in Org 1.2 must obey in fact norms 1, 7, 3 and 8.

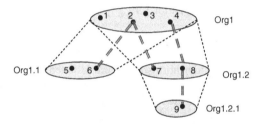

Fig. 2. Organization hierarchy

The reputations of the agents are evaluated according to the norms violated in the organizations where they are playing roles. The three reputation kinds defined in Section 3.3 (*local*, *role* and *norm* reputations) are used to evaluate the reputations of the agents in each organization. Each organization evaluates the three reputation types considering its own norms and the norms defined in their super-organizations. These reputations do not include the violations performed in their sub-organizations. In order to consider those violations while evaluating the reputation of an agent, three others reputation types are available: (i) $\text{globalRep}_{Orgx}(a_j)$ represents the average of the reputations evaluated in Org_x and in all its sub-organizations, as stated in equation (13); (ii) $\text{globalRoleRep}_{Orgx}(a_j^r)$ represents the average of the reputations evaluated while the agent is playing a given role in Org_x and in all its sub-organizations (if it is the case), as depicted in equation (14); and (iii) $\text{globalNormRep}_{Orgx}(a_j, n_i)$ represents the average of the reputations evaluated according to the violation of a given norm in Org_x and the same norm[1] in all its sub-organizations, as stated in equation (15). For organizations that do not have sub-organizations, for instance Org 1.1, the global reputations are equal to the local reputations, as depicted in equations (16, 17 and 18).

$$\text{globalRep}_{Orgx}(a_j) = \{ \text{localRep}_{Orgx}(a_j) + [\textstyle\sum_{0<m<=n}\text{globalRep}_{Orgm}(a_j) / i] \} / 2 \qquad (13)$$

$$\text{globalRoleRep}_{Orgx}(a_j^r) = \{\text{roleRep}_{Orgx}(a_j^r) + [\textstyle\sum_{0<m<=n}\text{globalRoleRep}_{Orgm}(a_j^r) /i]\}/2 \quad (14)$$

---

[1] Such norm is of course a norm defined in Org_m or in its (super-...)super-organization.

$$\text{globalNormRep}_{\text{Orgx}}(a_j, n_i) = \{ \text{ normRep}_{\text{Orgx}}(a_j, n_i) +$$
$$[\textstyle\sum_{0 < m <= n} \text{globalNormRep}_{\text{Orgm}}(a_j, n_i) / i] \}/2 \quad (15)$$

$$\text{globalRep}_{\text{Orgx}}(a_j) = \text{localRep}_{\text{Orgx}}(a_j) \quad (16)$$

$$\text{globalRoleRep}_{\text{Orgx}}(a_j) = \text{roleRep}_{\text{Orgx}}(a_j) \quad (17)$$

$$\text{globalNormRep}_{\text{Orgx}}(a_j, n_i) = \text{normRep}_{\text{Orgx}}(a_j, n_i) \quad (18)$$

Norms defined in organizations that are not in the same hierarchy do not influence the reputation of agents playing roles in those organizations. For instance, while evaluating the reputation of an agent in Org 1.2 the violations that this agent may have done in Org 1.1 do not influence its reputation in Org 1.2 but will influence its reputation in the Org 1 point of view.

4 Case Study: Cargo Consolidation and Transportation

To illustrate the use of reputation subsystems, in this section we present some aspects of the cargo consolidation and transportation system. This example is used to demonstrate the evaluation of agents' reputations according to violations of three norms from the perspective of two different organizations.

Cargo consolidation is the act of grouping together small shipments of goods (often from different shippers) into a larger unique unit that is sent to a single destination point (and often to different consignees), in order to obtain reduced shipping rate. Importers and exporters that want to ship small cargos may look for consolidators agents that provide cargo consolidation services to ship their goods.

An open multi-agent system approach is entirely adequate for developing applications on this domain because such applications mostly involve interactions between different autonomous partners playing different roles in order to accomplish similar objectives. This approach may also provide support for the automation of the negotiation between the agents looking for reducing the prices and the delivery time. In addition, such applications are particular, governed by several rules that are used to regulate the behaviour of the heterogeneous and independently designed entities that reinforce the open characteristic of the systems. Since these rules are adequately modeled as norms in governance multi-agent systems, we will use the cargo consolidation and transportation system to illustrate our reputation model.

In this business, exporters and importers frequently use standardized contracts called Incoterms (International Commercial Terms) [7]. Those contracts establish a set of norms that determine the obligations of the involved parties. In addition, a cargo and consolidation system is divided into several subsystems that deal with its different categories. Table 2 illustrates some of the norms defined in the (main) system (independently of any category) and in two different subsystems (Org 1.1 and 1.2). In Org 1.1 the importers are responsible for contracting the transports (or consolidators) and in Org 1.2 the ones responsible for contracting the transports are the exporters.

Table 2. Norms defined in the contacts

Organization / Norms	Ref Norm	Norm Power	Total Time
Org1 – Cargo Consolidation and Transportation			
01. Consolidator needs to deliver the cargo to the importer(s) at the determined location and by the established deadline		1.0	60
02. Exporter(s) need(s) to deliver the cargo to the consolidator at the determined location and by the established deadline		0.5	30
Org1.1 – Importers responsibility			
03. Exporter(s) need(s) to deliver the cargo to the consolidator at *the cargo terminal* and by the established deadline	2	0.5	30
04. Importer(s) is(are) responsible for contracting the consolidator		0.2	10
Org1.2 – Exporters responsibility			
03. Exporter(s) need(s) to deliver the cargo to the consolidator at *the cargo terminal* and by the established deadline	2	0.5	30
05. Exporter(s) is(are) responsible for contracting the consolidator		0.5	30

By analyzing the above norms we can see that both Org 1.1 and Org 1.2 specializes norm 2 while defining norm 3. Figure 2 depicts such specialization.

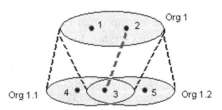

Fig. 3. Specialization of the norm 2 while defining norm 3

On the one hand, in negotiations where importers are responsible for contracting the consolidators, the agents play roles in Org 1.1 and obey norms 1, 3 and 4. On the other hand, when the exporters are responsible for contract the consolidator, the agents play roles in Org 1.2 and obey norms 1, 3 and 5.

Suppose that agent abc has violated norm 3 while playing role in Org 1.1 and in Org 1,2, and has also violated norm 5 while in Org 1.2. Table 3 shows the details of such violations. We will use this example to evaluate: (i) the global reputation of agent abc in the point of view of Org 1.2, (ii) the global reputation of agent abc in the point of view the main organization Org 1, and (iii) the norm reputation of agent abc by considering norm 3 and the Org 1 point of view. Those reputations are evaluated in the same day of the last violation, 25/09/2006.

Table 3. Norms Violations

organization	Violation date	agent	Role	Violated norm	Blame %	Relapse	confession
Org1.1	20/09/06	abc@platform1.1	exporter	3	100	1	False
Org1.2	24/09/06	abc@platform1.2	exporter	3	100	1	False
Org1.2	25/09/06	abc@platform1.2	exporter	5	80	1	True (0,3)

4.1 The Global Reputation of an Agent from the Point of View of a Sub-Organization

In this section we will evaluate the reputation of agent abc in the point of view of the organization 1.2. Since Org 1.2 does not have sub-organizations, the global and local reputations of the agents playing role in Org 1.2 are the same. In addition, since agent abc has never told a lie in Org 1.2, its witnessRep is equal to 1 and, thus, its $globalRep_{1.2}$ only depends on its $defendantRep_{1.2}$.

$globalRep_{Org1.2}(abc) = localRep_{Org1.2}(abc) = [defendantRep_{Org1.2}(abc) + 1] / 2$

$defendantRep_{Org1.2}(abc) = 1 - [defRepInf_{Org1.2}(abc,n_3) + defRepInf_{Org1.2}(abc,n_5)]$

$i)\ defRepInf_{Org1.2}(abc,n_3) = normPower^{rc}(n_3)*blamePercentage(abc,n_3)*$
$$remainingDays(abc,n_3)$$

$normPower^{rc}(n_3) = normPower(n_3)* (1/relapse(n_3))*confession(n_3) = 0,5*(1/1)*1=0,5$

$remainingDays(abc,n_3) = [totalTime (n_3) - passedDays(abc,n_3) / totalTime (n_3)]$
$$= 29 / 30 = 0,96$$

$defRepInf_{Org1.2}(abc,n_3) = 0,5 * 1 * 0,96 = 0,48$

$ii)\ normPower^{rc}(n_5)\ = normPower(n_5) * (1/relapse(n_5)) * confession(n_5)$
$$= 0,5*(1/1)*0,3=0,15$$

$remainingDays(abc,n_5) = [totalTime(n_5) - passedDays(abc,n_5) / totalTime(n_5)]$
$$= 30 / 30 = 1$$

$defRepInf_{Org1.2}(abc,n_5) = 0,15 * 0,8 * 1 = 0,12$

$iii)\ defendantRep_{Org1.2}(abc) = 1 - [defRepInf_{Org1.2}(abc,n_3) + defRepInf_{Org1.2}(abc,n_5)]$
$$= 1 - [0,48 + 0,12] = 0,4$$

$iv)\ globalRep_{Org1.2}(abc) = [defendantRep_{Org1.2}(abc) + 1] / 2 = [0,4 + 1] / 2 = 0,7$

4.2 The Global Reputation of Agent from the Point of View the of Main Organization

The global reputation of abc in the point of view of Org 1 (the main organization) is equal to the average of the global reputations of abc in Org 1.1 and in Org 1.2 plus the local reputation of agent abc in Org 1. Since abc has not violated any norm in Org 1, its local reputation is equal to 1.

$globalRep_{Org1}(abc) = \{ 1+ [globalRep_{Org1.1}(abc) + globalRep_{Org1.2}(abc)] / 2 \} / 2$

$globalRep_{Org1.1}(abc) = [(1 - defRepInf_{Org1.1}(abc,n_3)) + 1] / 2$
$= [(1 - 0,41) +1] / 2 = 0,79$

$globalRep_{Org1.2}(abc) = 0,7$

$globalRep_{Org1}(abc) = \{ 1 + [0,79 + 0,7] /2 \} / 2 \{ 1 + 0,74 \} / 2 = 0,87$

4.3 The Global Norm Reputation of an Agent

In order to evaluate the global norm reputation of an agent it is necessary not only to choose an agent but also a norm. In this section we will evaluate the reputation of agent abc while considering norm 3. The reputation of agent abc considering only the violations of norm 3 is evaluated through the average of the violations of norm 3 while the agent was playing roles in Org 1.1 and in Org 1.2.

$globalNormRep_{Org1}(abc,n_3) = [normRep_{Org1.1}(abc,n_3) + normRep_{Org1.2}(abc,n_3)] / 2$

$globalNormRep_{Org1}(abc,n_3) = [0,79 + 0,74] / 2 = 0,76$

By using the agents reputation it is possible to know, for instance, (i) if someone can trust a given exporter while negotiating cargos in categories where the export is responsible for contracting the consolidator by analyzing the $globalRep_{Org1.2}(exporter)$ that provides the reputation of the exporter in an organization what deals with this negotiation category and (ii) if the exporter usually delivers the cargo to the consolidator at the cargo terminal by the established deadline by analyzing the $globalNormRep(exporter, n_3)$ since n_3 describes this restriction.

5 Related Work

Centralized reputation systems used by eBay[4], Amazon Auctions [2] and Sporas [15] were developed in order to inform buyers about the performance of sellers in previous negotiations. Such systems represent the sellers' performance by attributing to each seller a single global reputation value. The system receives from buyers their personal evaluations about the performance of the sellers during the interactions. The system combines this information to update the reputation of the sellers.

The main differences between our centralized approach and those are:

i. The reputations provided by the centralized system are not biased by the agents' point of view. The centralized system does not receive the evaluations made by one agent about the performance of its partner. Our centralized reputation system receives testimonies about norm violations. The judgement subsystem [11] judges these testimonies and advises the reputation subsystem of their veracity. The reputation subsystem uses the verdict provided by the judgement subsystem to update the reputation of the sellers.

ii. The system can provide different reputations for each agent according to different contexts. Three distinct contexts have been defined, so far: global, norm and role context. These different reputations help agents to anticipate the behaviour of agents in different situations.

iii. Our approach provides the possibility of grouping the agents in several sub-systems that can together provide a more stable basis of support for the evaluation of the reputations.

As stated before, our reputation model is a hybrid one. To implement the decentralized reputation part any published decentralized reputation model can be used. The implementation of the decentralized reputation part does not affect the centralized one. In decentralized models such as [1], FIRE [6], Regret [9,10], and [13,14] agents are endowed with the capacity to evaluate the interactions and to store then individually. In such models the agents themselves use different information sources to evaluate the trust and reputation of others. Socio-cognitive models such as [3] where trust is considered an agent mental state can also be used to implement the decentralized subsystem.

The most important advantage of our approach is the use of a centralized reputation mechanism, implemented by the organizations, together with the decentralized one. The organizations can provide trustful and unbiased agents' reputations that are accessible by any system agent. This is extremely important when considering two situations:

i. Agents that want to know the reputation of other agents with whom they have had no previous interaction.

ii. Agents that want to update the reputation of partners with whom they have not interacted for long time.

In both cases agents can use the reputations provided by the centralized system. Based on theses reputations, an agent can decide if it wishes to interact with another agent or not.

6 Conclusions and Future Work

The most important characteristics of the centralized reputation system presented in this paper as part of a hybrid reputation mechanism are:

i. It is based on testimonies about norm violations. It considers uncertainty while evaluating the agents' reputations and these reputations are not biased by the agents' point of view.

ii. The reputations of agents are influenced by the norms they have violated. Different norms influence the reputation of the agents in different ways.

iii. Three different reputation contexts are defined: global, norm and role context.

iv. It considers relapses and the duration of norm influences on the agent's reputation.

Currently, when an agent has a reputation equal to *1.0,* three completely different conclusions can be reached: the agent has already entered the system, the agent has never violated a norm or the norms violated by the agent are no longer influencing its reputation. The centralized model should be revised in order to differentiate these situations.

In order to improve our approach it is also necessary to apply it to real case scenarios and analyze the impact of the reputations provided by the centralized system in the evaluations done by the agents about the reputation of their partners.

References

1. Abdul-Rahman, A., Hailes, S.: Supporting Trust in Virtual Communities. In: Proceedings of the 33rd Hawaii International Conference on System Sciences, vol. 6 (2000)
2. Amazon Site. World Wide Web (2006), http://www.amazon.com
3. Castelfranchi, C., Falcone, R.: Social Trust: A Cognitive Approach. In: Castelfranchi, C., Tan, Y. (eds.) Trust and Deception in Virtual Societies, pp. 55–90. Kluwer Academic Publishers, Dordrecht (2001)
4. eBay Site. World Wide Web (2006), http://www.ebay.com
5. Grandison, T., Sloman, M.: A Survey of Trust in Internet Applications. IEEE Communications Surveys & Tutorials 3(4) (2000)
6. Huynh, T.D., Jennings, N.R., Shadbolt, N.R.: FIRE: An Integrated Trust and Reputation Model for Open Multi-Agent Systems. In: Proceedings of the 16th European Conference on Artificial Intelligence (ECAI), pp. 18–22 (2004)
7. Incoterms Site. World Wide Web (2006), http://incoterms.atspace.com/index.html
8. Resnick, P., Zeckhauser, R., Friedman, E., Kuwabara, K.: Reputation Systems. Communications of ACM 43(12), 45–48 (2000)
9. Sabater, J.: Trust and Reputation for Agent Societies. PhD thesis, Universitat Autonoma de Barcelona (UAB) (2003)
10. Sabater, J., Sierra, C.: Reputation and Social Network Analysis in Multi-Agent Systems. In: Falcone, R., Barber, S., Korba, L., Singh, M.P. (eds.) AAMAS 2002. LNCS (LNAI), vol. 2631, pp. 475–482. Springer, Heidelberg (2003)
11. Silva, V., Lucena, C.: Governance in Multi-Agent Systems Based on Witnesses. Pontifical Catholic University of Rio de Janeiro (PUC-Rio). Rio de Janeiro - Brazil (2005)
12. Skogsrud, H., Benatallah, B., Casati, F.: Model-Driven Trust Negotiation for Web Services. IEEE Internet Computing 7(6), 45–52 (2003)
13. Yu, B., Singh, M.P.: Distributed Reputation Management for Electronic Commerce. Computational Intelligence 18(4), 535–549 (2002)
14. Yu, B., Singh, M.P.: An Evidential Model of Distributed Reputation Management. In: Proceedings of First International Joint Conference on Autonomous Agents and Multi-Agent Systems, vol. 1, pp. 294–301 (2002)
15. Zacharia, G., Maes, P.: Trust management through reputation mechanisms. Applied Artificial Intelligence 14(9), 881–908 (2000)

Towards Agent-Based Scenario Development for Strategic Decision Support

Maarten Mensonides[1], Bob Huisman[2], and Virginia Dignum[1]

[1] ICS, Utrecht University, The Netherlands
maartenmensonides@gmail.com, virginia@cs.uu.nl
[2] Strategic Development, NedTrain, The Netherlands
b.huisman@nedtrain.nl

Abstract. Scenario planning is a method for learning about the future by understanding the nature and impact of the most uncertain and important driving forces affecting that future. However, most scenarios, being mostly stories, lack validation, dynamism and fail to acknowledge all relations between actors, activities and resources. In this paper, we propose an agent-based model for scenario development that tackles these problems by specifying scenarios as agent organizations which makes possible the representation of the global organization strategy, and global goals together with the objectives and requirements of different stakeholders. As a concrete example of agent-based scenario planning, the OperA model for agent organizations is used to create a model scenario for NedTrain, a rolling stock maintenance provider in the Netherlands.

1 Introduction

The purpose of strategy is to create a good fit between the organization and its business environment. As organizations seek to adapt in a world of rapid change, strategic planning becomes increasingly dynamic and complex. This usually happens in situations that are uncertain and ambiguous, which means that there are multiple equally possible futures to be reckoned with. Strategic planning typically involves establishing or validating an organizational vision identifying corporate values, stake-holders and their goals, objectives and dependencies, and perhaps specifying critical success factors or tactics in support of the goals and objectives. It may also include identification of processes and value chain links or business processes for business process re-engineering [17].

Scenario planning is a method for learning about the future by understanding the nature and impact of the most uncertain and important driving forces affecting that future. It has been advocated as a suitable way to describe views of the future within the context of a business organization [21]. Scenario planning is a group process that encourages knowledge exchange and development of mutual deeper understanding of central issues important to the organization. The goal is to craft a number of diverging stories by extrapolating uncertain and heavily influencing driving forces. Scenarios are powerful planning tools precisely because the future is unpredictable. Unlike traditional forecasting or market

M. Kolp et al. (Eds.): AOIS 2006, LNAI 4898, pp. 53–72, 2008.
© Springer-Verlag Berlin Heidelberg 2008

54   M. Mensonides, B. Huisman, and V. Dignum

research, scenarios present alternative images instead of extrapolating current trends from the present. Nevertheless, classical scenario planning suffers from some pitfalls, one of which being the fact that scenario planning lacks validation tools that enable the evaluation of the proposed scenario, and therefore it will be difficult to reach hard business decisions based solely on scenarios, unless the scenarios are underpinned by facts and sound analysis [7]. Furthermore, being mostly stories, scenarios often lack a clear internal logic (credibility), dynamism, and fail to acknowledge all relations between heterogenous actors, activities and resources [18].

The development of organizational scenarios calls for models, languages and methodologies to represent interaction, roles and other concepts that character ize societies. That is, such models must depart from the global requirements and objectives, and an organizational view on the environment reflecting the orga nizational strategy [10]. Agent models offer an appropriate route for describing a complex system, by enabling its specification in terms of autonomous com ponents and their interactions. Agent-based models are increasingly recognized as powerful tools for simulating social systems, as they can represent impor tant information about the world not easily captured by traditional models [16]. Agent-based models enable to connect the (heterogeneous) micro behaviour of individual entities to different patterns of macro, or organizational, behaviour. In the same way as scenarios, agent models can be seen as support tools for decision making by proving powerful 'what-if' images of the future. Agent based modelling of organizations provides a natural framework for tuning the complex ity of the organization and its components: roles, rules, interactions, individual behaviour, degree of rationality, ability to learn and evolve [1]. Furthermore, agent models enable the identification of unexpected or hidden complexity that would never be revealed by traditional scenario planning.

Nevertheless, most traditional agent models are mostly concerned with the individual agents' perspectives. Those models mostly assume an individualistic perspective in which agents are taken as autonomous entities pursuing their own individual goals based on their own beliefs and capabilities In this perspective, global behaviour emerges from individual interactions and cannot easily be man aged or specified externally. However, in the case of scenario planning (as in the case of institutions and other formal organizations), the behaviour of the global system is leading, and structural characteristics of the domain must be consid ered and incorporated in the model. Furthermore, agent-based models have the capability to overcome some of the problems with scenario planning, due to the ability of agent models to represent dynamics and enable (formal) validation of systems. That is, the use of agent models enables the generation of meaningful insights and the evaluation of policies and strategies [5]. From the above consid erations, we have identified the following requirements for agent-based scenario planning and organizational modelling systems [13]:

- Support and direct the analysis of the organizational structure of the domain in order to determine society norms and facilitation roles

- Include explicit formalisms for the description, construction and control of the organizational and normative elements of a society (roles, norms and goals) instead of agent beliefs and states.
- Provide mechanisms to describe the environment of the society and the interactions between agents and the society, and to formalize the expected outcome of roles in order to verify the overall animation of the society.
- Provide methods and tools to verify whether the design of an agent society satisfies its design requirements and objectives.

Although the OperA model for agent organizations has not been developed with a scenario planning application in mind, but it aims at generic organizational modelling, OperA meets the above requirements which have been the guidelines to its development [10]. As such, we advocate in this paper that OperA can be used for scenario developement. Using OperA enables the formal specification and validation of scenarios, which, as described above, lacks is most of the scenario development approaches.

OperA takes a collectivist view on agent societies that places the global characteristics of the domain in the first place. The framework consists of three models that make the conceptual separation between organizational and individual perspectives possible. The organizational model describes agents societies in terms of roles, constraints and interactions rules. In this paper, we present a practical application of OperA as scenario planning tool to the development of strategy at NedTrain, a rolling stock maintenance provider in the Netherlands. OperA is used to develop a scenario for the organization of rolling stock maintenance and operational services for transportation along a decentralized, client-oriented view (trains are responsible to determine their status and request maintenance), replacing the current centralized view (planning based on centrally managed time tables). The agent-based scenario represents and evaluates the desired, possible future, situation and is used to guide the discussion around strategic decision making and adoption of change.

The paper is organized as follows: in section 2 we briefly introduce the OperA model for agent organizations, which is the basis for scenario development method proposed in section 3. Section 4 provides an overview of NedTrain and the goals this company has for the project. Section 5 presents the agent-based model for the rolling stock maintenance scenario. Current and future research on the evaluation of the model and its implications for the decision making process at Nedtrain are described in section 6. In section 7 we briefly introduces related work in MAS modelling and the specific features of Agent Organization design. Finally, we conclude and present some directions for future work in section 8.

2   The OperA Model

The OperA model for agent organizations enables the specification of organizational requirements and objectives, and at the same time allows participants to have the freedom to act according to their own capabilities and demands.

OperA considers agent organization models as having at least two description levels. At the *abstract* level, which can be seen as a receipt for collective activity, organizations are described in terms of roles, their dependencies and groups, interactions and global norms and communication requirements. The *concrete* level is a possible instantiation of the abstract organization, by populating it with real agents that play the roles and realize interactions [22], [19]. Organizational design starts from the identification of business strategy, stakeholders, their relationships, goals and requirements and results in a comprehensive (agent) organization model including organizational roles, interactions and planning rules, that fulfil the requirements set by the business strategy. Organizational instantiation is the process that accepts an abstract organization model and a set of agents, and resources and generates a concrete organization by assigning responsibilities and organizational goals to each agent. Organizational roles and responsibilities represent general, long-term guidelines while operational control involves specific short-term agreements among agents to perform specific activities for specific time periods [20].

The OperA framework consists of three interrelated models. The organizational structure of the society, as intended by the organization designers, is described in the **Organizational Model** (OM). The OM specifies an agent society in terms of four structures: social, interaction, normative and communicative. The *social structure* specifies objectives of the society, its roles and the model that governs coordination. The interaction structure gives a partial order of the scene scripts that specify the intended interactions between roles. Interaction scene scripts are specified in terms of landmarks, which describe how a result should be achieved, that is, describe the states that must be part of any protocol that implements the interaction scene in the Interaction Model. Society norms and regulations are specified in the normative structure, expressed in terms of role and interaction norms. Finally, the communicative structure specifies the ontologies for description of domain concepts and communication illocutions. The way interaction occurs in a society depends on the aims and characteristics of the application, and determines the way roles are related to each other, and how role goals and norms are 'passed' between related roles. For example, in a hierarchical society, goals of a parent role are shared with its children by delegation, while in a market society, different participants bid to the realization of a goal of another role.

The **Social Model** (SM) specifies the interaction scenes that describe the possibilities for negotiation of role enactment by agents joining the organization. As a result, the agent population of an OM is specified in the (SM) in terms of social contracts that make explicit the commitments regulating the enactment of roles by individual agents. Note that whereas the social structure in the OM describe organizational requirements and expectations concerning roles and their dependencies, in the social model, the requirements and capabilities of the specific individual agents that populate the organization are taken in account. Social contracts describe the capabilities and responsibilities of an agent within the society, in a way that includes the desires of the agent. The use of contracts to describe the activity of the system allows on the one hand for flexibility in the balance between organizational aims and agent desires and on the other hand for verification of the outcome of the system. For example, consider the case of two different agents fulfilling the role of Program Committee member: while one will accept the number of papers intended by the organization, the other may negotiate to review less papers or to get an extension on the reviewing deadline. Both fulfil the same role as described in the OM, but their specific contracts fixed in the SM describe their individual differences.

Finally, given an agent population for a society, the **Interaction Model** (IM) specifies possible interaction protocols between agents that implement the functionalities described in scene scripts in the OM. After all models have been specified, the characteristics and requirements of the society can be incorporated in the implemented software agents themselves. Agents will thus contain enough information and capabilities to interact with others according to the society specification.

Table 1. Overview of OperA methodology

	Step	Description	Result
OM	Coordination Level	Identifies organization's main characteristics: purpose, relation forms	Stakeholders, facilitation roles, coordination requirements
	Environment Level	Analysis of expected external behavior of system	operational roles, use cases, normative requirements
	Behavior Level	Design of internal behavior of system	Role structure, interaction structure, norms, roles, scripts
SM	Population Level	Design of enactment negotiation protocols	Agent entrance scripts, Role enactment contracts
IM	Interaction Level	Design of interaction negotiation protocols	Scene script protocols, Interaction contracts

A generic methodology to analyze a given domain and determine the type and structure of an application domain resulting in a OperA agent organization model is described in [11]. The methodology provides generic facilitation and interaction frameworks for agent societies that implement the functionality derived from the co-ordination model applicable to the problem domain. Standard society types such as market, hierarchy and network, can be used as starting point for development and can be extended where needed and determine the basic norms and facilitation roles necessary for the society. These coordination models describe the different types of roles that can be identified in the society and issues such as communication forms, desired social order and co-operation possibilities between partners. A brief summary of the methodology is given in table 1. In the next section, we describe how we have adapted the OperA methodology to the development of scenario planning models. The resulting adapted methodology has been used to develop a scenario planning model to support strategic decisions at NedTrain, described in sections 4 and 6.

3   A Methodology for Scenario Modelling

Multi-agent models have been only sparsely used for decision support and policy-making. However, the ability of agent models to connect heterogeneous individual behaviour to different patterns of collective behaviour, makes agent organizations particularly useful to model uncertain situations, such as scenarios, involving different parties with different expectations and needs [16]. Traditional policy analysis aims at efficiency or optimality of strategy given environment conditions.

Scenarios represent interaction among stakeholders and incorporate their different perceptions and requirements. Furthermore, in order to be legitimized in their eyes, the development method must ensure the participation of all stakeholders such that the resulting model integrates their particular perceptions, capabilities and requirements. The very nature of scenario planning, suggests that agent organizations incorporating intelligent adaptive agents that model the different stakeholders, are valuable to predict, understand and interpret on the one hand the collective behaviour of the organization as described by the scenario, and on the other hand the consequences of the change to the different component system and entities that form the organization [4].

Work on agent-based models of organization scenarios is very much in the exploratory phase and there has been so far hardly any methodological or tool support. Methodologies to support the structured development of scenarios are needed, that (1) enable the systematic analysis and incorporation of different perspectives, (2) assess the robustness of insight to the particular way agents and interactions are represented, and (3) guides and interprets results achieved [6]. Due to its strong foundation on organizational perspective, that exactly enables this incorporation of different perspectives, the OperA model is appropriate for the development of organizational models [11]. Therefore, the OperA methodology and framework was chosen for the construction of Organizational Model for NedTrain. Several approaches have been proposed to support scenario development. By making a correspondence between an existing scenario design approach and the OperA methodology, we are able to use the formalization and validation capabilities of OperA to scenario development, which is one of the aspects that lack in traditional scenario development approaches. In this project, we use a methodology derived from the environmental simulation field [2] and adapted to the OperA framework, consisting of three phases:

1. **Model construction:** during this phase analysis of the environment, stakeholders, perceptions and business strategies takes place, resulting in an OperA Organizational Model (OM).
2. **Model validation:** different agents representing possible stakeholder attitudes and requirements can specified to enact roles specified in the OM, resulting in different possible Social Models (SM) implementing different scenarios. This enables a thorough evaluation of the OM by the stakeholders, e.g. using role playing approaches, that enable each stakeholder to 'enact' its

role in the system, facilitating discussion on the impact and completeness of the model.

3. **Scenario animation:** corresponds to the implementation of an Interaction Model corresponding to each of the different possible SMs. Using computational simulation techniques, these scenarios can be animate to illustrate the activity and effects of the different scenarios.

The challenge of the first phase is to identify stakeholders, requirements and interactions, describe a coherent possible future that incorporates strategic changes with individual considerations. The resulting OM model for NedTrain is described in section 5. An important result of phases 2 and 3 above is the generation of common understanding of the future organizational forms (resulting from the chosen scenario) and realize consensus about its consequences for current activities. Besides its objectives of evaluation and refinement of the model, the second phase also aims at generating consensus among the stakeholders and ensuring their understanding and acceptance of the strategic changes. Finally, during the third phase, the effects of different ways of realizing strategy are generated and analyzed. In section 6, we look at how phases 2 and 3 are currently taking place at NedTrain.

4 The NedTrain Situation

NedTrain is a rolling stock Maintenance Provider, owned by Dutch Rail (NS). It runs 2 workshops, 5 depots and 25 service locations around the Netherlands, employing more than 3000 people. Clients include national, local and international Train Operators. Originating from a state owned monopolist, NedTrain now faces strong competition and has to adapt itself to the requirements of the European market. Changes in political and business environment made clear that the current organizational model must be reconsidered. Moving from state owned monopolists, railway companies are increasingly becoming competitors over a shared infrastructure and maintenance services.

At the same time the technology used for railway transportation is changing rapidly. Modern trains are composed of subsystems requiring various maintenance strategies. Some components are maintained at regular intervals based upon distance or time. Other components are only inspected at regular intervals, while repair or replacement depends on the individual technical condition. The second group asks for continuous automated monitoring and dynamic job scheduling to prevent in-service failures (failure during operations) and to minimize means of production. Since traditional railways are optimized for the first group of subsystems, the existence of the second disturbs smooth logistics fundamentally. Especially in the Netherlands it puts high pressure on rolling stock availability and costs, due to the geographic structure of the network and the locations of maintenance facilities.

The challenges faced by NedTrain can be summarized as follows:

– From rigid operations driven by timetables to dynamic scheduling of operational services and maintenance jobs triggered by events.

- From homogeneous processes for a single client to heterogeneous processes to comply with a number of different contracts.
- From top down planning and scheduling to dynamic negotiation between companies with conflicting interests.
- From rigid maintenance job allocation based on depot planning to dynamic negotiation based on train-centered automatic evaluation of technical condition

Operators uses different trains for their services. Trains and other rolling stock has been delivered by various manufacturers over time and represents different generations of technology. So Fleet management has to deal with sub-fleets. For older sub-fleets Operators bear full responsibility and can decide upon use and maintenance independently. In contrast, manufacturers guarantee reliability, availability and costs in more recent contracts. In return operators are obliged to comply with the maintenance plans which are supplied by manufacturers. Since sub-fleets may be contracted in different ways, Fleet management and maintenance providers have to deal with rather heterogeneous maintenance processes. This introduces an extra level of required coordination, in order to manage the various sub-fleets according to their contracts within the overall interest of the operator. Furthermore, operators must respect the agreements made (usually) with their country's government about the transportation, fixed in a Service Level Agreement (SLA), which includes agreements about travelling frequencies, rolling stock types, number of seats that should be available, etc.

Facing the complexity of managing dynamically (sub)fleets of individual trains according to condition based maintenance, different contracts and conflicting interests between Operators, NedTrain initiated a study to analyze future scenario's and to support strategic decision making using the concept of agent organizations. In particular, the project aims at supporting fleet management solving the question of how to allocate individual trains to operational services and to maintenance. The project reported in this paper is part of this plan, and was meant to evaluate the possibilities of MAS technology to solve these challenges.

NedTrain operates as a Maintenance Provider, receiving orders from Fleet Managers serving different Operators. In some cases NedTrain provides all maintenance for an Operator. In other cases NedTrain is one of the Maintenance Providers that is contracted by an Operator. Individual Train Units aim for an optimal mixture of reliability, availability and costs. Information from different sources as inspection staff, train borne control systems and track-side sensors, enables a Train Unit to determine its technical condition. However, extra coordination is necessary in order to assure the interests of the Fleet Manager. Usually the Fleet Manager has some kind of SLA with the Operator to deliver a daily set of trains and so is usually called Daily Seat Provider. That is, the behaviour of the group of intelligent agents representing trains, besides determining the best solution for each individual train, must also comply with the SLA of the Fleet Manager. Proposals for maintenance plans are then determined by the Train Unit through intelligent reasoning aiming at in-service failures prevention.

Given these plans of proposed maintenance tasks assigned to individual trains, the availability of means of production at the Maintenance Provider and the expected flow of the transportation process, optimal depot assignment and job scheduling will be calculated. Due to the nature of operations and the characteristics of rolling stock, scheduling becomes fairly dynamic.

The envisioned model of operation is not deterministic as its results are dependent on independent discrete decisions (by Fleet Management and Maintenance Provider) with a stochastic system (the set of Train Units). In this situation, statistic decision support is not usable. A simulation model is however a good analysis tool as it enables to represent operational management decisions. Moreover, an agent-based simulation model was chosen due to its possibilities to represent and relate heterogeneous, autonomous entities with different information and decision rules, to the global behaviour of the overall system [16]. In addition, agent models are able to represent the capabilities, requirements and objectives of different stakeholders, and provide as such a means for discussion and validation. In the following, we describe the (simplified) agent-based simulation model developed at NedTrain.

5   Organizational Model

As discussed previously, the aim of this project is to develop and specify reliable operation scenarios, resulting for the envisioned strategic changes at NedTrain. The project so far has focused on the development of an agent organization model representing the organization that results from the strategic changes. This organizational model is to be used in later phases of the project as a basis for the generation of different operational scenarios (this is described in section 6. To facilitate the study, a simplified operation model of the company was used. In this model, the rail network consists of two main national lines with their own depot each, a local line and an international line. Both national lines are serviced by commuter and intercity trains, operated by the same Fleet Manager of a single Operator (Operator1). Both depots belong to NedTrain. One of the depots has also contracted all maintenance of a second, local Operator (Operator2). The other depot may be called by a third, international Operator (Operator3) who also has the opportunity to use another, competing Maintenance Provider (MP2). This geographically simplified model of operation is depicted in figure 1 where Train types A, B, C or D are different train types served by the Depots.

We have used the OperA methodology [11] to analyze the NedTrain situation and design the organization model, OM, as described in the first phase of the scenario modelling process presented in section 3. Facilitation aspects of the case are analyzed at Coordination Level by considering the nature of the main activities within the domain. The objectives of the participants in the NedTrain agent organization reflect the interests of the stakeholders in the real world, which leads to complex decision making for maintenance and operational services scheduling because of two facts: (1) differences between interests of stakeholders, and (2) stakeholders that are not willing to share private information. Another reason

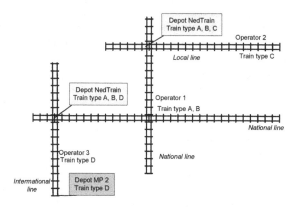

Fig. 1. Simplified model of operation

for complex decision making results from the increasing need of dynamically anticipating to the environment. The NedTrain case is characterized by two main goals: (1) scheduling maintenance, and (2) allocating trains to operational services. Scheduling of maintenance is defined by two different types of contracts: **Fixed Maintenance Volume**, defining in advance the daily volume of maintenance an Operator can make use of; and **Maintenance On Demand** contracts, defining the way parties can negotiate about the volume of maintenance on a daily basis.

With respect to relation forms, activities related to scheduling fixed maintenance volume and allocating the trains to operational services are organized in a hierarchy reflecting the traditional paradigm of railway organizations, that enable a global view on fleet level on the risk for in-service failures. However, negotiation about maintenance on demand follows a network structure reflecting the collaboration aspect between equal partners. Facilitation requirements resulting from these relation forms are the need for negotiation features together with a global control on fleet reliability. This is necessary to be able to allocate the most reliable trains to operational services and to determine the required maintenance on fleet level. The negotiation feature is needed to let parties negotiate about maintenance jobs. The following facilitation roles result from the Coordination Level analysis:

- **Notary:** It keeps track of a collaboration contract between agents.
- **Monitor:** It is responsible for controlling and supporting the contract.
- **Fleet Management:** responsible for a global view on allocation and fleet risk.

At Environment Level, the analysis of stakeholders and their requirements leads to the identification of roles describing the expected functionality of the society. The social structure results from those roles and their dependencies. For this case, stakeholders and their corresponding roles are as follows. The social structure describing roles and their dependencies is depicted in figure 2.

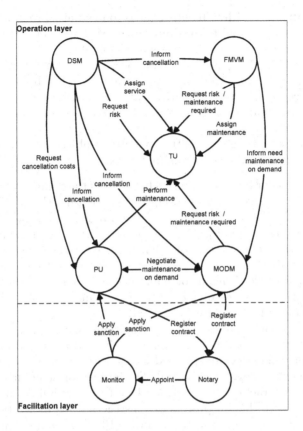

Fig. 2. Social structure

- **Train Unit (TU):** Its objective is to maximize reliability against minimal costs.
- **Daily Seat Management (DSM):** Its objective is to allocate Train Units to operational services according to the contracted requirements and to minimize the overall risk for in-service failures.
- **Maintenance Management:** Its objective is to maximize fleet reliability within the limits of the contracted availability by assigning maintenance jobs to Train Units. It is represented by two roles:
    - **Fixed Maintenance Volume Management (FMVM):** Uses the Fixed Maintenance Volume contract.
    - **Maintenance On Demand Management (MODM):** Negotiates with the Planning Unit to contract vacant maintenance capacity.
- **Fleet Management** (which encloses Daily Seat Management and Maintenance Management): Its objective is to supply Train Units to operational services according to the contracted requirements and against minimal costs.
- **Operator:** Its objective is to maximize profitability by providing operational services with respect to the SLA with the Government.

- **Maintenance Provider:** Its objective is to maximize profitability by maintaining Train Units and to maximize Fleet Management satisfaction by offering high quality, cost effectiveness and reliability.
- **Planning Unit (PU)** (which is part of a Maintenance Provider): Its objective is to maximize Maintenance Provider earnings by assigning vacant maintenance capacity to requests by Maintenance On Demand Management, taking into account the scheduled use of the contracted Fixed Maintenance Volume.
- **Government** (not included in this model): Its objective is to offer sufficient public transportation against minimal costs.

Finally, at Behavior Level the internal behavior of the organization is designed. For each role, a role description is specified that identifies the activities and services necessary to achieve its (social) objectives. In general, a role is described in terms of its objectives, sub-objectives, norms and rights. As an example, in table 2, we show the description of the role Maintenance On Demand Management to clarify the dynamic characteristic of maintenance. MODM serves the Operator in managing a variable demand for maintenance volume that is not captured within a fixed maintenance volume contract or managing different offers when more Maintenance Providers are contracted.

The social structure relates the role definitions to their dependencies. The dependencies between roles reflect the interactions of roles to realize their objectives. The dependencies are specified by interaction scenes, which capture a certain multi-agent dialogic activity [14]. The interaction structure describes the partial order of interaction scene scripts. Due to space limitations, we are not able to describe here the full process of constructing the interaction structure. A more detailed description can be found in [10]. The interaction structure is depicted in figure 3.

The schedules for maintenance and allocation to operational services are based on the technical condition of a Train Unit. The Train Unit is able to express its condition in terms of a risk value for in-service failure (operational risk) and to determine the required maintenance, both deduced from the technical condition. Based on this information schedules are created. DSM allocates the operational services to the Train Units in a hierarchical fashion (where DSM has control over the assignments) on the basis of the lowest operational risks and with respect to the operational time table (scene *Allocate Services*). FMVM determines which maintenance tasks are scheduled for the entire fleet also on the basis of a hierarchical relation (scene *Assign Fixed Maintenance Volume*). Scheduling maintenance on demand requires negotiating between the PU and MODM, by which the PU represents the interests of the Maintenance Provider (increase turnover by extending profitable maintenance volume) and the MODM represents the interests of the Operator (increase reliability with minimum costs). This is handled in the network-related interaction scene *Negotiate Maintenance On Demand*. The interaction scenes that follow take care of the compliance with the agreements for the negotiators.

The schedules are created some time in advance. The technical condition of the Train Units frequently changes. Therefore, schedules are subject to change and require a dynamic approach. This model includes a rescheduling mechanism. A new schedule is accepted if the associated costs for cancellation are compensated by overall better results.

In OperA interaction scenes are specified as scene script descriptions. To study the example of the MODM in more depth, the interaction scene *Negotiate Maintenance On Demand* is given in table 3. This scene describes the creation of extra production capacity. It is initiated when the fixed maintenance volume is not sufficient to guarantee a reliable fleet. Alternatively, for the operators that have not signed contracts in which the maintenance volume is contracted in advance, such as the international Operator in the example, the scene is initiated to schedule all maintenance tasks. The negotiation requires a common base to compare the bids of the different parties (MODM and PU). For this purpose, we introduced a cost factor. The negotiation mechanism that was chosen for this scene prescribes the buyer (i.e. the MODM) as the initiator of the negotiation.

Behavior Level design results in the complete Organization Model for the domain. Due to space limitations, we are not able to present the complete model, but present examples of relevant role and scene script descriptions. The design of

Table 2. Example of a role: MODM

Role: Maintenance On Demand Management	
Objectives	Maximize fleet reliability by assigning maintenance jobs to TU by negotiating with PU to contract vacant maintenance capacity
Sub-objectives	Determine available Train Units for maintenance Request maintenance required Request fixed maintenance volume availability Determine need for variable maintenance volume Determine maintenance volume Request operational risk Determine profitable tasks Determine logistics Determine bidding possibilities Negotiate volume Schedule maintenance Register contract
Rights	Decide need for variable maintenance volume Decide negotiable maintenance tasks
Norms	**If** parties have made agreements about maintenance volume **then** MODM **is** obliged **to do** register agreements with notary **If** offer is profitable **then** MODM **is** permitted **to do** accept offer **If** DSM cancels maintenance **then** MODM **is** obliged **to do** comply with cancellation **and** determine new need variable volume

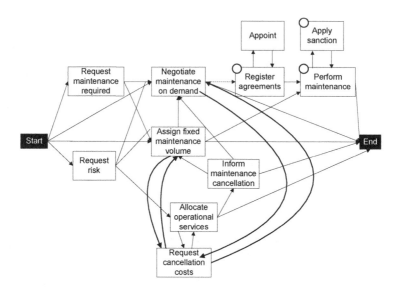

Fig. 3. Interaction structure

the Social and Interaction Models are the next steps in the OperA methodology, corresponding to phases 2 and 3 in the scenario development framework proposed in section 3. In the following section, we will describe the second and third phases of the methodology for scenario modelling for the NetTrain case.

6   Model Validation and Animation

According to the scenario development model presented in section 3, the model construction phase (1) is followed by the phases model validation (2) and scenario animation (3). The **validation phase** involves a thorough analysis of the model and its components. This verification is supported by the formal semantics of OperA models, which is based on the LCR logic [12]. At the present, we are working on tools that support the (semi) automatic verification of OperA models, but for the project reported in this paper, verification has been done by hand.

Furthermore, it is necessary to provide a means to analyze the perceptions and interactions of the different stakeholders and to convert the envisioned future into common knowledge and shared goals. The model described in section 5, was used to promote the awareness of stakeholders for the situation forthcoming from the strategic changes. Even though, after strategic changes take place, all stakeholders will profit from the optimal value chain, the outcomes of change were not clear to the people involved. The model made possible to understand the complexity of the different roles and of the interactions between them, and the highly dynamic processes derived from the environment changes.

Role playing games have been proposed to decision making process and strategy change [8]. The role descriptions resulting from the organizational model can

Table 3. Example of a scene script: *Negotiate maintenance on demand*

Scene Script: Negotiate variable volume	
Roles	Planning Unit, Train Unit, Maintenance On Demand Management
Results	Obtain list of maintenance tasks scheduled by MODM, which a PU executes for a TU
Patterns	MODM obtains minimum reliability / availability **and** MODM obtains realisation fixed volume **and** MODM requests TU for operational risks **and** MODM determines need variable volume **and** MODM requests available TU for required maintenance tasks and decrease failure costs **and** MODM obtains track hours and maintenance volume for the maintenance tasks **and** MODM obtains logistic costs **and** MODM creates list of the most valuable tasks arranged on ratio **and** MODM determines first offer and maximum price for product **and** PU determines minimum price and counteroffer **and** PU and MODM negotiate until reached consensus or could not agree **and** MODM negotiates the valuable tasks **until** fleetRisk = minimumReliability **or** fleetAvailability = minimumAvailability **and** MODM is informed about rescheduling **and** MODM and PU register maintenance
Norms	**If** fleetRisk > minimumReliability **or** fleetAvailability < minimumAvailability **then** MODM **is** obliged **to do** start negotiation **If** fleetRisk ≤ minimumReliability or fleetAvailability ≥ minimumAvailability **then** MODM **is** obliged **to do** stop negotiation **If** offer is acceptable **then** obliged **to do** accept offer **If** PU and MODM agreed **then** PU and MODM **is** obliged **to do** register maintenance

support stakeholders to understand their expected future behavior and scope of action. By analysing their own role and its interactions to other roles, stakeholder came up with many different possible interaction scenarios. For instance, from the perspective of a Maintenance Provider, it is important to understand the difference between scenarios that maximalize fixed volume maintenance, or maximalize on demand maintenance, or scenarios in which they are free to buy and sell each others' maintenance quotes. This will result in different sceanrio instances of the maintenance model described in section 5 by varying the objectives and plans of the agents that enact the different roles and by negotiating different ways to realize the interaction scenes. Role enactment negotiation is specified in OperA as a special interaction scene script that describes the possible negotiable aspects (such as deadlines, results, capabilities) and generates a social contract describing the activities of a role enacting agent. As any other scene script, a role enactment negotiation script can provide more or less interpretation freedom to the agents through the level of specification described by its landmarks. For example, the script for the role enactment negotiation for the Train Unit role enables agents, representing specific trains, to specify contract clauses fixing issues such as maximum waiting time, preference for depot, and possibility for phased maintenance (different parts at different moments). Another example, the role enactment negotiation script for the MODM role (cf. table 2) enables different agents to use different values for operational risk, profitable tasks, volume, etc.

The different scenario instances generated by the stakeholders evaluation of their roles is implemented during the third phase of the scenario development method, **scenario animation**, in which the agent-based model will be instantiated to represent those different possible situations. We are currently working on a simulation framework that is able to generate simulations from a given OperA model instantiation. By allowing populations of agents to negotiate different parameters, different scenarios are achieved. For instance, a possible scenario aims at minimizing cost and optimizing maintenance planning, while giving a lower priority to reliability. That is, what happens if we try to plan maintenance to optimize the use of depots, if this means that trains will in some cases have to operate at higher risk levels? Another scenario considers the case in which risk must be minimized even if this means higher operation costs due to non-optimal use of depots, or recurse to competitor maintenance providers.

Unpredictability of maintenance jobs to be executed will become manifest as technical advances enable trains to sense more aspects of their state, and economical pressures demand longer operation of rolling stock or better allocation of depots. By analyzing the results of the different scenarios, decision makers at NedTrain will be able to discuss and measure the effects of different strategic choices derived from these changes. For instance, if the volume of the Maintenance Provider's means of production equals the average demand by the Fleet Managers, variations in the volume of maintenance jobs over time result in waiting queues of rolling stock in front of the depots. Therefore the fleet availability decreases. The Fleet Management has to choose between two unwanted effects: To accept lower operational capacity or higher investments in rolling stock. On the other hand, asking for high fleet availability by Fleet Management can only be answered by introducing peak capacity of production means at the Maintenance Provider. This effect is amplified by the growing length of expensive train sets. Capital costs of the operator and the costs of maintenance are communicating vessels. These are issues represented in the scenario described in section 5. However, the consequences of this strategic move are difficult to understand and even more to adapt to, which results in reluctance by different parties to adjust.

7   Related Work on MAS Models

A *multi-agent system* (MAS) is commonly defined as a system composed of several agents, capable of mutual interaction. However, the exact nature of the agents and their interaction can vary greatly across different existing models.

In fact, even if autonomy is commonly accepted as a defining characteristic of agents, current definitions differ in terms of characteristics such as intelligence, rationality, sociability or mobility. Furthermore, the organization of a MAS is also assumed in different ways. Some approaches, see organization as a feature that should be *designed* to exhibit specific characteristics, whereas others see organization as an *emergent* property of the system. Models of agent systems, as well of any other (distributed) system, are based on the assumption that there is a system which behavior and functionality can be controlled, and an external world (the environment) which is largely uncontrolled. When developing distributed systems, engineers are faced with two basic types of designs with respect to interaction between system components and environment. On the one hand, design can be realized by specifying the individual components and their possible interactions and on the other hand, models are achieved by fully specifying the coordination context and the roles of the entities in the domain. The first design type is the one followed by most existing AOSE (Agent Oriented Software Engineering) methodologies, resulting in MAS systems composed of specific agents designed to the purpose of the application on hand. Following the second type, agent organizations and institutions can be modelled that fully adhere to certain global objectives and requirements without the need to control the specific agents in the system. That is, Agent Organization modelling differs from traditional MAS modelling by integrating organizational and individual perspectives into one model and enabling dynamic adaptation to organizational and environment changes [10].

Existing MAS design methodologies such as Tropos [3] or Gaia [23] consider specific agents as being explicit to be part the model. Design starts therefore from the analysis of the overall system, while the resulting software consists mainly (if not exclusively) of the agents, together with a communication (messaging) infrastructure. The main concepts that are used in these methodologies center around goals, plans and interaction protocols. Although organizational concepts like "roles" are used, they have a different meaning in this context. They refer to specific types of functionalities that can be bundled into agent types. Some of these methodologies provide a graphical design tool for MAS models and support semi-automatic generation of agents.

Methodologies for agent organizations, such as OperA [11] or MOISE+ [15] acknowledge the concept of organization as first class entity. In this context roles are seen as positions in an organizational structure that can be fulfilled by agents. Important is the balance between the organizational goal and the goals of the agents (or global, system goal vs. local goals). OperA clearly distinguishes between the concept of role (specified in the OM) and the concept of agent (as a role enacting entity as described in the SM). This enables the abstraction from specific agents in the model, makes it more relevant for the development of scenarios and other organizational models. Besides the fact that OperA models are explicitly geared to the development of agent organizations, the fact that OperA is funded on a formal representation, presents an advantage over e.g. Tropos. This formal semantics enable the formal verification of OperA models in terms of completeness (e.g. are the specified roles sufficient to eventually achieve the organizational goals) and liveliness (e.g. successful termination of interaction scenes)[1]. Space limitations do not allow us to extend here the discussion of related work on Agent-oriented Software Engineering frameworks. Such an extended comparison has been reported in [9].

8   Conclusions

In order to achieve rich scenarios, it is important to be able to represent multiple and contrasting viewpoints. OperA enables to represent many different populations of agents for the same organization. Organization being specified in the OM and different populations in the SM and IM. This means that organization scenarios can be animated to study instantiations based on different priorities and capabilities of the stakeholders. For example, the needs and goals of the Operators (optimal planning of train units) are often in conflict with those of the Maintenance Provider (constant, well balanced workload at the depots). Furthermore, agent models have proved to be useful tools to involve stakeholders in a collective design on management plans [16,2].

At the present, we have fully specified the organizational model of the agent-based scenario at NedTrain. This model has increased the awareness of the different stakeholders to the consequences of the strategic changes taking place, and to lead the decision-making process, as described in section 6. A follow up to this project will result in an implemented agent-based scenario simulation system for the model described in this paper. In this system, the different visions of the future, can be visualized and analyzed by weighting differently the priorities of each stakeholder.

The results of application of the agent-based scenario planning methodology at NedTrain demonstrate the validity of the use of agent models as specification tool for organization systems, as well as a basis for discussion, validation and acceptance of strategic changes. Future work will concentrate on generalizing the results obtained at NedTrain to other scenario planing situations. The method must be further applied to other domains, tested and refined in order to be able to draw wider conclusions. This project also served as an evaluation of the possibilities of agent modelling and agent technology for the system needs at NedTrain. From the experience so far, agent technology will be a likely option at NedTrain for the support of the implementation of real life planning prototypes.

References

1. Bonabeau, E.: Agent-based modeling: Methods and techniques for simulating human systems. PNAS 99(3), 7280–7287 (2002)
2. Bousquet, F., et al.: Multi-agent systems and role games: collective learning processes for ecosystem management. In: Bousquet, F. (ed.) Complexity and ecosystem management: The theory and practice of multiagent systems, Edward Elgar, pp. 248–285 (2002)

---

[1] See [10] for the formal semantics of OperA.

3. Bresciani, P., Giorgini, P., Giunchiglia, F., Mylopoulos, J., Perini, A.: Tropos: An agent-oriented software development methodology. Journal of Autonomous Agents and Multi-Agent Systems 8, 203–236 (2004)
4. Carley, K., Lee, J., Krackhardt, D.: Destabilizing networks. Connections 24(3), 79–92 (2002)
5. Carley, K.: Computational organization science: a new frontier. PNAS 99(3), 7257–7262 (2002)
6. Chang, M.-H., Harrington Jr., J.E.: Agent-based models of organizations. Handbook of Computational Economics II (2006)
7. Chermack, T.J.: A theoretical model of scenario planning. Human Resource Development Review 3(4), 301–325 (2004)
8. D'Aquino, P., Le Page, C., Bousquet, F., Bah, A.: Using self-designed role-playing games and a multi-agent system to empower a local decision-making process for land use management: The selfcormas experiment in senegal. Journal of Artificial Societies and Social Simulation 6
9. Dastani, M., Hulstijn, J., Dignum, F., Meyer, J.: Issues in multiagent system development. In: Kudenko, D., Kazakov, D., Alonso, E. (eds.) Adaptive Agents and Multi-Agent Systems II. LNCS (LNAI), vol. 3394, pp. 922–929. Springer, Heidelberg (2005)
10. Dignum, V.: A Model for Organizational Interaction: based on Agents, founded in Logic. SIKS Dissertation Series, -1. Utrecht University, 2004. PhD Thesis (2004)
11. Dignum, V., Dignum, F., Meyer, J.J.: An agent-mediated approach to the support of knowledge sharing in organizations. Knowledge Engineering Review 19(2), 147–174 (2004)
12. Dignum, V., Meyer, J.J., Dignum, F., Weigand, H.: Formal specification of interaction in agent societies. In: Hinchey, M.G., Rash, J.L., Truszkowski, W.F., Rouff, C.A., Gordon-Spears, D.F. (eds.) FAABS 2002. LNCS (LNAI), vol. 2699, Springer, Heidelberg (2003)
13. Dignum, V., Dignum, F.: Modeling agent societies: co-ordination frameworks and institutions. In: Brazdil, P.B., Jorge, A.M. (eds.) EPIA 2001. LNCS (LNAI), vol. 2258, pp. 191–204. Springer, Heidelberg (2001)
14. Esteva, M., Padget, J., Sierra, C.: Formalizing a language for institutions and norms. In: Meyer, J.-J.C., Tambe, M. (eds.) ATAL 2001. LNCS (LNAI), vol. 2333, Springer, Heidelberg (2002)
15. Hübner, J., Sichman, J., Boissier, O.: S-moise+: A middleware for developing organised multi-agent systems. In: Boissier, O., Padget, J., Dignum, V., Lindemann, G., Matson, E., Ossowski, S., Sichman, J.S., Vázquez-Salceda, J. (eds.) Coordination, Organizations, Institutions, and Norms in Multi-Agent Systems. LNCS (LNAI), vol. 3913, pp. 64–78. Springer, Heidelberg (2006)
16. Lempert, R.: Agent-based modeling as organizational and public policy simulators. PNAS 99(3), 7195–7196 (2002)
17. Orwig, R., Chen, H., Nunamaker, J.F.: A multi-agent view of strategic planning using group support systems and artificial intelligence. Group Decision and Negotiation 5, 37–59 (1996)
18. Schoemaker, P.: Twenty common pitfalls in scenario planning. Learning from the future: competitive foresight scenarios (1998)
19. Sichman, J., Dignum, V., Castelfranchi, C.: Agent organizations. JBCS 11(3) (2005)
20. Sims, M., Corkill, D., Lesser, V.: Separating domain and coordination knowledge in multi-agent organizational design and instantiation. In: Proc. Agent Organizations: Theory and Practice vol. WS-04-02. AAAI (2004)

21. van der Heijden, K.: Scenarios, Strategies and the Strategy Process. Nijenrode University Press, The Netherlands (1997)
22. Vazquez-Salceda, V.J., Dignum, V., Dignum, F.: Organizing multiagent systems. JAAMAS 11(3), 307–360 (2005)
23. Wooldridge, M., Jennings, N., Kinny, D.: The Gaia methodology for agent-oriented analysis and design. Journal of Autonomous Agents and Multi-Agent Systems 3(3), 285–312 (2000)

Preliminary Validation of MOBMAS
(Ontology-Centric Agent Oriented Methodology):
Design of a Peer-to-Peer Information Sharing MAS

Quynh-Nhu Numi Tran[1], Ghassan Beydoun[2], Graham Low[1],
and Cesar Gonzalez-Perez[3]

[1] School of Information Management and Technology Management,
University of New South Wales, Australia
{g.low,numitran}@unsw.edu.au
[2] Faculty of Informatics, University of Wollongong, Australia
beydoun@uow.edu.au
[3] Faculty of Information Technology, University of Technology of Sydney, Australia
cesargon@it.uts.edu.au

Abstract. Most existing AOSE methodologies ignore system extensibility, interoperability and reusability issues. Ontologies have been found to play a significant role in facilitating interoperability, reusability, MAS development activities (including MAS analysis and agent knowledge modelling) and MAS run-time operation (including agent communication and reasoning). However, most of the existing AOSE methodologies do not provide support for ontology-based MAS development. In light of this shortcoming of the existing AOSE work, we have developed MOBMAS – a "*Me*thodology for *O*ntology-*B*ased *MAS*s". In this paper, as part of its ongoing evaluation, we demonstrate MOBMAS on a peer-to-peer (P2P) community-based information sharing application. MOBMAS is used by an experienced software developer, who is not an author of the methodology.

Keywords: Multi-agent system, methodology, validation.

1 Introduction

Ontologies are an explicit formal specification of a shared conceptualization [1]. They have been successfully used to enhance extensibility, reusability, interoperability and verify various products of software development e.g. [2-4]. In Agent-Oriented Software Engineering (AOSE), existing methodologies do not implement these important potentials of ontologies and very few MAS methodologies include ontologies in their workproducts and processes (as shown in the recent survey of existing AOSE methodologies [5]).

When AOSE methodologies use ontologies, this use tends to be confined to the early phase of the development (the *analysis* phase). For example, GRAMO [6] specifies how a domain model that includes goal and role analyses is developed from an initial ontology. Another example, MASE [7] uses ontologies to mediate the transition

M. Kolp et al. (Eds.): AOIS 2006, LNAI 4898, pp. 73–89, 2008.

between the goal and the task analyses. Our use of ontologies in developing MAS is perhaps closest to recent work in [8] which recognizes the role of using ontologies for verification of models during the analysis phase. Outside the analysis phase, ontologies currently are mainly used to express a common terminology for agent interactions in an MAS e.g. [9].

Towards enhancing reusability and interoperability of MAS components, Tran et al. [10] proposed a framework that supports the creation of methodologies supporting and making use of ontologies throughout much of the development lifecycle. To illustrate the use of the framework, an ontology based AOSE methodology, MOBMAS – a "*Methodology for Ontology-Based MASs*" [11] was instantiated that explicitly and extensively investigates the diverse roles of ontology in MAS development and provides support for these roles. It has an ontology-based MAS development process and ontology-based MAS model definitions. MOBMAS provides support for the following key areas of MAS development: analysis, agent internal design, agent interaction design, organizational design and architecture design. MOBMAS takes advantage of existing AOSE methodologies, by reusing and enhancing their techniques and modelling definitions where appropriate. It endeavours to combine the strengths of the existing methodologies into one methodological framework [5, 11, 12].

In this paper, we overview MOBMAS [11, 13] and demonstrate its use for a community-based peer-to-peer (P2P) information sharing application. An experienced software developer who was not an author of the MOBMAS methodology was its user. The domain has been chosen for its current importance and it being a common application area of MAS. The case study shown in this paper is part of a wider comparative study to evaluate how various software developers respond to MOBMAS. After we overview MOBMAS and its use in sections 2 and 3, we conclude the paper with a discussion of limitations of the current verification of MOBMAS and future evaluation work to address some of the limitations.

2 MOBMAS Methodology

Using MOBMAS, the MAS development starts with a domain ontology which is initially used to identify goals and roles of the system to index an appropriate set of problem solving capabilities from an appropriate existing library of capabilities. Individual ontologies corresponding to the knowledge requirements of each capability are then extracted from the initial common ontology, to provide knowledge representation and allow reasoning by individual agents. Those ontologies form the basis for an iterative process to develop a common communication ontology between all agents and verify the knowledge requirements of chosen capabilities. Individual localised ontologies may also require incremental refinement during the iterative process. Appropriate ontology mappings are needed between local ontologies and the communication ontology. The development of MAS using MOBMAS has five activities. Each focuses on one of the following key area of MAS development: Analysis, Organization Design, Agent Internal Design, Agent Interaction Design and Architecture Design (Fig. 1). The development process of MOBMAS is highly iterative. MOBMAS activities are detailed in this section.

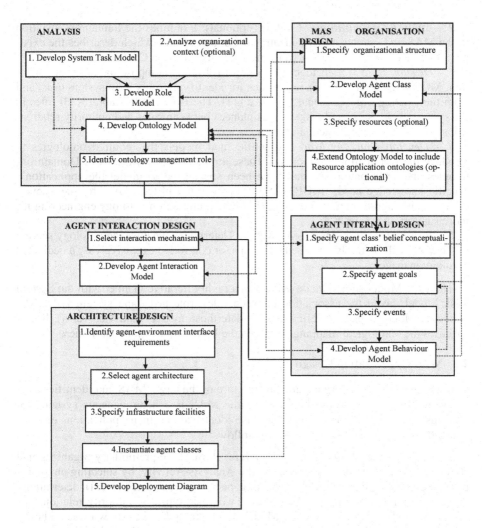

Fig. 1. MOBMAS development process: The solid arrows represent the flow of steps within and across activities, while the dotted arrows indicate the potential iterative cycles of steps. Models produced or refined by each step are shown in square brackets.

2.1 Analysis Activity

The Analysis activity aims to form a conception for the target MAS from the domain ontology and the system requirements, giving a first-cut identification of the roles and tasks that compose the MAS. This activity consists of the five following steps:

1 – Develop System Task Model: Takes as input specifications of the desirable functionality of the MAS and constructs a System Task Model showing system tasks, their functional decomposition, and any conflicts amongst them.

2 – Analyze Organizational Context (optional): Examines the human organization of the MAS and outputs an Organizational Context Model, which describes the existing structure of the contextual organization via Organization Context Charts.

3 – Develop Role Model: Identifies a set of roles that compose the MAS organization. MOBMAS offers various techniques for identifying roles from system tasks and from the existing organizational structure [11]. The Role Model captures all roles in the system, their associated tasks, acquaintances between roles and authority relationships governing inter-role acquaintances.

4 – Develop Ontology Model: Identifies and models the required ontologies to produce the Application Ontologies . These are basically a synthesis of Domain ontologies and Task ontologies that have been specialised to model the application's specific knowledge needs. MOBMAS offers some useful techniques for their development , although it refers the developers to the literature on ontology engineering for more support on this task.

5 – Identify Ontology-Management Role: Determines whether the ontology servers in the MAS will be freely accessed by agents, or controlled exclusively by a dedicated ontology manager.

The Role Model should be developed in a highly iterative manner with the System Task Model, given the association between roles, role tasks and system tasks. The Ontology Model is used to refine and validate those models (and vice versa). It also specifies the ontological mappings between the MAS Application Ontologies.

2.2 MAS Organization Design

This activity refines the organizational structure of the target MAS and identifies a set of agent classes composing the MAS. If the MAS is a heterogeneous system that contains non-agent resources, these are also identified and their applications conceptualized. Four steps in this activity are as follows:

1 – Specify MAS Organizational Structure: Refines the preliminary organizational structure of MAS previously shaped by the Analysis Activity, by selecting an appropriate organizational style for the MAS (e.g. peer-to-peer or hierarchical), determining the authority relationships between roles. Two basic types of authority relationships are "peer" and "control". The Role Model should be updated to show these authority relationships between roles, and to include any new roles and/or inter-role acquaintances (e.g. Mediator or Broker role).

2 – Develop Agent Class Model: Identifies agent classes from roles. Generally, roles are assigned to agent classes via one-to-one mappings, but multiple roles can be mapped onto a single agent class for convenience, taking into account modularity and efficiency considerations. The developer should determine at design time whether the assignment of roles to agent classes is dynamic or static; that is, whether instances of an agent class may change their roles at run-time or not. In this sense, MOBMAS recognizes implicitly the notion of *'participation'* that ROADMAP makes explicit [14]. The Agent Class Model is depicted by Agent Class Diagrams and an Agent Relationship Diagram. The former defines each agent class in terms of its internal constructs (e.g. beliefs, goals, events), while the latter shows the acquaintances between agent classes, instantiation cardinality of each agent class, and the resources wrapped by agent classes (if any). Both Agent Class Diagrams and Agent Relationship Diagrams are developed in an incremental manner.

3 – Specify Resources (optional): Identifies and models non-agent resources that provide application-specific information and/or services to the agents, e.g. information sources or legacy systems. The output of this step is a Resource Model that describes each resource via a Resource Diagram. Two basic dimensions for describing a resource are its type and its Resource Application Ontology. The Resource Application Ontology is integrated in the Application Ontology developed during the Analysis Phase. The Agent Relationship Diagram should also be updated to show newly identified resources and their connections with wrapper agent classes.

4 – Revisit the Ontology Model: This updates, if required, the Ontology Model to add ontologies that conceptualize the resources' data, domains and/or services. Generally, each resource should be conceptualized by a separate Resource Application Ontology. The developer should also specify the mappings between Resource Application Ontologies and relevant MAS Application Ontologies, so as to enable the integration of these resources into the MAS application, as well as to support the interoperability between heterogeneous resources.

2.3 Agent Internal Design

For each agent class, this activity specifies belief conceptualization, agent goals, events, plan templates and reactive rules. It consists of four steps:

1 – Specify Agent Class' Belief Conceptualization: Identifies which (part of) application ontologies in the Ontology Model are needed by an agent class to conceptualize its run-time beliefs. These ontologies are those providing the necessary and relevant vocabulary for an agent instance to formulate and interpret factual knowledge about its world at run-time. The developer should update the Agent Class Diagram of each agent class to show the name of these application ontologies.

2 – Specify Agent Goals: Identifies the states of the world that an agent class aims to achieve or satisfy. Agent goals can be derived from role tasks as specified in the Role Model. Different agent classes may pursue an identical goal if they are mutually in charge of a joint role task (c-f. Section 2.2). The Agent Class Diagram of each agent class should be updated to list the identified goals.

3 – Specify Events: Identifies significant occurrences in the environment that agents need to respond to at run-time. These include events that activate agent goals and/or affect the agent's course of actions in fulfilling the agent goals. The Agent Class Diagram of each agent class should be updated to list the identified events.

4 – Develop Agent Behaviour Model: Specifies how each agent class behaves to achieve or satisfy each agent goal. We consider two behavioural style of agents: First is *planning behaviour*, where Agent Plan Templates are used to define the input information required by built-in planners to formulate actual plans for agents at run-time. These input information include: the target agent goal, potential sub-agent goals (if any), actions, events that may affect the agent's course of actions, commitment strategy and conflict resolution strategy. The second is *reactive behaviour* where Rule Specifications should be documented to specify the "if-then" rules linking the events and the required actions. Note that an agent class may adopt hybrid behaviour. The resulted Agent Behaviour Model should be validated for consistency against the Ontology Model and vice versa.

2.4 Agent Interaction Design

This activity models the interactions between agent instances, by selecting a suitable interaction mechanism for the target MAS and modelling the interactions. It has two steps: firstly, to decide upon which interaction mechanism is best suited to the target MAS. Two basic mechanisms considered by MOBMAS are "direct" (where agents directly exchange ACL messages following interaction protocols) and "indirect" (where agents indirectly exchange tuples). MOBMAS offers guidelines for selecting between these two mechanisms. Secondly, to define how agents interact depending on the selected interaction mechanism. In the direct interaction scheme, the developer should specify the interaction protocols governing the ACL message exchanges between agent instances. The Agent Interaction Model in this case is represented by a set of Interaction Protocol Diagrams. For the indirect interaction scheme, the developer should model the exchanges of tuples between agents and the shared tuplespace. In both cases, the developer should validate the Agent Interaction Model against the Ontology Model and vice versa, because the datatypes of all arguments in the ACL messages or tuples must be equivalent to the ontological concepts defined in the application ontologies. This requirement helps to ensure that the semantics of all information conveyed in ACL messages or tuples are consistently understood by the interacting agents. The Agent Class Model should also be checked to ensure that all communicating agent classes share the same application ontologies that govern their interactions. Lastly, the Agent Relationship Diagram should be updated to show descriptive information about each interaction pathway between agent classes.

2.5 Architecture Design

This activity deals with various design issues relating to agent architecture and MAS architecture. Its five steps produce different notational components that constitute the Architecture Model Kind. They are as follows:

1 – Identify Agent-Environment Interface Requirements: Investigates the requirements and characteristics of the agent perception, effect and communication mechanisms, so as to facilitate implementation of MAS. The requirements should be listed in an Agent-Environment Interface Requirement Specification.

2 – Select Agent Architecture: Decides upon the most appropriate architecture(s) for agents in the MAS. We suggest various factors to be considered when making the decision, e.g. the desirable style of agent behaviour, style of control, knowledge representation mechanism or scalability requirements. The selected agent architecture(s) should be graphically modelled in an Agent Architecture Diagram.

3 – Specify MAS Infrastructure Facilities: Identifies system components that are needed to provide system-specific services. All necessary infrastructure facilities should be listed in an Infrastructure Facility Specification.

4 – Instantiate Agent Classes: Determines the cardinality of instances in each agent class. This cardinality should be shown as an annotation next to the agent class name in the Agent Relationship Diagram.

5 – Develop MAS Deployment Diagram: Describes how the logical MAS architecture can be actuated in the operational environment. A MAS Deployment Diagram should be constructed to show the physical agent platforms, nodes, agent instances at each node and their acquaintances, and connections between nodes.

3 Community-Based P2P Information Sharing MAS

In this section, we illustrate the use of MOBMAS on a P2P information sharing application by an experienced system developer. The application and its specifications are based on Klampanos and Jose [15] and Mine et al.'s [16] conception of a P2P information sharing architecture.

3.1 Application Description

Each human user is represented by an agent in the network to act on his/her behalf. This agent locates files and responds to queries by other similar agents. The collection of all these agents and agents assisting them in their tasks form the P2P community based searching MAS (Fig. 2). An agent representing the human user has access to a knowledge base containing electronic files that the user is willing to share with other users. Each file is identified by its title and type (e.g. HTML, pdf, music or video).

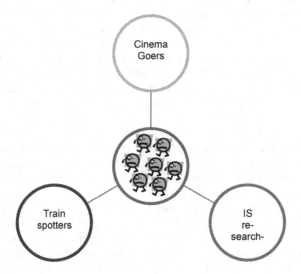

Fig. 2. The P2P Multi agent system is the collection of the agent assistants and any supporting specialized agents

As agents interact on behalf of their users, communities of interest begin to emerge. These communities may overlap (Fig. 3). A human user may belong to more than one community, for instance an IS researcher may also be a cinema goer. Agents develop an awareness of the communities to which users belong and use this awareness to fulfil their users' search requests efficiently and effectively, by interacting with the agents in the communities most likely to be able to serve their requests.

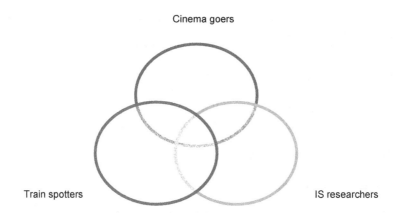

Fig. 3. A human user may belong to more than one community

A human user can pose a query to request files. Each query is made up of one or more keywords. The P2P system is responsible for locating sites where files matching the queries may reside, based on the behaviour of the users at those sites (as represented by their agents). The mediation between the human users is always done by the system and is initiated by the agent representing the human making the request. The agent of the like-minded user responds either by providing details about the files it can supply, or by refusing the service. When all responses are received, the agent combines and refines the results to compose a list of files that satisfy the query. The agent initiating the query can then select which file(s) it wants to download to the human it represents and initiates the file transfer process. After a successful transfer the knowledge base, located where the query was made, is updated to contain the received file(s).

For all agents involved in processing the query, their knowledge base is also updated with1 additional information reflecting the interests of the agent that initiated the query. This information is used in future queries. That is, as agents interact they develop awareness of the files possessed by their peers and which peers may be interested in the files that they themselves have.

At each node in the network, each user-agent keeps a record of its history of information sharing. The history contains two records: one of the past queries that it made on behalf of the human user and its respective responders, and one of the past queries received and their respective agent senders (acting on behalf of other human users). The former needs to be updated every time the user-agent receives a result list from the system, while the latter requires updating every time the user-agent replies to a query sent by the system. The history is used to produce short lists of candidate nodes for future queries, by calculating the similarity between the current query and a past query [16]. If no nodes can be short-listed, or if all candidate user-agents cannot provide the service required, the agent-user broadcasts the query to a wider circle of user-agents in the community, in order to identify new candidate providers. In a fully evolved P2P system, agents may use their knowledge about other users interests to request/negotiate for information from their peers when they do not know who has the files of interest. Any new providers are eventually added to the history, thereby expanding the user-agent's contact circle.

This strategy of information sharing can be applied to any domain. We limit our analysis to an application for the Movies domain. This simplifies the requirements of the system by focusing on one community, and details of how a community emerges or connect to another community (using a global ontology) is left out for future extension. Accordingly, the information to be shared amongst user-agents is assumed to only be movie-related files, such as movie trailers, movie posters or movie web pages.

3.2 P2P Analysis

The first step of the Analysis activity was to identify the required system tasks and their functional decomposition (Figs. 4 and 5). The optional step in the Analysis activity to investigate the MAS organizational context is omitted in this application. A preliminary Role Model was developed to show tentative roles in the system and their tentative acquaintances. The developer identified roles by grouping closely-related system tasks in the System Task Model. For example, he assigned all the tasks dealing with interactions between the human user and his representing agents to a "User Interface" role (Fig. 8). The tasks relating to user query processing and file transferring (including file downloading and uploading) were allocated to three separate roles, "Searcher", "Downloader" and "FileServer". The tasks relating to maintaining transfer histories are implicitly handled by the roles "Downloader" and "FileServer".

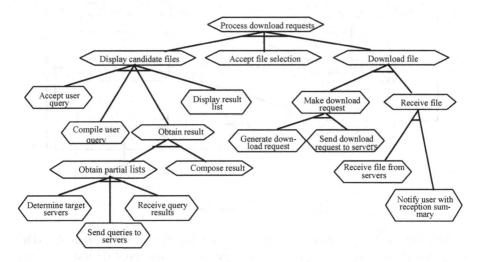

Fig. 4. System Task Diagram #1

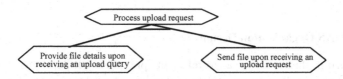

Fig. 5. System Task Diagram #2

An Ontology Model was then constructed to define the necessary application ontologies for the MAS. Only MAS Application Ontologies were initially examined, an ontology for conceptualising the information sharing domain is identified (Fig. 7). Resource Ontologies were identified later in the Organization Design activity (see Section 3.3) including an ontology for Movies information sharing (Fig. 6).

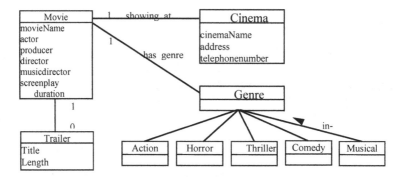

Fig. 6. Movie Ontology (from www.cse.dmu.ac.uk/~monika/Pages/ Ontolgies/)

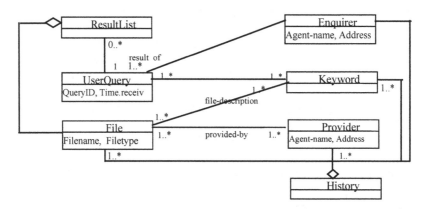

Fig. 7. Information Sharing Ontology

All agents in the system are expected to know about the two MAS Application Ontologies and they are not expected to change, so the developer decided that they should be stored at publicly-accessed ontology servers and can be accessed by all agents. No particular new role or agents was needed to manage and control these servers.

3.3 P2P MAS Organization Design

The first step in this activity was to refine the preliminary Role Model developed in Section 3.2 to specify authority relationships between roles (Fig. 8). Agent classes were then identified from roles. The Developer associated two roles "Searcher" and "Downloader" into one single agent class "Client".

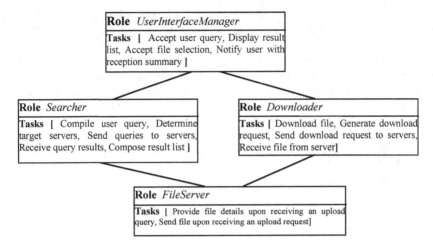

Fig. 8. Role Diagram, all roles defined are in peer-to-peer relationships

Remaining roles were assigned to respective agent classes via one-to-one mappings. A preliminary Agent Relationship Diagram was constructed to show the tentative agent classes, their roles and their interaction pathways (Fig. 9). The Agent Class Diagram for each agent class was mostly empty at this stage, since no internal details were yet apparent. Note that the explicit separation of the "Client" and "Server" agent classes in the solution helped to clearly model that each user in the P2P network can be both a client and a server. Each user can be represented by a "Client" agent at one time, and by a "Server" agent some other times.

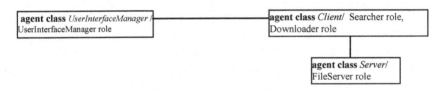

Fig. 9. Preliminary Agent Relationship

Non-agent software resources were identified: knowledge sources containing movie-related electronic files, e.g. web servers of HTTP files, directories of multi-media files. Each knowledge source needed to be managed and controlled by a specialized wrapper agent which provides an interface to the resource when requested by other agents in the system. Accordingly, the Role Model was extended to add a "Wrapper" role, and the Agent Class Model was updated to show the newly identified "Wrapper" agent class (Fig. 15).

The ontology conceptualizing each knowledge source was defined and thereafter added to the Ontology Model. Fig. 10 presents a Resource Application ontology for a knowledge source containing movie trailer files (which is one of the knowledge sources in the system) [and possibly many other domain ontologies for information sharing in a fully fledged deployed P2P system]. Mappings between concepts of this ontology (named "MovieTrailer Resource Ontology") and the "Movie Ontology" were also specified. In Fig. 10, the "Movie Ontology" is re-shown in grey (c.f. Fig. 6). Relationships annotated with predicate "equivalent" represent the semantic mappings between the concepts of "MovieTrailer Resource Ontology" and those of "Movie Ontology". Note that other knowledge sources in the system would have their own resource ontologies and would be mapped differently to the "Movie Ontology".

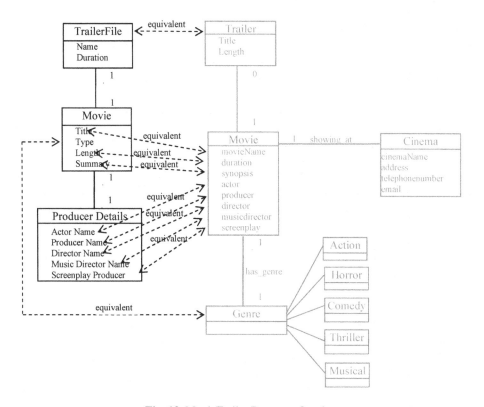

Fig. 10. MovieTrailer Resource Ontology

3.4 P2P Agent Internal Design

The internal design of each agent class begins with the identification of ontologies conceptualizing the agent's run-time beliefs. Agent goals are identified directly from role tasks. However, while role tasks were specified using imperatives, agent goals were specified as "something is achieved". For instance, the task "Provide file details upon receiving an upload query" of the role "FileServer" (Fig. 8) revealed an agent goal "File details are provided upon receiving an upload query".

Events affecting agents' courses of actions were also identified. The Agent Class Model, particularly the Agent Class Diagrams, was then updated to show the listing of belief conceptualization, agent goals and events for each agent class. Fig. 11 illustrates the updated Agent Class Diagram for the "Server" agent class.

agent class *Server* / FileServer role
belief conceptualization   Movie Ontology   Information Sharing Ontology   MovieTrailer Resource Ontology
agent-goals   File details are provided upon receiving an upload query   File is sent upon receiving an upload request
Events   Reception of upload query   Reception of upload request

Fig. 11. Agent Class Diagram for the "Server" agent class

An Agent Behaviour Model was developed to define plan templates and reactive rules for each agent class. The developer considered both planning and reactive behaviour for each agent class, depending on the target agent goal. For example, the "Server" agent class required planning behaviour to fulfil the agent goal "File details are provided upon receiving an upload query". The Agent Plan Template and Agent Plan Diagram for these behaviours is illustrated (Figs. 12 and 13 respectively). The Agent Behaviour Model was also validated against the Ontology Model and Agent Class Diagram.

Initial State: any   **Agent Goal:** File details provided upon receiving an upload query
Commitment Strategy: single-minded
Action 1: ValidateQuerySyntax (q : UserQuery)
    Pre-condition: true *Post-condition:* Query q is valid OR refusal message is sent to cl: *Client*
Action 2: ExecuteQuery (q : UserQuery)
    Pre-condition: q is valid *Post-condition:* File queried in q is found or no result is found
Action 3: ReplyToQuery (filepointer: File)
    Pre-condition: true *Post-condition:* f.Filename and f.Filetype are sent to cl: *Client*
Event 1: Reception of upload query q

Fig. 12. Agent Plan Template for the "Server" agent class

3.5 P2P MAS Agent Interaction Design

The first step here was to select a suitable interaction mechanism for the MAS. The developer chose the direct interaction mechanism using ACL, rather than "indirect" mechanism because he believed that the speech-act performatives provided by ACL can better support the high level of communication semantics required by this application than primitives provided by an indirect mechanism. The target application can also reuse many interaction protocols provided by existing catalogues, such as FIPA's Protocol Library [17]. An Agent Interaction Model was then developed to define interaction protocols between agents. Each protocol was represented by an AUML Interaction Protocol Diagram (Fig. 14). The developer also checked the Agent Interaction Model against the Ontology Model for consistent use of constructs.

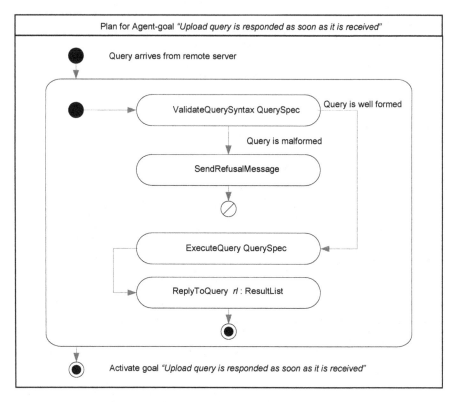

Fig. 13. Agent Plan Diagram (for the *Server* agent class)

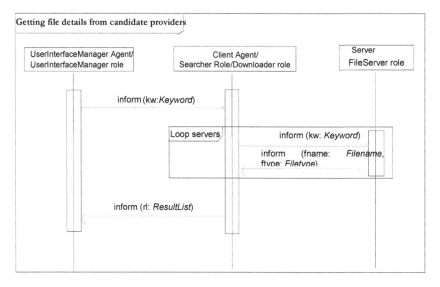

Fig. 14. Interaction Protocol Diagram

The Agent Relationship Diagram gets finally updated to show descriptive information for each interaction pathway between agent classes specifying the Interaction Protocol and the used ontology.

4 Discussion, Limitations and Future Work

We have demonstrated the first four phases of MOBMAS – a methodology for ontology-based MAS development – on a P2P community-based information sharing application. (Due to space restrictions the results of the last phase, MAS Architecture Design are not reported here). This work is part of an on-going evaluation of MOBMAS as reported in [13]. The MOBMAS methodology was initially reviewed and refined based on the feedback of two experts in AOSE. The refined methodology was then used by two different developers to design a peer to peer community-based information sharing application (this paper reports the results from one developer; the results from the other developer are reported in [18]). The feedback from the developers was used to refine MOBMAS into its final version. Both the expert reviews and test-uses by developers were conducted in a sequential order. Evaluation of the first expert/developer was used to refine MOBMAS before the second expert/developer was asked to evaluate/use the refined version. This sequential and independent procedure prevented the possibility of two experts/developers identifying the same areas for improvement, and helped to identify new areas of improvement that might arise from the refinement of the methodology after the first review/test-use. In addition, the refinements made to MOBMAS as a result of the second expert's/developer's feedback were also discussed with the first expert/developer to ensure that no conflicts of opinions occurred. A feature analysis was the conducted on the final version of MOBMAS to verify MOBMAS' ability to support important AOSE methodological features, steps and modelling concepts.

In both case studies the use of MOBMAS was conducted by experienced software developers, who were not authors of the MOBMAS methodology but was given detailed documentation of the methodology. Both case studies included developers responses to a detailed questionnaire regarding the usage of MOBMAS. Existing surveys indicate that they valued the step-by-step development process of MOBMAS and the provision of many heuristics and techniques to support each step.

It must noted that even with the set of case studies and the questionnaires, without comparing MOBMAS against other methodologies limits on the evaluation will remain without a direct comparison with other methodologies across a number of application types. We expect this next phase of evaluation to highlight in addition to its ease of use, its interoperability and its extensibility. MOBMAS supports interoperability for agents with heterogeneous local knowledge can communicate by sharing a common MAS Application Ontology, and by using this ontology to formulate and interpret their exchanged messages. This also leads to extensibility since new knowledge sources and agents can be easily added to the MAS. MOBMAS also supports reusability since the core models of MOBMAS are composed of ontologies and ontological concepts (namely, Agent Belief Conceptualization, Agent Behaviour Model and Agent Interaction Model), hence the design can be adapted to a new application by simply changing the ontologies involved. This feature of MOBMAS will be tested by attempting to reuse developed work products in significantly different applications.

Finally MOBMAS provided verification and validation: The steps of MOBMAS enforce extensive consistency checking amongst the major model kinds. For example, the Ontology Model is used to verify and validate the System Task Model, Agent Class Model, Agent Behaviour Model and Agent Interaction Model. Currently, we do not have a tool to enforce this checking. We are in the process of formalizing the current manual checking. Beydoun et al. recently in [19] completed a preliminary framework which checks the early requirements against role models. This will be usable as a stepping stone to develop a supporting tool (as suggested by one of the reviewers).

References

1. Gruber, T.R.: Automated Knowledge Acquisition for Strategic Knowledge. Machine Learning 4, 293–336 (1989)
2. Shave, M.J.R.: Ontological Structures for Knowledge Sharing. New Review of Information Networking 3, 125–133 (1997)
3. Uschold, M., Grueninger, M.: Ontologies: Principles, Methods and Application. Knowledge Engineering Review 11, 93–195 (1996)
4. Fensel, D.: Ontologies: A Silver Bullet for Knowledge Management and Electronic Commerce. Springer, Heidelberg (2001)
5. Tran, Q.N., Low, G.: Comparison of Methodologies. In: Henderson-Sellers, B., Giorgini, P. (eds.) Agent-Oriented Methodologies, pp. 341–367. Idea Group Publishing, USA (2005)
6. Girardi, R., Faria, C.G.: Ontology-based Domain Modelling of Multi-Agent Systems. In: OOPLSA Workshop, pp. 295–308 (2004)
7. Dileo, J., Jacobs, T., Deloach, S.: Integrating Ontologies into Multi-Agent Systems Engineering. In: AOIS2002. 4th International Bi-Conference Workshop on Agent Oriented Information Systems, Italy (2002)
8. Brandao, A.A.F., Silva, V.T.d., Lucena, C.J.P.d.: Ontologies as Specification for the Verification of Multi-Agent Systems Design. In: Object Oriented Programmings, Systems, Languages and Applications Workshop (2004), California (2004)
9. Esteva, M.: Electronic Institutions: From Specification To Development. In: UAB - Universitat Autònoma de Barcelona, Barcelona. Artificial Intelligence Research Insitute (2003)
10. Tran, Q.N., Low, G., Beydoun, G.: A Methodological Framework for Ontology Centric Agen oriented Software Engineering. Computer Science Systems and Engineering 21, 117–132 (2006)
11. Tran, N.: MOBMAS: A Methodology for Ontology-Based Multi-Agent Systems Development. In: School of Information Systems, Technology and Management, Vol. PhD. UNSW, Sydney (2005)
12. Tran, Q.N.N., Low, G.C., Williams, M.A.: A preliminary comparative feature analysis of multi-agent systems development methodologies. In: Bresciani, P., Giorgini, P., Henderson-Sellers, B., Low, G., Winikoff, M. (eds.) AOIS 2004. LNCS (LNAI), vol. 3508, pp. 157–168. Springer, Heidelberg (2005)
13. Tran, Q.N.N., Low, G.C.: MOBMAS: A Methodology for Ontology-Based Multi-Agent Systems Development. Information and Software Technology (2007)

14. Juan, T., Pearce, A.R., Sterling, L.: ROADMAP: extending the gaia methodology for complex open systems. In: First International Joint Conference on Autonomous Agents and Multi-Agent Systems (AAMAS2002), Italy (2002)
15. Klampanos, I.A., Jose, J.M.: An Architecture for Peer-to-Peer Information Retrieval. In: SIGIR 2003, pp. 401–402 (2003)
16. Mine, T., Matsuno, D., Kogo, A., Amamiya, M.: Design and Implementation of Agent Community Based Peer-to-Peer Information Retrieval Method. In: Klusch, M., Ossowski, S., Kashyap, V., Unland, R. (eds.) CIA 2004. LNCS (LNAI), vol. 3191, pp. 31–46. Springer, Heidelberg (2004)
17. FIPA: FIPA Query Interaction Protocol Specification (2003)
18. Tran, N., Beydoun, G., Low, G.C.: Design of a Peer-to-Peer Information Sharing MAS Using MOBMAS (Ontology-Centric Agent Oriented Methodology). In: Information Systems Development (ISD 2006), Budapest (2006)
19. Beydoun, G., Krishna, A.K., Ghose, A., Low, G.C.: Towards Ontology-Based MAS Methodologies: Ontology Based Early Requirements. In: Information Systems Development Conference (ISD 2007), Galway (2007)

A Methodology to Bring MAS to Information Systems

Emmanuelle Grislin-Le Strugeon, Abdouroihamane Anli, and Emmanuel Adam

LAMIH-UMR-CNRS 8530, Le Mont Houy, F-59313 Valenciennes cedex 9, France
{`emmanuelle.grislin,abdouroihamane.anli,emmanuel.adam`}@univ-valenciennes.fr

Abstract. Agents have been used to provide qualities of adaptation to the Information Systems (IS) since the Nineties. Apart from agent-based IS, existing IS can benefit from additional services provided by agents. We focus on personalization services, which aim is to give specific and customized responses to individual user requests. This paper describes a methodology to design the adaptation part of an IS with the help of a multi-agent system (MAS). An initial multi-agent architecture with an application-independent organization and interaction protocols is provided. On this base, the methodology proposes a guide into the design of the specific knowledge and skills that allow adaptation of the agents behaviour to the characteristics of the application, and into realization of the integration between IS and MAS. An example taken in the transport information field illustrates our proposition.

1 Introduction

Due to the similitude between architectures of multi-agent system (MAS) and distributed Information System, MAS have been used to provide qualities of adaptation to the Information Systems (IS) since the Nineties. Agents are used for the possibilities they offer mainly in terms of: distribution; autonomy; user assistance; information recommendation; information personalization including searching, filtering, content-matching, and presentation of information.

In a context of management of information integrating multiple modes of transport (e.g. train, bus, subway), we focus on the information personalization performed by a MAS. Above all, we study the possibility of adding a MAS having this task to an IS that is already used. So we have developed a method, described in this article, to design an Information Multi-Agent Systems, in the aim to specify and build a MAS linked to an existing IS.

After an overview of the agents abilities used by Information Multi-Agent Systems and the usual approaches in Section 2, we describe our methodology in Section 3. Section 4 illustrates how we have applied it to personalize transportation information.

M. Kolp et al. (Eds.): AOIS 2006, LNAI 4898, pp. 90–104, 2008.

2 IS Based on MAS

In our works, we consider an Information Multi-Agent System (IMAS) as a Multi-Agent System that is designed to make the kernel of an IS. The multi-agent approach brings facilities of adaptation to distributed, dynamic, open or evolving environments such as Internet and remote databases. Specific changes of IS environment are formed by its users. Adaptation to the users is another ability of the agents. They can perform personalization tasks in the aim to provide the information that is relevant to the user.

The behaviours required by the agents to achieve the tasks of the information system are described in a first section. The way they are organized to compose IMAS is described in the second section.

2.1 Agents Abilities in IMAS

The agents in IMAS share fundamental features, such as: the ability to communicate; social knowledge about the skills of each other; and the coordination methods used to achieve common tasks. On this fundamental and shared layer, the agents differ by the skills they possess. Indeed, three categories of skills are required to perform the information providing task (for a detailed classification see for instance [14]), in the aim to:

1. interact with users, i.e. to understand their needs and to adapt the responses from the system ;
2. interact with data sources, i.e. to search and access internal or external data bases and web sites, to retrieve and collect the relevant data ;
3. process the data, i.e. the retrieved information and the data about the users, in order to make the information match the users' needs.

The *interface agents* that interact with the users have knowledge about the available presentation formats, interaction material and software. The ability for the agents to be physically distributed on several platforms can be used to support various types of interaction. Via an agent, the communication with the system is also richer than simple request/response transactions, because the agent can include specific contextual information in the request to the IS and it can apply specific formatting to the response. A part of the research for better interactions with the user is done in the field of the avatar assistants, as, for example, the embodied conversational agents [5].

The *assistant agent* possesses generally further functionalities than these ones, taking part into the information processing and/or the management of the user profiles. One of the best known examples of this kind is given by Letizia [16].

The *wrappers agents* are dedicated to the interaction with the data sources required to know where the relevant data are and how they can be retrieved. The distribution characteristic of the agents is well-adapted to the distribution of the sources. Mobile agents can be used to migrate from one net source to another one. The pro-activity feature of the agents that run remotely allows to keep a useful activity even when the connection with a central system is interrupted.

Finally, information is processed by the *information agents* that are able to perform gathering, filtering, fusion, etc. The process of generating a solution can be made by integrating partial solutions. The management of the data about the users requires learning abilities to make the user profiles evolve progressively with the transactions.

In addition to the three categories of abilities above, there is another one that consists in mediating or even coordinating the actions of the others. When it appears to be too expensive (in terms of time costs or complexity of the required social knowledge) to make the agents interact and coordinate directly and themselves, a design solution is to use *mediator agents*, or even *brokers*, whose task is to create links between offers and demands of services [11]. The mediation activity requires some knowledge about the other agents' abilities and capacities.

The way these abilities are distributed among the agents in the IMAS results from a software engineering choice.

2.2   Software Engineering Approaches of Information Multi-Agent Systems

The global architecture of the IMAS includes generally the three main parts previously cited, related to (i) the interaction with the users, (ii) the interaction with the data sources, and (iii) the data processing. This is the common point but distinct features must be studied to go further in the description and to classify the SE approaches used for agent-based IS and IMAS. As it is said about recommender agents on the Internet in [17]: "[...]most systems have been developed following ad hoc approaches to satisfy specific application requirements." However, two ways of designing a IMAS can be distinguished, which are the functional and the distributed solving approaches ([10]; [21]).

The functional approach consists in reproducing the functional division of the system into the multi-agent architecture. Each agent has a distinct role, it is in charge of one of the three tasks described above. There is sometimes a fourth task which results from dividing the data processing task in two parts: a first one that is concerned by the users profiling and a second one that is dedicated to the information filtering, the content-matching, etc. The InfoSleuth [19] and IMPS [7] systems can be classified in this approach.

In the second approach, information gathering from multiple data sources on behalf of the users is considered as a distributed solving problem. The focus is put on the interaction between several agents in order to merge heterogeneous data. The RETSINA architecture and its application to web information in WebMate [6], and the systems BIG [15] and CIA [10] belong to this approach.

In our opinion, these two approaches are not really antagonist. They differ essentially by the way the abilities of the agents are distributed. According to the first approach, the emphasis is put on the roles and abilities of the agents, but these notions can result in various abstraction levels. Indeed, the system analysis can manipulate high-level roles and abilities, information processing for example, that can lead to multiple finer roles and abilities with the more detailed design of them, as information processing can be divided into information filtering, fusion and preferences applying, for example. Then these notions can be encapsulated as high-level ones in agents, or being implemented as detailed elements in fine-grain interacting agents. According to the second approach, the emphasis is put on the communication and the shared ontologies used to collaborate or negotiate. From an abstract view of the second approach, the distributed solving is realized by a set of interacting agents that can be seen, together, as a coarse-grain data processing agent. The realization of a common goal such as information processing results from a coordination of the agents, which can be achieved for example, with the help of distributed partial plan exchanges.

According to these two SE approaches, our proposition stands in the functional approach at a global level, but it allows the use of distributed methods by the agents to achieve common goals. Our objective is not to develop a full new IMAS, but to propose development of specific parts enabling the MAS to provide new functionalities to an existing IS. Our main objectives are on the one hand, to avoid ad-hoc developments as much as possible, and on the other hand, to facilitate modifications of the behaviour of the system in order to adapt to new requirements. The scope of this study is limited to the set of functionalities that concern the personalization of the information, i.e. the adaptation of the response of the information system to the users' needs and preferences.

3   A Methodology to Bring MAS to IS

The proposed methodology, called *PerMet* (Personalization Methodology), is aimed at providing personalization services, i.e. sets of particular functionalities, to IS by using the adaptation capacities of a MAS. PerMet is aimed at responding to a double adaptation goal:

- the adaptation to future modifications of the system. Especially, the idea is to facilitate modifications in the services provided by the system. Toward eventual modifications, the principle is to use the facilities the agents offer in terms of reorganization and adaptation of their behaviour. This is described in the first section below.
- the adaptation to already existing IS. The idea is to allow some improvement of the IS behaviour with only few adaptation of it. This is detailed in the second section.

3.1   MAS Adaptation

The adaptation of the system relies upon the MAS. In the present approach, the agents adapt themselves as for the quantitative adaptation and requires an explicit human intervention for the qualitative adaptation. The quantitative adaptation comes from the organization of the agents. The qualitative adaptation is done by the management of the agents' behaviours.

Organization of the MAS. The organization of the agents in PerMet can be classified with the functional approaches, because the agents are specialized in one specific and rather fine-grained task. However, they are not ad hoc designed, all of them derive from a common model that supports different instantiations of knowledge and behaviours according to their role. They can solve common problems using task delegation.

The agents are organized in hierarchies. Each personalization demand is processed by one hierarchy managed by a *mediator agent* that supervises and coordinates a *profile* management *agent* and a *search agent*. This one can coordinate the actions of several other agents, each of which being a specialist for some specific data sources (Figure 1). The hierarchies are created "on-demand": the fundamental hierarchy is copied every time it is required, and each of its clone is deleted when it has achieved its task. Consequently, at a given time, the system includes a set of two or three-level hierarchies, each of them processing a distinct information demand.

Fig. 1. Example of a hierarchy, member of the organization of agents

At a more precise level of description, a role is composed of "behaviours" that can be considered as fine-grain skills or abilities. In the above hierarchy, the three kinds of roles - the *Mediator*, *Profile* and *Search* roles - subdivide in smaller and more specialised parts defined as behaviours. Every time one of these "heavy" agents needs to proceed with one of its own behaviours, it creates an appropriate "light" agent, that have only this required behaviour. The light agents realize only the temporary activation of the heavy agents' behaviours. In concrete terms, this action is realized by creating threads on the fly to run the methods that implement the agents' behaviours. At the end of their task, the light agents kill themselves. If the agent needs a behaviour that is owned by another agent, it propagates its need via the links of the organisation. If no other agent have the required skill, it creates the appropriate (heavy) agent, by instantiating the predefined model.

This method is closely linked to the principles which are implemented in the multi-agent platform we use, the Magique platform [20], and is quite similar, concerning the development of IMAS, to the AMOMCASYS method, which allows to specify MAS for cooperative work [1].

Some roles share common behaviours ; some of them require the call to other behaviours. In the UML models, we propose that this need of a call by a behaviour to another one will be shown as a dependency link with the new stereotype "require" attached to it. The client and the supplier of such a dependency link are "behaviour" classes.

This model of organization and interaction among the agents provides us a common fundamental element, which is application-independent, to base the MAS development.

Management of the Agents behaviours. The qualitative adaptation of the agents can be performed in modifying their behaviours. For example, the learning method used to make the user profiles evolve is encapsulated in a behaviour that one or more agents possess. In condition of preserving its interface, the content of this behaviour can be modified.

Similarly, it is possible to add behaviours to specific agents or to retrieve behaviours in the system. As explained before, the light agents agentify the behaviours, thus their quantity and their behaviour can be adapted to the circumstances, like a MAS adapt its composition when it is required.

The adaptation of the behaviours is designed in the view to be managed by the system administrator. It is not a self-adaptation of the system but a possibility to make it evolve manually, according to new requirements. However, it is a dynamic adaptation because it can be realized at runtime.

3.2   Methodology

A main characteristic of *PerMet* consists in the separation of the MAS parts from the IS ones, in order to allow reuse and distinct modification of each of them. The design is then made in two parallel and independent phases: one for the IS part design, which is also the starting point of the process, and one for the MAS part design. The two phases follow traditional software engineering steps and they join in a third phase, resulting in the global representation that forms a "Y" (see Figure 2). The third phase that joins the results of the IS and MAS parts consists in the creation of the conditions necessary for the dialogue between these two parts based: on the knowledge for asking a service from the IS part; on the knowledge of appropriate services providing from the MAS part. The last phase is the evaluation phase that can lead to a new iteration. Indeed, the process is iterative and incremental: each cycle aims at including a new functionality.

The separation principle is not new, other approaches separate the IS design from the personalization system design. For example, the methods proposed by [13], [22], or [9], make this distinction.

The first reason for an approach that separates IS and MAS designs, is to allow to add easily new functionalities to existing IS. Compared to existing agent-oriented methodologies (see [2] for a detailed analysis of them), the position of this work is not to study how information systems can be developed on the base of MAS but rather to study how MAS can be used to enhance traditional IS. When the IS already exists, the design consists either in creating the MAS that will provide personalization functionalities, or in connecting it to an existing one that is already dedicated to provide personalization treatments.

The second reason for the separated approach is that the independence of the two design parts allows to enhance the behaviour of the system by modifying

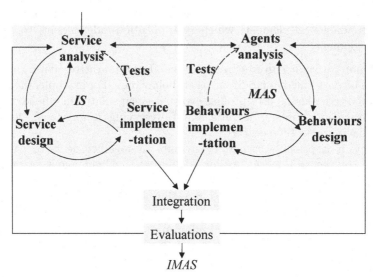

Fig. 2. Overview of the PerMet methodology to design Information Multi-Agent System

only the agents methods, provided that no change is done in the communication interface (it keeps the same in/out content). An integrated design would fix it or, at least, would make it difficult to modify.

The third reason for the separated approach is to facilitate multi-application personnalization. It should be possible, for example, to design a service that allow a Single Sign-On process, provided by one MAS to several distinct IS.

However, the integration operations this approach requires may be seen as an inconvenient. Indeed, the results of the analysis steps must be coherent, a work must be done in order to precise which kinds of services are expected from the IS side and, conversely, which ones can really be offered by the MAS. The aim is to ensure that the IS will send the data required by the MAS and vice-versa, the data the IS get from the MAS must fulfil its needs and must be included in the information process the right way. Then, this approach requires an integration step to detail the communication between both parts. The technologies exist that enable the data exchange between them, like the web services standards.

It is also important to notice that the method does not guide the full development of the IS and the MAS. It is focused on the steps which are specific to the design of the personalization functionalities as improvements made to an existing IS. The MAS is not really developed from scratch as we give the fundamental organization and agent models described in section 3.1. The design work consists in adapting the models to the particular application requirements. The AUML notation [3] is used to describe the system at the different design steps, with one additional dependency stereotype (≪ require ≫), used to represent that one agent behaviour requires the execution of another behaviour (see example in part 4).

The specific steps to design the IS part of the system concern the service that will be added to the IS. The notion of service differs here from the one described in the Gaia methodology [23] by the level at which it is used. In PerMet, a service is defined at a global level, as a global functionality provided by the MAS, whereas in Gaia, a service is linked to a specific role. From the IS side, the goal is to analyse the particular requirements related to this service and to enable its integration to the existing elements by specific developments or modifications.

Service analysis. The objective of this step is to analyse the functionalities of the system, taking into account the specific requirements of the IS users in terms of personalized services. This analysis is going then to pilot the symmetrical step of analysis in the agents part of the design. The data that will be exchanged between the IS and the MAS are also specified during this step. The output of this step is the specification of the expected service taking into account the personalization actions performed by the MAS.

Service design. On the base of the above specification, the aim is to detail the architecture of the system, to do technical choices, to design the user interface, etc. In the case of the adaptation of an existing service, the main point is the design of the user interface. The output of this step is a set of models describing the modification or the development that will be realized in the IS to integrate the new service.

Service implementation. During this step, the service is developed according to the conceptual models defined during Service Design step. Tests of service can be made on the base of data samples. The output of this step is the software of the service.

The base of the multi-agent organization is provided, as described above. The analysis steps of the methodology consists in the specification of the roles played by the agents, and in the application dependent adjustment of their interactions and behaviours. Our proposition is driven by the underlying hierarchical organization and interaction model previously described. The IS, the data sources and the users form the environment of the MAS. The specific steps to design the MAS are the following.

Agents analysis. The aim in this step is to model the agents that will be useful for the personalization required by the users. It consists mainly in describing the tasks of the MAS and to specify the related roles of the agents to which they are assigned. The specification must detail, for each role, the goals, skills and knowledge of the agents. We propose to start with the three categories of tasks described in Part 2.1: interaction with the users, interaction with the data sources and data processing. The agents prototypes being given, the work consists in adapting them to the specific needs of the IMAS (see the example given in Part 4). The output of this step is the specification of the agent models for the defined service. When it seems necessary, it is then possible to loop back toward the Service Analysis to propose additional functionalities.

Behaviour design. It concerns the design of the methods and knowledge to achieve the expected behaviour for each agent model specified in the previous step. The aim is to detail what each agent model must be able to do and what it must know in order to perform its task. The interaction protocols are written in this step. Then the technical solutions regarding to each behaviour must be studied. The output of this step is the agents' detailed contents and the activity representations, including the interaction models.

Behaviour implementation. The behaviours are realized and tested during this step. The agents are created and deployed. The behaviour of the agents and their interaction are tested.

Once the service and the agents are implemented, they must communicate with each others. The goal of the next step is to create the conditions for this communication.

Integration. It is the step of the integration of the IS and the MAS to obtain the IMAS. The objective is to create the required links to allow the IS and the MAS to communicate and to exchange data. We propose to use the web services paradigm to generate the communication link between them. From the IS side, an application interface must be developed to be able to use the services that are proposed by the MAS.

Evaluation. In the last step, final evaluations are performed, with possible back influence to the IS or the MAS design. The evaluation can be of three different types: ergonomic, technical or qualitative. Ergonomic evaluation consists to evaluate the usability [18] of the IMAS. Technical evaluation verifies the implementation conformity of the system compared to the existing standards. And qualitative evaluation consists to computer user satisfaction degree about the personalisation provided by the system. Each of them can lead to modify the models produced in the previous steps of the design.

A first application of our methodology PerMet has been led in the transportation information field.

4   Application to an IS Dedicated to Transportation Information

We used the PerMet methodology to personalize transportation information. The aim of the personalization is to recommend relevant routes for each user and to inform from disturbances in taking into account the data, the user and his/her interaction platforms. The itinerary information are proposed as complementary services linked to an electronic agenda. The agenda is designed to be used via web pages or PDA (Personal Digital Assistant).

In this aim, we have connected an existing web application, a transportation Information System, with a MAS, following the steps of the methodology.

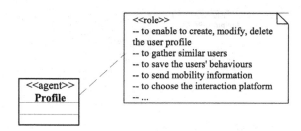

Fig. 3. Agents Analysis step: Example of agent role description in a note

The *Service Analysis* is used to detail the goal and the expected functionalities. Among them, the emphasis has been put on the interaction with the user's personal agenda. We focus on integrating transportation information to the users' daily organization. The expected service consists in retrieving relevant transport data and recommend the routes and means that are susceptible to be preferred by the user. It has been described by a use case diagram.

The *Service Design* describes the behaviour of the system in taking into account the information given by the MAS. For example, it includes the possibility to see route recommendations linked to an event in the agenda. Every use case resulting from the analysis step has been detailed by an activity diagram. Communication diagrams have been used to describe the interaction with the user.

The *Service Implementation* is the step during which some developments are realized. For example, an agenda was already existing, but we extend the XML format used by this one to include itinerary data. In this step, the use of a LDAP dictionary has been adopted to manage users who must be identified to provide them personal recommendations.

The *Agents Analysis* lead to identify five roles of agents according to the sets of expected functionalities provided by the service analysis results. These roles are: to assist the users and adapt the presentation to the interaction platform; to create and maintain the user profiles; to process the routes and disturbances; to manage the interaction with agendas and their constraints; to coordinate and integrate the results of the agents. The aim is to detail the tasks each of them must be able to perform, in order to create the required skills for the agents. As an example, the Profile role, is described in Fig. 3: its tasks are detailed in a textual form in a note associated to the role class, that will be useful to determine agent behaviours in the behaviour design step. Like others methodologies (PASSI [4], for example) agent structure is modelled by a class diagram with stereotype "agent". But our representation mentions neither attribute, nor method: an agent can change his behaviour, it is thus not appropriate to fix his behaviour in a method. Once the roles have been described, the aim is to find coherent sets and eventual common skills among them.

During the *Behaviour Design*, the agent roles are realized by sets of behaviours and the activities of each role are detailed. Each role is defined by the skills the agents must possess to perform their tasks. The skills are modeled as independent units of behaviours that can be associated to the roles. As an example, the

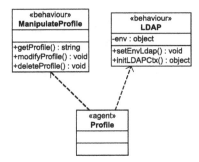

Fig. 4. Behaviours Design step: Two of the behaviours used by the Profile agents

realization of the users' profiling role is given in Figure 4: the Profile agents include two behaviours that enable them to manage the users profile and to use LDAP data.

To complete the design of the roles, the activity models describe their internal dynamic process. For example, the activity model of the profile management agents is described in Figure 5: the process selects one filtering method among three, according to the knowledge of the system about the user and the request.

The *Behaviour Implementation* is applied to all of the specified and designed models of agents. For example, the development of the Profile agents described above requires to develop the following behaviours:

– `KSocialLastFilteringSkill`: To personalize the itineraries according to an activity model like the one presented in Figure 5,
– `LDAPSkill`: To access the LDAP directory service to get the user's personal data, for example a phone number to warn him/her of a disturbance via an SMS during a trip, using then the `DisturbanceSkill`
– `ManipulateProfileSkill`: To allow the user to manage his/her own profile: profile visualization, deleting, or modification of the weights which are associated to the criteria,
– `SaveChoiceSkill`: To save the choice made by the user,
– `DisturbanceInfoSkill, DisturbanceSkill`: To personalize the disturbance information,
– `MailSkill`: To enable sending mails (to warn the user of eventual disturbance).

On Figure 6, each class represents a behaviour. The public methods correspond to the callable tasks: any agent can ask to the agents having the behaviour `ManipulateProfileSkill` to carry out the task `getProfile`. The agents having this behaviour perform internal actions, represented by the private methods, using internal states represented by the attributes. As it has been explained previously, a link($\ll$ require $\gg$) between two classes means that at least one task or internal action carried out by the origin behaviour requires the execution of the target behaviour, either by the same agent or by a call to another agent.

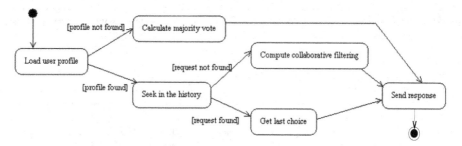

Fig. 5. Example of activity diagram realized during the Behaviours Design step

In our example, the *Integration* of the IS and the MAS (called *PerSyst*) is based on SOAP (Simple Object Access Protocol) communications. For example, the user adds a new event to its agenda. This action triggers the creation of an XML file that includes information about the sequence of the events of the day. The IS sends the file as the parameter `Request` in the call to the MAS:

```
Response=perSyst.request("searchItinerary",Request)
```

The research agents look at the available transportation means and their time data. The solutions are ordered according to the user's preferences and formatted

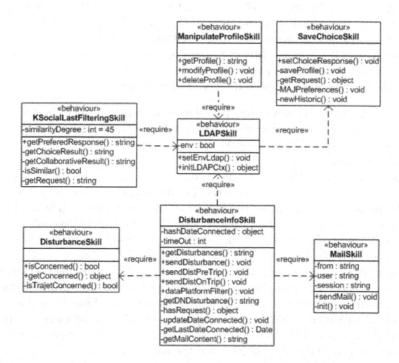

Fig. 6. Example of class diagram realized during the Behaviours implementation step

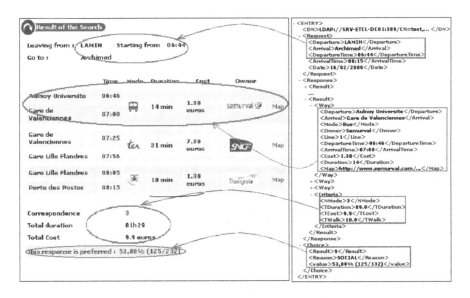

Fig. 7. Example of display based on the data file exchanged by the IS and the MAS in the XML format

to complete the solution part of the XML file, that forms the response to the request. The response is transformed by the IS to be displayed by the user interface as in Figure 7, where the first result given by the MAS is proposed to the user by the IS. The last line of the display gives the reason for the system to choose the above itinerary solution.

The *Evaluation* step has been divided into three parts:

– The technical tests were aimed at detecting eventual defaults due to the implementation steps. Especially, the integration tests focused on the interaction between the IS and the MAS.
– The evaluation of the personalization method was aimed at checking that the personalization method correctly answers to the users requests, according to quantitative and qualitative criteria. The quantitative aspect we evaluated is the response times of the methods used by the profile agents. The qualitative aspect we evaluated is the rate of the prediction errors of two collaborative filtering methods. We chose the one that decreased the quicker while the number of requests increased.
– The evaluation of the software ergonomy is aimed at gathering users opinion about the content and the display of the personalization provided by the IMAS. It is not finished but some preliminary tests have been done that report a satisfying behaviour of the system according to the users preferences and the support (PDA or PC) they used, and a need of improvements in the adaptation to the user's abilities and the context of use.

5 Conclusion

In this paper, we have presented PerMet, a methodology to design Information Multi-Agent Systems. The originality of the approach is the division of the design into two distinct branches, the first one being dedicated to the IS and the other one to the MAS. The aim is both to facilitate the integration of adaptation services like the personalization to existing IS, and to allow the reuse of personalization services provided by existing MAS.

The methodology has been applied to an IS dedicated to transportation information. To go further in the reusability aspect of our proposition, we will study whether the methods that allow the identification of the reusable parts in agent-oriented systems can apply in the context of IMAS, like in [12].

Acknowledgements

The present research work has been supported by the *Region Nord-Pas de Calais* and the PREDIM program (project *MOUVER.PERSO*). The authors gratefully acknowledge the support of these institutions.

References

1. Adam, E., Mandiau, R.: Design of a MAS into a human organization: application to an information multi-agent system. In: Giorgini, P., Henderson-Sellers, B., Winikoff, M. (eds.) AOIS 2003. LNCS (LNAI), vol. 3030, Springer, Heidelberg (2004)
2. Arazy, O., Woo, C.: Analysis and design of agent-oriented information systems. Knowl. Eng. Rev. 17 (3), 215–260 (2002)
3. Bauer, B., Muller, J.P., Odell, J.: Agent UML: a formalism for specifying multiagent interaction. In: Ciancarini, P., Wooldridge, M. (eds.) Agent-Oriented Software Engineering, Springer, pp. 91–103. Springer, Heidelberg (2001)
4. Burrafato, P., Cossentino, M.: Designing a multi-agent solution for a bookstore with the PASSI methodology. In: Bussler, C.J., McIlraith, S.A., Orlowska, M.E., Pernici, B., Yang, J. (eds.) CAiSE 2002 and WES 2002. LNCS, vol. 2512, pp. 27–28. Springer, Heidelberg (2002)
5. Cassell, J., Vilhjálmsson, H.: Fully Embodied Conversational Avatars: Making Communicative Behaviors Autonomous. Autonomous Agents and Multi-Agent Systems 2(1), 45–64 (1999)
6. Chen, L., Sycara, K.: WebMate: A Personal Agent for Browsing and Searching. In: Proc.of AGENTS 1998, pp. 132–139. ACM Publishers, New York (1998)
7. Crow, L., Shadbolt, N.R.: IMPS - Internet agents for knowledge engineering. In: Gaines, B.R., Musen, M. (eds.) Proc. of the 11th Workshop on Knowledge Acquisition, Modelling and Management, SRDG Publ, Calgary (1998)
8. Demazeau, Y.: From interactions to collective behaviour in agent-based systems. In: European Conference on Cognitive Sciences (1995)
9. Dickinson, I., Reynolds, D., Banks, D., Cayzer, S., Vora, P.: User Profiling with privacy: A framework for Adaptive Information Agents. In: Klusch, M., Bergamaschi, S., Edwards, P., Petta, P. (eds.) Intelligent Information Agents. LNCS (LNAI), vol. 2586, pp. 123–151. Springer, Heidelberg (2003)

10. Dignum, F.: Agent Communication and Cooperative Information Agents. In: Klusch, M., Kerschberg, L. (eds.) CIA 2000. LNCS (LNAI), vol. 1860, pp. 191–207. Springer, Heidelberg (2000)
11. Gleizes, M.P., Glize, P.: ABROSE: Multi Agent Systems for Adaptive Brokerage. In Giorgini, P., et al (eds.) AOIS 2002. Agent-Oriented Information Systems, Proceedings of the Fourth International Bi-Conference Workshop on Agent-Oriented Information Systems (AOIS-2002 at CAiSE*02), CEUR Workshop Proceedings. 57 (2002)
12. Henderson-Sellers, B., Debenham, J., Tran, N., Cossentino, M., Low, G.: Identification of Reusable Method Fragments from the PASSI Agent-Oriented Methodology. In: Kolp, M., Bresciani, P., Henderson-Sellers, B., Winikoff, M. (eds.) AOIS 2005. LNCS (LNAI), vol. 3529, pp. 90–105. Springer, Heidelberg (2006)
13. Kobsa, A., Pohl, W.: The User Modeling Shell System BGP-MS. User Modeling and User-Adapted Interaction 4, 59–106 (1995)
14. Klusch, M.: Information agent technology for the Internet: A survey. Data and Knowledge Engineering 36, 337–372 (2001)
15. Lesser, V., Horling, B., Klassner, F., Raja, A., Wagner, T., Zhang, S.X.: BIG: An agent for resource-bounded information gathering and decision making. Artificial Intelligence 118, 197–244 (2000)
16. Lieberman, H.: Letizia: an agent that assists web browsing. In: Proc. of the Int. Joint Conf. on Artificial Intelligence, pp. 924–929. Morgan Kaufmann, San Francisco (1995)
17. Montaner, M., Lopez, B., De la Rosa, J.L.: A Taxonomy of Recommender Agents on the Internet. Artificial Intelligence Review 19, 285–330 (2003)
18. Nielsen, J.: Usability Engineering. Academinc Press, San Diego (1993)
19. Nodine, M.H., Fowler, J., Ksiezyk, T., Perry, B., Taylor, M., Unruh, A.: Active Information Gathering in InfoSleuth. Int. Jnl.of Cooperative Information Systems 9, 3–28 (2000)
20. Routier, J.C., Mathieu, P., Secq, Y.: Dynamic skill learning: A support to agent evolution. In: Proc. of the AISB 2001 Symp. on Adaptive Agents and Multi-Agent Systems, pp. 25–32 (2001)
21. Shakshuki, E., Ghenniwa, H., Kamel, M.: An architecture for cooperative information systems. Knowledge-Based Systems 16, 17–27 (2003)
22. Trousse, B., Jaczynski, M., Kanawati, R.: Using user behavior similarity for recommandation computation: The broadway approach. In: HCI 1999. Proceedings of 8th international conference on human computer interaction, pp. 85–89. Lawrence Erlbaum Associates, Mahwah (1999)
23. Wooldridge, M., Jennings, N., Kinny, D.: The Gaia methodology for agent-oriented analysis and design. Jnl. of Autonomous Agents and Multi-Agent Systems. 3(3), 285–312 (2000)

On the Evaluation of Agent-Oriented Software Engineering Methodologies: A Statistical Approach

Abdel-Halim Hafez Elamy[1] and Behrouz Far[2]

[1] Department of Electrical and Computer Engineering, University of Alberta
Edmonton, Alberta T6G 2E1, Canada
elamy@ualberta.ca
[2] Department of Electrical and Computer Engineering, University of Calgary
Calgary, Alberta T2N 1N4, Canada
far@ucalgary.ca

Abstract. Agent-based computing is one of the fastest growing areas of research and development in information technology. A large number of Agent-Oriented Software Engineering (AOSE) methodologies have been evolved in order to assist in building intelligent software. Nevertheless, the immaturity of this emerging technology can result in difficulties for a developer when deciding which methodology can best fit a prospective application. A limited number of studies have been conducted to address the comparison and evaluation of AOSE methodologies. However, such studies lack a reliable framework that can be implemented and generalized effectively; most of the proposed approaches are not capable of providing sufficient knowledge to support accurate decision-making. In this paper, we present a reliable framework based on adopting state-of-the-art statistical procedures to evaluate AOSE methodologies and come up with a set of metrics that can help in selecting the most appropriate methodology, or assembling more than one, to accommodate the anticipated features.

Keywords: Multi-agent Systems (MAS), Methodologies, Balanced Incomplete Block Design (BIBD), Analysis of Variance (ANOVA), Software Metrics.

1 Introduction

1.1 Research Problem

As a result of the growing interest in multi-agent systems (MAS), a large number of AOSE methodologies and modelling techniques have been evolved in order to support the development of agent-based applications in all of their life cycle phases. From the literature, we have enumerated more than thirty methodologies; despite this large number, AOSE still lacks maturity. One of the reasons is that most of the available methodologies differ in their concepts, premises, development phases and models; such divergences mean that methodologies lack adequate capabilities to model the anticipated properties of all types of agents. Furthermore, some methodologies are developed for special purposes, some do not have sufficient

M. Kolp et al. (Eds.): AOIS 2006, LNAI 4898, pp. 105–122, 2008.

documentation and some methodologies have not been presented in a commonly-used language, such as English. Moreover, the lack of consensus between the different AOSE methodologies is one of the open problems in order for a methodology to become "mainstream" [26]. Deciding what methodology is the best to adopt for developing a potential MAS depends on which aspects are considered more important for the prospective application. Up till now, there is no industry-wide agreement on the kinds of concepts a methodology should support.

1.2 Literature Review and Related Works

In order to strengthen our research work, we considered several views from most of the related works established and presented in various refereed sources. For space limitation, we will just exhibit here two of the leading works. For further reading, we addressed this topic thoroughly with different views in [7].

1.2.1 Tran et al.'s Work

Tran *et al.* [28], [29] present a preliminary comparative Feature Analysis framework, which they used to compare ten AOSE methodologies. They actually considered the three major components of a system development methodology (process, models, and techniques) as defined by one of the leading public-domain and process-focused full lifecycle methodologies - Object-oriented Process, Environment and Notation (OPEN). *Tran et al.* came up with a new framework to evaluate AOSE methodologies based on identifying four groups of criteria: (1) Process-related criteria, (2) Technique-related criteria, (3) Model-related criteria, and (4) Supportive feature criteria.

This framework has the advantage that it provides a broad coverage of an integrated set of features describing an AOSE methodology. However, we have some comments that we believe worthy of consideration. Since it is hard to reflect on all the described features when evaluating a methodology, the framework may eliminate some methodologies from being qualified for evaluation. For instance, assessing the methodology's robustness, in terms of providing techniques to analyze system performance for all configurations and to detect/recover failures seems to be more hypothetical than realistic, and not easy to perform. In actual fact, some of these features can be recommended in order to examine the final product of the developed MAS or to evaluate the agent-oriented tool that can be used for the physical design of the desired MAS, rather than evaluating the methodology itself. Moreover, the framework supports the process of setting the criteria upon which methodologies will be evaluated, but it lacks the empirical tool to quantify the subjective/qualitative evaluation responses in a computational manner, which is indispensable during the evaluation process. Furthermore, the Feature Analysis framework can be recommended to adopt as an analytical tool to exhibit various detailed features involving agents and MAS. Yet, it is not a purely evaluation framework. For instance, in the process-related criteria, the development lifecycle is assessed by the question "What development lifecycle best describes the methodology?" In fact, this cannot be considered as an evaluation question because it does not show the degree of usefulness or effectiveness of the life cycle used. Rather, it is a traditional comparison question whose answer identifies the type of lifecycle used, without carrying sufficient information about the efficiency of such a lifecycle.

1.2.2 Shehory et al.'s Work

Shehory and Sturm [17] carried out an experimental study to compare and evaluate the modelling technique existing in three agent-based methodologies (AOM, ADEPT, and DESIRE) against two major criteria by examining some features from software engineering (such as ease of use and understanding, expressiveness, refinability, complexity management, testability, modularity, analyzability and open system architecture) as well as characteristics of agent-based systems (such as autonomy, complexity, adaptability, concurrency, distribution and communication). The authors examined the evaluation criteria via a case study of an existing application that utilizes a single-agent, auction agent, which participates and bids in web-based auctions on behalf of its user in order to perform several tasks to purchase specific items based on some given parameters. Our argument here is that Shehory and Sturm's study provides partial feedback when selecting a limited number of evaluation criteria to compare a small number of AOSE methodologies. However, the study does not cover many other criteria that affect the final feedback. Also, this approach does not adopt a computational tool to quantify the evaluation data, which in turn reduces the evaluation accuracy. In addition, the adopted qualitative measurement scale, which is nominal, is incapable of providing adequate information in the case of scaling up the study.

1.3 Research Questions

The ambiguity and lack of standardization associated with existing AOSE methodologies makes it hard to take ad-hoc decisions to select the most appropriate methodology that best fits a particular agent-based application. Unfortunately, most of the available works about methodologies just pay attention to the best features of the one presented. Moreover, in some cases the authors cannot see any negative aspects with their own developed methodologies. Furthermore, some authors simply compare their methodologies to object-oriented methodologies. However, object orientation is not a main competitor when we talk about the analysis and design of agent-based systems [2]. Finally, in some situations the recommendation may be to adopt more than one methodology to achieve the specific requirements of a potential multi-agent system that cannot be designed by means of a single AOSE methodology [16]. However, assembling several methodologies requires better understanding of the differences and the effectiveness of the attributes characterizing each methodology.

In this paper, we describe an empirical approach to evaluate the effectiveness of a number of AOSE methodologies and come up with a set of metrics that rates their common characteristics. We express four broad research questions to address this issue:

(1) What are the criteria upon which we can describe and evaluate a methodology?
(2) What are the different attributes that must be included under each criterion?
(3) How can we quantify and assess the evaluation criteria of a methodology?
(4) How can we rank the evaluated methodologies to easily select the most qualified one, or assemble several in order to accommodate the anticipated characteristics of an agent-based application?

The following sections describe a number of steps that will be adopted to answer these research questions.

2   Selecting Methodologies and Participants

We started by conducting a primarily comparative survey to review a large number of AOSE methodologies to select the most qualified ones. We defined a qualified methodology as the one that fulfils the following three prerequisites: (a) has reasonable documentation, (b) is fairly well known to the agent community and (c) is not a special-purpose methodology; rather, it has a reasonable domain of applicability. After reviewing 31 methodologies against these assumptions, the following nine methodologies were selected: Gaia [25], MaSE [6], Tropos [14], Agent-SE [12], MASSIVE [18], Prometheus [22], [5], MESSAGE [11], MAS-CommonKADS [15] and PASSI [4].

Participants. There were 12 participants in our experiment, all of whom are graduate students in Software Engineering at the University of Calgary who have adequate knowledge and experience in developing agent-based software. They were provided with sufficient documentation about the methodologies, clear instructions about the experiment and an equal amount of time to complete their tasks by utilizing the concepts of their assigned methodologies in designing an online university registration system, and then assessing the methodologies using a well-prepared survey questionnaire.

3   Evaluating the Methodologies

We based our evaluation upon the applyication of the Multidimensional Weighted-Attributes Framework (MWAF) [7], [8]. The main idea of MWAF is to define the most common and important criteria (or dimensions) of the methodology being evaluated, identifying the attributes that describe each of these dimensions, and then evaluating each dimension through its attributes against all the potential methodologies that are selected for evaluation. As shown in Fig. 1, MWAF consists of the following three main components:

1) Dimensions: the framework comprises a number of dimensions, each of which represents one of the major evaluation criteria.
2) Attributes: are the different features pertaining to each criterion (i.e. dimension) to describe it using a set of definite questions.
3) Parameters: the numerical values that are given to measure the attributes.

The participants were asked to give two parameters to each of the evaluated attributes: a *weight* to identify the importance of the attribute, and a *rate* to measure its strength or effectiveness. *Weight* is a subjective parameter, as it is entirely reliant upon the evaluator's personal opinion. On the other hand, *Rate* is an objective parameter because it is measured according to the degree of availability or effectiveness of the examined property as represented by the evaluated attribute. The values given to these two parameters are numeric and range from 0 to 10. A value of '0' implies full absence of the measured attribute, whereas a value of 10 reflects its maximum availability and strength. In order to take a broad view of the final conclusions, each methodology will be evaluated by several participants (four in our study).

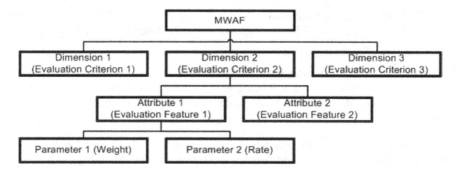

Fig. 1. General hierarchy of the Multidimensional Weighted-Attributes Framework (MWAF)

3.1 Identifying Dimensions

We studied the selected nine methodologies comprehensively to identify the most important/common measures that will be used as evaluation criteria and we came up with the following eight primary criteria that we represent by the following dimensions:

1. Dimension 1: Agency-related attributes
2. Dimension 2: Modelling-related
3. Dimension 3: Communication attributes
   Dimension 4: Process-related attributes
5. Dimension 5: Upgradeability attributes
6. Dimension 6: Application attributes
7. Dimension 7: Support-related properties
8. Dimension 8: User-perception attributes

These dimensions will be treated statistically as *independent factors*, each of which encompasses a number of *attributes* or *levels* i.e., *modelling* is a factor with seven levels. We use the terms *dimensions*, *criteria*, or *factors* to mean the same thing.

3.2 Identifying Attributes

We broke down each dimension into a number of relational attributes that describe its main features. Furthermore, we assumed that an attribute is low-weighted if it receives an average weight of less than 7 (i.e. 70%) on a 10-point scale. By examining the collected data against this assumption, we noticed that a number of attributes have been given low weights. We investigated these attributes to validate the reasons for being low weighted, and to assure that the recorded weights are accurate and not inferred by random chance. As a result, we came up with the following six dimensions that represent the set of criteria upon which we can describe and evaluate AOSE methodologies. This answers the first question we stated in Section 1.3.

3.2.1 Dimension 1: Agency-Related Attributes
This dimension comprises attri- butes that address features involving the internal properties and basic architecture of agents. The conceptual hierarchical structure of this dimension is given below.

      1. Architecture properties
          1.1 Organization   1.2 Mobility
      2. Basic properties
          2.1 Autonomy 2.2 Reactivity   2.3 Reasoning   2.4 Temporal continuity

3. Advanced (mental) properties
   3.1 Beliefs   3.2 Desires (goals)   3.3 Intentions (actions)
4. Learning ability

3.2.2 Dimension 2: Modelling-Related Attributes

This dimension consists of the following seven attributes that address and examine specific features to describe the most common and important aspects for modelling agents.

1. Notation   2. Expressiveness   3. Abstraction   4. Consistency
5. Concurrency   6. Traceability   7. Derivation and reusability

3.2.3 Dimension 3: Communication-Related Attributes

This dimension addresses features that are related to different possible interactions and interfacing of agents. Following is the conceptual hierarchical structure of this dimension:

1. Local communication (Basic Sociability)
   1.1 Cooperation   1.2 Coordination 1.3 Competition 1.4 Negotiation
2. Wide Communication (Advanced Sociability)
   2.1 Interaction with the external environment
   2.2 Agent-based user interface   2.3 Subsystems interaction

3.2.4 Dimension 4: Process-Related Attributes

This dimension encompasses attri- butes that address and examine several issues invol- ving the development process of agents and MAS. Following is the hierarchical structure of this dimension:

1. Development lifecycle
   1.1 Architectural design   1.2 Detailed design
   1.3 Verification and validation
2. Refinability   3. Managing complexity

3.2.5 Dimension 5: Application-Related Attributes

This dimension includes the following four attributes that address and assess aspects involving the methodology's applicability and examine some relevant socio-economic factors:

1. Applicability   2. Field history   3. Maturity   4. Cost concerns

3.2.6 Dimension 6: User Perception Attributes

In order to make a decision on whether to adopt a particular methodology, perception is crucial and substantial due to the effect of the natural intentionality in human behaviour [13]. As a result, we are not just concerned about how effective a methodology is, but how users are satisfied and agree on its effectiveness in the way that makes them satisfied and obliged to using it. User perception will be assessed using the following three attributes:

1. Perceived ease of use 2. Perceived usefulness 3. Intention to use the methodology

By identifying the attributes of the previously described dimensions, we answer the second research question specified in Section 1.3. The complete definitions of the proposed attributes of these dimensions are described thoroughly in [7] and [9].

3.3   Identifying Experimental Variables

Before selecting the statistical model that best fit our data, or even setting up our hypotheses, it is essential to define the experimental variables and the appropriate scale of measurement [10]. In our study, the effectiveness of the methodologies' characteristics, as described by the weighted rate given to each dimension attribute, is the dependent variable (i.e. response). In order to be tested, a dependent variable is usually quantitative and measurable. Methodologies and participants are, on the other hand, independent variables that influence and regulate the response; these variables are discrete in their nature and work through a nominal (i.e. categorical) scale. When applying ANOVA, the independent variables are usually called factors or treatments.

3.4   Identifying the Scale of Measurement

Our dependent variable will be measured by the selected 12 participants in the way that a block of three methodologies is assigned at random to each participant. However, due to the overlap among blocks and participants, each methodology will be evaluated by four participants, and thus will have four replicates. The dependent variable will be measured using the Universal Leveled Scale of measurement (ULS) of Elamy [7]. This scale is a modified version of Stevens' scales [23] to support the objectives of Likert's [21] in representing attitude data. The ULS contributes to measuring attitudes based on assigning approximate numeric values to the examined attributes. We assumed that our data represent a continuous random variable whose values include a true zero to represent the absence of the measured property. Consequently, we will use the highest level of the ULS as a measurement scale, which is closely equivalent to the ratio scale of Stevens. Using the ULS capability in quantifying qualitative data, and weighting the rates collected by the average weights from the participants answers the third research question in Section 1.3.

3.5   Selecting the Appropriate Statistical Model

Our experiment includes nine methodologies that will be treated statistically as *treatments*. We decided to have at least four replicates for each treatment. Thus, if we used the One-way ANOVA model for a Complete Random Design (CRD), we will need 36 participants to evaluate the nine methodologies, so that each participant will receive one methodology at random to evaluate it, and each methodology will be evaluated by four participants. However, we have two limitations here. Firstly, we believe that there is heterogeneity among participants for many reasons (e.g. technical experience, academic background, response accuracy and personal satisfaction with the participation in the survey) that contribute to creating some sort of variability among participants. Although the randomization will tend to spread the heterogeneity around to reduce bias, we still have another strong limitation, the lack of resources - we have only 12 participants. One way to overcome this deficiency is to make use of each participant to assess more than one methodology. This solution led us to try considering a 2-way ANOVA model with blocking. In such a model, each block of treatments will be assigned at random to one participant. If we used a Randomized Complete Block Design (RCBD), each participant must assess a complete block, i.e. nine methodologies, and the design will probably be more effective because we will have more replications, $12 \times 9 = 108$, by assuming considerable variability within blocks. Unfortunately, this design has also a limitation that makes it hard to implement because we cannot guarantee that all the participants are familiar with the whole set of methodologies. After a thorough analysis and extended discussions, we finally adopted the following Balanced Incomplete Block Design (BIBD) model:

$$Y_{ij} = \mu + \tau_i + \beta_j + \varepsilon_{ij}$$

This model is referred to as "**balanced**" because each block will have the same number of treatments, "**additive**" because no interactions are considered between factors, "**incomplete**" because each participant will not evaluate a complete set of methodologies, and "**fixed**" because we narrowed down the selection of the qualified methodologies upon our own interest and not at random from a large number of methodologies; thus, if we repeated the experiment, the same methodologies we be used. By denoting the nine methodologies with letters from A to I and assigning each block of three methodologies - after selecting them in such a way to be as homogeneous as possible - to a participant, we can obtain 36 replicates that will sufficiently satisfy our goal of having four replicas per treatment as shown in Table 1.

Table 1. BIBD tableau for blocks and treatments

		Treatments (AOSE Methodologies), i								
		M1	M2	M3	M4	M5	M6	M7	M8	M9
	P1	A	B	C						
	P2				D	E	F			
	P3							G	H	I
	P4	A			D			G		
	P5		B			E			H	
	P6			C			F			I
	P7	A					F		H	
	P8		B		D					I
	P9			C		E		G		
	P10	A				E				I
	P11		B				F	G		
	P12			C	D				H	

M = Methodology; P = Participant

The rationale behind blocking here is to eliminate the effects of extraneous variation due to the noise that may result from the differences between participants. By eliminating the variability within blocks from the experimental error, we gain a substantial increase in the precision of the conducted experiment [1]. For this reason, we tried to make the treatment blocks as similar as possible, by trying to avoid assigning simple and complicated methodologies all together into the same block.

4 Statistical Hypotheses

In order to determine whether significant differences exist between the evaluated methodologies, we will conduct a separate experiment to each of the six dimensions that characterize the nine AOSE methodologies. In this context, each set of attributes representing a particular dimension will be investigated statistically over all the evaluated nine methodologies. This will help to determine whether the strength or effectiveness of this dimension differs among the evaluated methodologies or not. The following set of hypotheses describes this strategy in a statistical fashion.

Null hypothesis, $H_o : \tau_i = 0$, $i = 1$ to 9
There is no significant difference in the mean effectiveness of the examined dimension among the evaluated AOSE methodologies.

Alternative hypothesis, H_a : at least one $\tau_i \neq 0$
There is a significant difference in the mean effectiveness.

5   Applying the ANOVA Approach

We analyzed the data by means of statistical techniques based on applying the Analysis of Variances (ANOVA) procedure to the Balanced Incomplete Block Design (BIBD) model proposed by Yates [27] to test the significant differences in the mean effectiveness of each individual dimension among the evaluated methodologies. In this way, if significant differences are ascertained, we shall go further to perform pairwise comparisons to identify which pairs of methodologies significantly differ from which ones. As a result, the evaluated methodologies are ranked according to their mean effectiveness in each individual dimension. On the other hand, if the overall ANOVA test was insignificant, we will not apply any pairwise comparisons. In such a case, the conclusion to be made is that all the methodologies are statistically equal in their main effects against the attributes of the examined dimension.

6   Dimensional Analyses

For space limitation, we will demonstrate a brief analysis for one of the dimensions only (Dimension 1: agency-related). However, we shall present the results and conclusions of all six dimensions. To assure higher accuracy, we performed our computations manually; then, we validated the results with the computer output produced by MINITAB® based on applying the General Linear Models.

6.1   Detailed Analysis of Dimension 1

Step 1: Data Abstraction and Formulation We extract the data for this dimension from the collected row data; then we multiply the recorded rates by the corresponding average weights of their attributes.

Step 2: Constructing the BIBD tableau By adopting the BIBD arrangement given in Table 1, we can construct the BIBD tableau of this dimension as shown in Table 2.

Step 3: Testing the ANOVA assumptions We considered the following three main tests to examine the assumptions involving the adequacy of ANOVA. The graphical results of this procedure are shown in Fig. 2.

Test type	Instrument used
Outliers	a. Normal probability plot of residuals b. Individual value plot of residuals versus independent variable
Normality of residuals	Normal probability plot of residuals
Homogeneity of variances	a. Residual plots against fitted values b. Bartlett's test

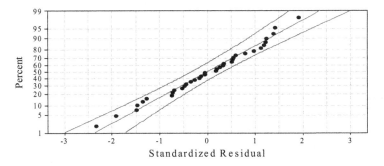

Fig. 2(a). Probability Plot of Standardized Residual, Normal - 95% CI

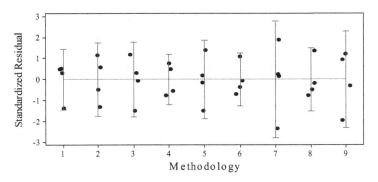

Fig. 2(b). Individual Value Plot of Standardized Residual vs. Methodology, 95% CI for Mean

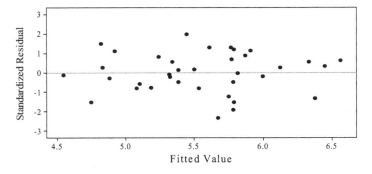

Fig. 2(c). Residuals Versus the Fitted Values, (response is Rate)

The plots of Fig. 2 do not suggest significant departures, either from the normality of the distribution of errors or the homogeneity of error variances. Also, there is no evidence of potential outliers; all the residuals appear to be bounded within a 95% confidence interval and all fall within the acceptable range of normality, $\pm 3\sigma$ [19].

Table 2. BIBD assignment for the average weighted rates of Dimension 1

| Block (Participants),j | Treatments (AOSE Methodologies), i | | | | | | | | | $Y_{.j}$ |
	M1	M2	M3	M4	M5	M6	M7	M8	M9	
P1	6.462	5.957	5.531							$Y_{.1}=$ 17.950
P2				5.371	4.817	5.047				$Y_{.2}=$ 15.234
P3							5.348	5.931	6.034	$Y_{.3}=$ 17.313
P4	6.212			5.034			5.734			$Y_{.4}=$ 16.980
P5		5.822			4.536			5.352		$Y_{.5}=$ 15.710
P6			6.146			5.300			5.932	$Y_{.6}=$ 17.377
P7	6.399					4.819		5.347		$Y_{.7}=$ 16.565
P8		5.718		5.009					5.828	$Y_{.8}=$ 16.556
P9			6.037		4.483		5.582			$Y_{.9}=$ 16.102
P10	6.667				4.991				5.518	$Y_{.10}=$ 17.176
P11		5.531				5.079	5.412			$Y_{.11}=$ 16.022
P12			5.841	5.325				5.452		$Y_{.12}=$ 16.617
$Y_{i.}$	$Y_{1.}=$ 25.74	$Y_{2.}=$ 23.03	$Y_{3.}=$ 23.55	$Y_{4.}=$ 20.74	$Y_{5.}=$ 18.83	$Y_{6.}=$ 20.25	$Y_{7.}=$ 22.08	$Y_{8.}=$ 22.08	$Y_{9.}=$ 23.31	$Y_{..}=$**199.603**

M = Methodology; P = Participant

Step 4: ANOVA computations and hypotheses testing

We applied the adjusted formulae of the BIBD described by the author of this design [27] to the data arranged in the BIBD tableau and came up with the analysis of variance components summarized in the ANOVA table (Table 3).

Table 3. ANOVA table for Dimension 1

Source of Variation	Degrees of Freedom, df	Sum of Squares, SS	Mean of Squares	Test Statistic, F_o
Adjusted Treatments	$a-1=9-1=8$	$SS_{TRT(adj)}=6.677$	$MS_{TRT(adj)}=.835$	$F_o = \dfrac{MS_{TRT(adj)}}{MS_{ERR}}$
Blocks (Participants)	$b-1=12-1=11$	$SS_{BLK}=2.214$	$MS_{BLK}=.201$	
Error	$N-a-b+1=16$	$SS_{ERR}=.810$	$MS_{ERR}=.05063$	$=16.49$
Total	$N-1=36-1=35$	$SS_{TOT}=9.701$		

The calculated F statistic ($F_0=7.25$) was larger than its critical value ($F_{crt}=2.59$). Thus, F_0 falls in the rejection region, and we have sufficient evidence to reject the null hypothesis at a 95% level of significance based on the available data. Consequently, there is a significant difference in the mean effectiveness of this dimension (Agency-related) among the evaluated nine AOSE methodologies.

Step 5: Identifying significant differences and ranking the evaluated methodologies against the attributes of Dimension 1.

Since the hypothesis test was significant, we shall go further to perform multiple comparison tests to identify which methodologies differ. Christensen [3], Neter [20], and others exhibit several methods for multiple comparisons, such as Bonferroni, Tukey, Scheffe, Duncan, and Fisher's LSD. However, Bonferroni and Tukey's HSD (Honestly Significant Differences) are suggested by many authors and statistical packages to be more suited for BIBD, based on the conservativeness and accuracy of various multiple comparisons methods. In this study, we shall adopt Tukey's HSD method. As a result, we obtained the following pairs of methodologies that show significant differences: [M1] with [M3, M4, M5, M6, M7, M8, M9]; [M2] with [M4, M5, M6]; [M3] with [M5, M6]; [M5] with [M7, M8, M9]; and [M6] with [M9].

Table 4. Binary representation of the evaluation results of Dimension 1

		M2	M3	M4	M5	M6	M7	M8	M9
Dimension 1: Agency	M1	0	1	1	1	1	1	1	1
	M2		0	1	1	1	0	0	0
	M3			0	1	1	0	0	0
	M4				0	0	0	0	0
	M5					0	1	1	1
	M6						0	0	1
	M7							0	0
	M8								0

In the same way, we applied the previous calculations and tests to the other five dimensions. Table 5 demonstrates the binary representation for the other dimensions.

Table 5. Evaluation results of Dimensions 2 to 6

		M2	M3	M4	M5	M6	M7	M8	M9
Dimension 2: Modelling	M1	0	1	0	0	0	0	0	0
	M2		1	1	0	1	0	0	0
	M3			0	0	0	0	0	1
	M4				0	0	0	0	1
	M5					0	0	0	0
	M6						0	0	1
	M7							0	0
	M8								0
Dimension 3: Communications	M1	0	0	0	0	0	1	1	0
	M2		0	1	0	1	0	0	0
	M3			0	0	0	1	1	1
	M4				0	0	1	1	1
	M5					1	1	0	0
	M6						1	1	1
	M7							0	0
	M8								0
Dimension 4: Process	M1	0	1	1	1	1	1	1	1
	M2		1	1	1	1	1	1	1
	M3			0	1	0	0	1	1
	M4				1	0	0	0	0
	M5					0	1	0	0
	M6						0	0	0
	M7							0	0
	M8								0

Table 5. (*continued*)

		M2	M3	M4	M5	M6	M7	M8	M9
Dimension 5: Application	M1	0	0	0	0	0	0	0	0
	M2		0	0	0	0	0	0	0
	M3			0	0	0	0	0	0
	M4				0	0	0	0	0
	M5					0	0	0	0
	M6						0	0	0
	M7							0	0
	M8								0
Dimension 6: User Perception	M1	0	1	0	0	1	0	0	0
	M2		1	1	1	1	0	0	0
	M3			0	0	0	0	0	0
	M4				0	0	0	0	0
	M5					0	0	0	0
	M6						1	1	0
	M7							0	0
	M8								0

M1:	Gaia	**M2:**	MaSE	**M3:**	Tropos	**M4:**	Agent-SE
M5:	MASSIVE	**M6:**	Prometheus	**M7:**	MESSAGE	**M8:**	MAS-Common
M9:	PASSI						

It is to be noted that an intersection of '0' in a cell implies that the corresponding two methodologies, as crossed by their rows and columns, are **not** significantly different. That is, when making a decision, both the methodologies are equal, although they may have different means of effectiveness. On the other hand, a value of '1' implies that they are significantly different and the one with the higher mean effectiveness is recommended. Tables 4 and 5 show that the mean effectiveness of all the evaluated dimensions, except Dimension 5, differs among the evaluated methodologies. In view of that, we ranked our methodologies against these dimensions according to their estimated adjusted mean of effectiveness $\hat{\mu}_i$ as shown in Table 6.

Table 6. Ranking the evaluated methodologies

Rank	Methodology	Est. Mean	Rank	Methodology	Est. Mean
	Dimension 1: Agency			**Dimension 2: Modelling**	
❶	M1: Gaia	$\hat{\mu}_1 = 6.494$	❶	M2: MaSE	$\hat{\mu}_2 = 6.593$
❷	M2: MaSE	$\hat{\mu}_2 = 5.861$	❷	M9: PASSI	$\hat{\mu}_9 = 6.428$
❸	M3: Tropos	$\hat{\mu}_3 = 5.835$	❸	M1: Gaia	$\hat{\mu}_1 = 6.037$
❹	M9: PASSI	$\hat{\mu}_9 = 5.713$	❹	M7: MESSAGE	$\hat{\mu}_7 = 5.777$
❺	M8: MAS-Common	$\hat{\mu}_8 = 5.549$	❺	M8: MAS-Common	$\hat{\mu}_8 = 5.560$
❻	M7: MESSAGE	$\hat{\mu}_7 = 5.524$	❻	M5: MASSIVE	$\hat{\mu}_5 = 5.271$
❼	M4: Agent-SE	$\hat{\mu}_4 = 5.192$	❼	M6: Prometheus	$\hat{\mu}_6 = 5.074$
❽	M6: Prometheus	$\hat{\mu}_6 = 5.049$	❽	M4: Agent-SE	$\hat{\mu}_4 = 4.755$
❾	M5: MASSIVE	$\hat{\mu}_5 = 4.684$	❾	M3: Tropos	$\hat{\mu}_3 = 4.580$

Table 6. (*continued*)

Dimension 3: Communication			Dimension 4: Process		
❶	M7: MESSAGE	$\hat{\mu}_7 = 6.945$	❶	M1: Gaia	$\hat{\mu}_1 = 6.932$
❷	M8: MAS-Common	$\hat{\mu}_8 = 6.847$	❷	M2: MaSE	$\hat{\mu}_2 = 6.830$
❸	M9: PASSI	$\hat{\mu}_9 = 6.560$	❸	M5: MASSIVE	$\hat{\mu}_5 = 5.839$
❹	M2: MaSE	$\hat{\mu}_2 = 5.805$	❹	M8: MAS-Common	$\hat{\mu}_8 = 5.477$
❺	M5: MASSIVE	$\hat{\mu}_5 = 5.760$	❺	M9: PASSI	$\hat{\mu}_9 = 5.460$
❻	M1: Gaia	$\hat{\mu}_1 = 5.446$	❻	M6: Prometheus	$\hat{\mu}_6 = 5.227$
❼	M3: Tropos	$\hat{\mu}_3 = 5.099$	❼	M4: Agent-SE	$\hat{\mu}_4 = 4.906$
❽	M4: Agent-SE	$\hat{\mu}_4 = 4.619$	❽	M7: MESSAGE	$\hat{\mu}_7 = 4.808$
❾	M6: Prometheus	$\hat{\mu}_6 = 4.575$	❾	M3: Tropos	$\hat{\mu}_3 = 4.502$
Dimension 5: Application			Dimension 6: User Perception		
❶	M2: MaSE	$\hat{\mu}_2 = 6.351$	❶	M2: MaSE	$\hat{\mu}_2 = 7.340$
❶	M1: Gaia	$\hat{\mu}_1 = 6.301$	❷	M1: Gaia	$\hat{\mu}_1 = 6.672$
❶	M9: PASSI	$\hat{\mu}_9 = 5.900$	❸	M7: MESSAGE	$\hat{\mu}_7 = 6.198$
❶	M7: MESSAGE	$\hat{\mu}_7 = 5.687$	❹	M8: MAS-Common.	$\hat{\mu}_8 = 6.118$
❶	M5: MASSIVE	$\hat{\mu}_5 = 5.527$	❺	M5: MASSIVE	$\hat{\mu}_5 = 5.376$
❶	M8: MAS-Common.	$\hat{\mu}_8 = 5.411$	❻	M9: PASSI	$\hat{\mu}_9 = 5.251$
❶	M3: Tropos	$\hat{\mu}_3 = 5.398$	❼	M4: Agent-SE	$\hat{\mu}_4 = 5.193$
❶	M4: Agent-SE	$\hat{\mu}_4 = 5.368$	❽	M3: Tropos	$\hat{\mu}_3 = 4.928$
❶	M6: Prometheus	$\hat{\mu}_6 = 5.187$	❾	M6: Prometheus	$\hat{\mu}_6 = 3.818$

It may look strange to find that the overall F test conducted by ANOVA is significant, while the pairwise comparisons of means conducted by Tukey's HSD test fails to reveal any significant differences among the methodologies evaluated against Dimension 5. In fact, this exceptional case occurs because the F test is simultaneously considering all possible contrasts involving the treatment means and not just the pairwise comparisons, which represent a special kind of contrasts in the form $\mu_j - \mu_i$. This is the statistical explanation. From the agent perspective, this case implies that the participants of the experiment could not reveal significant differences among the evaluated methodologies in the application-related attributes of Dimension 5.

6.2 Overall Outcome of the Evaluation Process

So far, we have concluded the results of evaluation through a number of tables that rank the methodologies and identify the significant differences among them. This solution is extremely helpful when assembling a number of methodologies to develop an agent-based application or proposing a unified AOSE methodology. However, it may not be feasible in many situations to assemble AOSE methodologies by just adopting the best modules from a set of methodologies. This is because of the technical difficulties associated with the compatibility between the different AOSE methodologies and the available features or modules that can be isolated or implemented away from each other. Above all, when we have a large number of dimensions the situation will be vague and we may not be able to come up with accurate decisions. To this point, this solution cannot clearly answer the fourth research question described in Section 1.3. In order to find a proper solution, let us first clarify the problem by compiling the ranking results as shown in Table 7. Now, we can view our case as an optimization problem to select the highly-ranked methodology from a set of methodologies based on the ranking of their effectiveness against the six dimensions describing their major features. The following two scenarios demonstrate different solutions to this problem:

Scenario 1:
We can rank the methodologies according to the accumulated proportional order of their dimensions. For example, the Gaia methodology, M1, has the following accumulated proportional order: $1(\leftarrow D1) + 7/9(\leftarrow D2) + 4/9(\leftarrow D3) + 1(\leftarrow D4) + 8/9(\leftarrow D6)$, where the arrow points to the dimension contributing the proportional value. In this way, we determined the accumulated proportional order of each methodology as shown in Table 8. By sorting these proportions (see Table 9), we come up with a clear solution to the fourth research question we raised in Section 1.3. Note that we discarded the proportional orders given to dimension D5 because no significant differences were detected when we evaluated this dimension against the nine methodologies.

Scenario 2:
In some situations we need to rank the evaluated methodologies based on maximizing the overall level of importance of each dimension. This is typically an optimization problem that can be solved by means of linear programming techniques. Graphical methods, and a widely used algorithmic technique, known as the Simplex method [24], can be used to solve this problem. The first step in this solution is to construct a mathematical model that consists of a set of constraints expressed in the form of a system of linear inequalities that will be solved under the condition of maximizing the following objective function:

$$Z_{max} = v_1 d_1 + v_2 d_2 + v_3 d_3 + v_4 d_4 + v_5 d_5 + v_6 d_6$$ where v_i is a constant that represents the overall weight assigned to dimension i ($i = 1$ to 6), and d_i is a variable given to each dimension i.

Table 7. Ranks of the six dimensions over the evaluated nine AOSE methodologies

	Order	Proportional Order	Dimension, D_i					
			D1	D2	D3	D4	D5	D6
Methodology, M_i	1	9/9	M1	M2	M7	M1	M2	M2
	2	8/9	M2	M9	M8	M2	M1	M1
	3	7/9	M3	M1	M9	M5	M9	M7
	4	6/9	M9	M7	M2	M8	M7	M8
	5	5/9	M8	M8	M5	M9	M5	M5
	6	4/9	M7	M5	M1	M6	M8	M9
	7	3/9	M4	M6	M3	M4	M3	M4
	8	2/9	M6	M4	M4	M7	M4	M3
	9	1/9	M5	M3	M6	M3	M6	M6

Table 8. Accumulated proportional order of the nine methodologies against the evaluated six dimensions

Methodology	Total weight
M1: Gaia	$[9 + 7 + 4 + 9 + 8] / 9 = 37 / 9$
M2: MaSE	$[8 + 9 + 6 + 8 + 9] / 9 = 40 / 9$
M3: Tropos	$[7 + 1 + 3 + 1 + 2] / 9 = 14 / 9$
M4: Agent-SE	$[3 + 2 + 2 + 3 + 3] / 9 = 13 / 9$
M5: MASSIVE	$[1 + 4 + 5 + 7 + 5] / 9 = 22 / 9$
M6: Prometheus	$[2 + 3 + 1 + 4 + 1] / 9 = 11 / 9$
M7: MESSAGE	$[4 + 6 + 9 + 2 + 7] / 9 = 28 / 9$
M8: MAS- CommonKADS	$[5 + 5 + 8 + 6 + 6] / 9 = 30 / 9$
M9: PASSI	$[6 + 8 + 7 + 5 + 4] / 9 = 30 / 9$

Table 9. Overall ranking of the evaluated nine AOSE methodologies

Rank	1	2	3	3	4	5	6	7	8
Methodology	M2	M1	M8	M9	M7	M5	M3	M4	M6

7 Conclusions

Based on the available data, we came up with a set of criteria that can be considered as empirical software metrics for evaluating AOSE methodologies. These criteria are organized in a hierarchy of dimensions and attributes as presented in Section 3.2. We then evaluated each of these dimensions against a set of nine AOSE methodologies by applying the ANOVA procedure to the BIBD model. Consequently, we were able to rank the evaluated methodologies according to the estimated mean effectiveness of the evaluation dimensions. The final results are extremely helpful in supporting the decision of selecting the most appropriate methodology, or assembling more than one, to develop a prospective agent-based application.

The approach we presented in this paper is reliable because it adopts state-of-the-art statistical procedures that makes use of the probability distribution of the data gathered from a number of stakeholders (participants) and validate the concluded results within specific confidence limits. The methodological analysis of this approach can actually help to bridge the gap between research and practice, as it addresses several issues that have largely been ignored by many researchers, especially adopting statistical methods in solving Software Engineering problems.

The greatest threat to the generalizability of the findings obtained from this research was the use of experimental subjects who are not strictly practitioners. This may be a significant drawback, which results from the limitation of selecting participants from a quite small population. However, because most of the participants are PhD candidates who are specialized in Software Engineering and have adequate knowledge and experience in the development of multi-agent systems, they can - to some extent - be assumed to be agent experts. This hypothesis was actually true, as supported by the reasonable normality and the consistency of the collected data. Even so, we still claim the limited generality of the concluding results of this research.

Following are some topics that we recommend for future work:

(1) Unifying AOSE Methodologies. Similar to the way the Unified Modeling Language (UML) was evolved, we would suggest looking at the comparative statistical analysis that we carried out in this research as a preliminary step towards unifying AOSE methodologies. In this context, we would suggest the following three primary steps to achieve this goal:

1) Identifying a whole set of dimensions and attributes that describe an integrated and ideal AOSE methodology that meets future business trends and technological advances.
2) Applying the proposed approach to evaluate the most common and mature AOSE methodologies (e.g. the nine methodologies we evaluated in this study) against the prospective dimensions of a future AOSE methodology.
3) Combining the strong attributes and dimensions that show higher average weights and higher mean effectiveness.

We would like also to comment that unifying methodologies is a vital project that requires adequate funding, time and expertise to propose the main components of a future AOSE methodology, as well as acquiring more accurate evaluation data.

(2) Proposing Agent-Based Software Metrics. In the time of giving birth to a unified AOSE methodology, we can easily deliver standardized scores that can be generalized as agent-based software metrics or benchmarks. Such metrics would be of great importance to support the process of evaluating any methodology by examining the rates it gives against these metrics. In this sense, we measure the relative efficiency of any AOSE methodology as compared to the unified methodology.

References

1. Antony, J.: Design of Experiments for Engineers and Scientists, Butterwort-Heinemann (2003)
2. Bayer, P., Svantesson, M.: Comparison of Agent-oriented Methodologies Analysis and Design. In: Programming, Blekinge Institute of Technology (BITSWAP) (2001)
3. Christensen, R.: Analysis of Variance and Regression. Chapman & Hall, Sydney (1996)
4. Cossentino, M.: From Requirements to Code with the PASSI Methodology. In: Henderson-Sellers, B., Giorgini, P. (eds.) Agent-Oriented Methodologies, Idea Group Inc, USA (2005)
5. Dam, K., Winikoff, M.: Comparing Agent-Oriented Methodologies. In: Giorgini, P., Henderson-Sellers, B., Winikoff, M. (eds.) AOIS 2003. LNCS (LNAI), vol. 3030, pp. 78–93. Springer, Heidelberg (2004)
6. DeLoach, S., Matson, E., Li, Y.: Applying Agent Oriented Software Engineering to Cooperative Robotics. In: Proceedings of the 15th Int'l FLAIRS Conference, Florida, pp. 391–396 (2002)
7. Elamy, A.A.: Statistical Approach for Evaluating Agent-Oriented Software Engineering Methodologies, MSc thesis, University of Calgary, Alberta, Canada (2005)
8. Elamy, A., Far, B.: Multidimensional Weighted-Attributes Framework (MWAF) for Evaluating Agent-Oriented Software Engineering Methodologies. In: CCECE'06. proceedings of the IEEE 19th Canadian Conference on Electrical and Computer Engineering, Ottawa, Canada (2006)

9. Elamy, A.: Perspectives in Agents-Based Technology. European Coordination Action for Agent-based Computing: AgentLink III 18, 19–22 (2005)

10. Elamy, A., Far, B.: Utilizing Incomplete Block Designs in Evaluating Agent-Oriented Software Engineering Methodologies. In: CCECE'05. Proceedings of the IEEE Canadian Conference on Electrical and Computer Engineering, Saskatoon, Canada, pp. 1412–1515 (May 2005)

11. Evans, R., Kearney, P., Stark, J., Caire, G., Garijo, F., Gomez Sanz, J., Pavon, J., Leal, F., Chainho, P., Massonet, P.: MESSAGE: Methodology for Engineering Systems of Software Agents, EURESCOM Project P907, EDIN 0223-0907

12. Far, B.: A Framework for Agent-Based Software Development. In: Proceedings of the 1st EurAsian Conf., Shiraz, Iran (2002)

13. Fishbein, M., Ajzen, I.: Belief, Attitude, Intention and Behavior: An Introduction to Theory and Research. Addison-Wesley, Boston (1975)

14. Giunchiglia, F., Mylopoulos, J., Perini, A.: The Tropos Software Development Methodology: Processes, Models and Diagrams. In: Giunchiglia, F., Odell, J.J., Weiss, G. (eds.) AOSE 2002. LNCS, vol. 2585, Springer, Heidelberg (2003)

15. Iglesias, C., Garijo, M., González, J., Velasco, J.: Analysis and Design of Multiagent Systems using MAS-Common KADS. In: Rao, A., Singh, M.P., Wooldridge, M.J. (eds.) ATAL 1997. LNCS, vol. 1365, pp. 313–327. Springer, Heidelberg (1998)

16. Juan, T., Sterling, L., Winikoff, M.: Assembling Agent Oriented Software Engineering Methodologies from Features. In: Giunchiglia, F., Odell, J.J., Weiss, G. (eds.) AOSE 2002. LNCS, vol. 2585, Springer, Heidelberg (2003)

17. Shehory, O., Sturm, A.: Evaluation of Modeling Techniques for Agent-Based Systems. In: Shehory, O., Sturm, A. (eds.) proceedings of the 5th Int'l Conf. on Autonomous Agents, Montréal, pp. 624–631 (May 2001)

18. Lind, J.: Agent-Oriented Software Engineering with MASSIVE. Informatiktage, Konradin Verlag (March 2002)

19. Montgomery, D.: Design and Analysis of Experiments, 6th edn. John Wiley & Sons, Chichester (2005)

20. Neter, J., Wasserman, W., Kutner, M.: Applied Linear Statistical Models, 5th ed., Irwin, USA (1996)

21. Oppenheim, A.: Questionnaire Design and Attitude Measurement, 2nd edn. Pinter Publications Ltd (1992)

22. Padgham, L., Winikoff, M.: Methodology for Developing Intelligent Agents. In: Alonso, E., Kudenko, D., Kazakov, D. (eds.) Adaptive Agents and Multi-Agent Systems. LNCS (LNAI), vol. 2636, Springer, Heidelberg (2003)

23. Stevens, S.: On the theory of scales of measurement. Science 103, 677–680 (1946)

24. Taha, H.: Operations Research: An Introduction, 7th edn. Prentice-Hall, Englewood Cliffs (2002)

25. Wooldridge, M., Jennings, N., Kinny, D.: The Gaia Methodology for Agent-Oriented Analysis and Design. Journal of Autonomous Agents and MAS 3(3), 285–312 (2000)

26. Wooldridge, M., Ciancarini, P.: Agent-Oriented Software Engineering: The State of the Art. In: Agent-Oriented Software Engineering. Lecture Notes in AI, Springer, Heidelberg (2001)

27. Yates, F.: Experimental Design: Selected Papers, Griffin, UK (1970)

28. Tran, Q., Low, G., Williams, M.: A Preliminary Comparative Feature Analysis of Multi-agent Systems Development Method-ologies. In: Proceedings of the 6th Int'l Bi-Conference Workshop on Agent-Oriented Information Systems, pp. 157–168 (2004)

29. Tran, Q., Low, G., Williams, M.: Comparison of Ten Agent-Oriented Methodologies. In: Henderson-Sellers, B., Giorgini, P. (eds.) Agent-Oriented Methodologies, Idea Group Inc, USA (2005)

From Early to Late Requirements: A Goal-Based Approach*

Alicia Martínez[1,2], Oscar Pastor[1], John Mylopoulos[3], and Paolo Giorgini[3]

[1] Valencia University of Technology, Valencia, Spain
{alimartin,opastor}@dsic.upv.es
[2] ITZ, Zacatepec, Mor. Mexico
[3] University of Trento, Italy
jm@cs.toronto.edu
paolo.giorgini@dit.unitn.it

Abstract. The Software Engineering community is placing increasing emphasis on understanding the organizational context of a new software system before its development. In this context, several research projects focus on mechanisms that facilitate the generation of a software system from early requirements specifications. However, none of these has proposed so far a systematic process for transforming an organizational model into a late requirements one. This paper presents a methodological approach to precisely this problem. In the proposed method, business goals constitute the basis for determining the relevant plans to be supported by the system-to-be. A pattern language is then used to systematically carry out the transformation from an organizational model into a late requirements model. The Tropos framework serves as baseline for this work. However, our work extends Tropos by proposing rules that support the model transformation process, thereby making organizational modeling an integral part of the software development process.

1 Introduction

In recent years, considerable attention has been paid to early phases of requirements engineering. This interest is motivated by the need for mechanisms that ensure a good fit between the functionality of the system-to-be and its organizational context. In this setting, social concepts and mechanisms (goals, beliefs, and intentions; communication and cooperation among agents) constitute powerful tools for capturing the semantics of an organizational setting. The Tropos method [1] uses such social concepts and mechanisms to support all phases of agent-oriented software development, from early requirements to implementation. In this work, we focus on the systematic transformation of an organizational model representing early requirements for a system-to-be into a late requirements model that prescribes functional and non-functional requirements.

* This work has been partially supported by the MEC project with ref. TIN2004-03534, the Valencia University of Technology, Spain, Care Technologies Enterprise Inc.; in addition the work was partially funded by the Provincial Government of Trento through a Fondo Unico project (STAMPS).

M. Kolp et al. (Eds.): AOIS 2006, LNAI 4898, pp. 123–142, 2008.

Current research approaches determine the functional requirements for the system-to-be (with an agent or non-agent orientation) directly from business plans/processes. However, we believe (along with others working on Goal-Oriented Requirements Engineering) that it is necessary to analyze not only the processes to be automated, but also business goals because they are the ultimate purpose to be fulfilled by the new system. We argue that this is the point where agent-oriented techniques can play an important role in modeling and analyzing complex organizational structures. Agent-oriented techniques, such as the Tropos framework, provide the modeling primitives needed to represent an organizational domain and analyze it from an agent perspective (e.g., with respect to autonomy, pro-activity, and sociality aspects). The social and intentional information captured by agent models should play an essential role in generating the inputs of the next modeling stage, namely that of late requirements.

One of the main tasks of any requirement engineer is to determine the functions the system-to-be needs to support in order to fulfill stakeholder objectives. In this sense, the main contribution of this paper consists in providing a methodological approach to determine the functionalities of the system from organizational models represented in the Tropos framework.

In order to make the model transformation process systematic, we propose a set of rules for identifying from stakeholder goals relevant plans to be supported by the system-to-be. The proposed approach also supports the delegation of plans to system actors. To accomplish this, we propose a pattern language where one can express what delegations are best under what circumstances. The proposed approach makes it possible to reduce the abstraction level of an early requirements model thereby bringing it closer to a late requirements one.

The rest of the paper is structured as follows: Section 2 presents an overview of the proposed method. Section 3 details our goal-based requirements elicitation process. Section 4 presents a process for generating a late requirements model, while section 5 discusses related works. Finally, section 6 concludes and sketches future work.

2 Method Overview

In our proposal we adopt the social and intentional concepts of Tropos to model and analyze enterprise behavior, and use this information to support design decisions about the system-to-be. It is true that not all the information captured in an agent-based early requirement phase is useful in the implementation of object-oriented systems. However, the value of agent-oriented modeling lies in the provision of precise justifications for each functional and non-functional requirement.

Our work has been conducted within the context of the OO-Method (http://oomethod.dsic.upv.es/). OO-Method is an industrial, model-transformation method that relies on a CASE tool [2] to automatically generate complete information systems from object-oriented conceptual models. The OO-Method can be viewed as a computer-aided requirements engineering (CARE) method where the focus is on properly capturing system requirements in order to manage the full software production process.

According to OO-Method, the software productions process starts with the specification of a conceptual model that consists of five complementary models (Fig. 1): object, dynamic, functional, presentation and navigation. These models allow the analyst to represent static and dynamic aspects of a software system. The resulting conceptual model specifies the problem to be solved (problem space). Then the graphical diagrams are formally represented in the OASIS formal language [3], which is the source for the abstract execution model provided to guide the translation of the elements of the conceptual model in a specific software development environment (solution space). The final software product is functionally equivalent to the requirements specification.

Despite major strengths of the OO-Method in automatically generating information systems, there are disadvantages as well. Specifically, there is currently no systematic method for acquiring requirements. Accordingly, a major challenge for the OO-Method is to add a new phase of organizational modeling, from which requirements can be derived. Our work is addressing this challenge. We have selected Tropos as a baseline for modeling early requirements because of the expressiveness of the modeling language (i*), as well as its methodological support for deriving late requirements. In fact, our work extends the Tropos method. Moreover, OO-Method focuses on functional aspects of the system-to-be and ignores completely non-functional requirements [4].

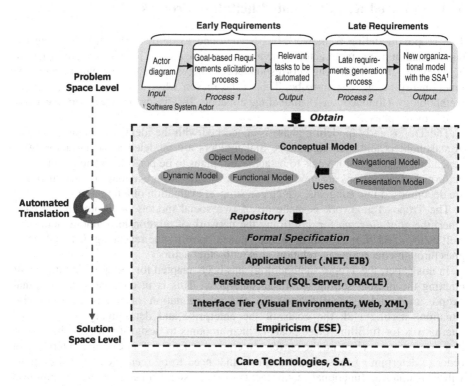

Fig. 1. Goal-oriented requirements elicitation process for the OO-Method approach

The proposed method starts with the definition of an organizational model that represents relevant actors (stakeholders) and their goals (Fig. 1). Following, a goal analysis process is carried out in order to identify plans that fulfill stakeholder goals. The result of this process consists of plans. In the next step, we use transformational rules (defined by a set of patterns) to generate a new organizational model. In this model, the software system is represented within its operational environment along with its functionality and relevant characteristics. This new model constitutes the final result of our proposed method. The approach proposed in this paper is an extension of the work presented in [5], where a first version of the proposed pattern language is presented. Some improvements have been done to this first specification in order to make explicit the steps needed to delegate plans to the system-to-be. Improvements are also proposed for the structure used in defining patterns. However the main contribution of this work is the integration of the pattern language with a goal-based elicitation process.

An evaluation of the proposed method has been conducted using an industrial case study involving car rental management. The case study dealt with the business processes of a car rental company in Alicante, Spain. These included processes for renting cars, chauffeurs services, telephone renting services, buying new cars, car maintenance and car repairs.

3 Goal-Based Requirements Elicitation Process

The Tropos modeling framework has been found to be effective in facilitating the representation of business actor behaviors and rationales [1] [6] [7]. This information is relevant in establishing correspondences between actor activities and the functionality of the system-to-be. This is the reason why, in this paper, the Tropos methodology (founded on i^* modeling concepts [8]) is used to support the early requirements phase.

The Tropos early modeling phase is concerned with the identification and analysis of stakeholders and their intentions. Stakeholders are modeled as social actors who depend on each other for goals to be achieved, plans to be performed and resources to be furnished. Intentions are modeled as goals which, through a goal-oriented analysis, are decomposed into subgoals, which can support evaluation of alternatives.

The Tropos framework is made up of two social models that complement each other: the *goal diagram* for describing the network of relationships among actors, as well as the *actor diagram* for describing and supporting the reasoning that each actor goes through concerning its relationships with other actors.

In this paper, the Tropos methodology has been adapted for the specific purpose of eliciting the present setting within an enterprise. This is in contrast to the original Tropos methodology that focuses on the representation of a desired enterprise situation, starting with the goals of the enterprise and determining the space of alternatives for fulfilling these goals (which amounts to design-from-scratch). In our case, we focus on eliciting the current enterprise situation of an existing enterprise in order to determining those business plans that need to be reengineered. These plans will constitute the functional requirements of the system-to-be. Two phases compose the goal-based elicitation process: (1) goal refinement, and (2) analysis of contributions.

Phase 1: Goal Analysis

The objective of this phase is to analyze each high-level goal that represents strategic interests, to determine the current plans that can operationalize these goals.

As a first step of this process, an actor diagram is created depicting stakeholder goals and dependencies among actors (stakeholders or otherwise). Fig. 2 presents a fragment of the actor diagram for the *car rental management* case study, where the goals (ovals) of *customer*, *employee*, and *mechanic* actors (circles) are shown.

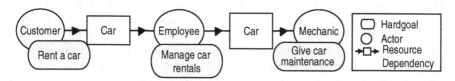

Fig. 2. Fragment of the actor diagram for the car rental case study

The arrows of Fig. 2 indicate dependency relationships between actors. For example, the *employee* depends on the *mechanic* for having the car ready to be rented. It is important to point out that for simplicity, this actor diagram only represents one of many goals of the business actors.

During the next step, each goal defined in the actor diagram must be refined in order to create a goal diagram that shows finer grain goals and plans for satisfying root-level goals. In this modeling stage, a specific goal model for each actor must be constructed to represent actor objectives. To create this model, we use goal refinement and abstraction strategies based on *AND/OR decomposition, means-ends,* or *contribution* links.

According to the refinement strategy, goal analysis starts with the elicitation of high level goals of the enterprise. Then, subgoals are introduced that can lead to the satisfaction of their parent goal. The refinement process ends when fine-grain goals have been introduced for which there are actions that the system-to-be or external actors can perform to fulfill them.

In the abstraction strategy, goal analysis starts by eliciting the plans that the business actors need to perform to fulfill their activities and own goals. Later on, the objectives of these plans need to be elicited in order to match them with the goals defined previously in actor diagram. The abstraction process ends when current plans and low-level goals can be matched with goals represented in the actor diagram. In the case of *softgoals,* the refinement process ends with the determination of means that help to satisfy them. This information is used to construct the low levels of goal models.

Usually, both refinement and abstraction approaches need to be used when eliciting goal diagrams in real cases studies where managers do no have complete information about the plans that operationalize the goals and where employees do not have information about business objectives.

In our framework, *softgoals* are used to represent quality factors that the enterprise wants to fulfill. The quality factors help an organization improve the performance of its business processes and management systems. In the literature, there are many authoritative quality attribute taxonomies [9] [10]. However, we selected only a set of quality factors that are relevant to the context of our case study:

- *Competitiveness*: This quality factor refers to the characteristics (profitability, costs, and quality) that permit an enterprise to compete effectively with other firms;
- *Performance*: This quality factor refers to the response and processing times of the business processes;
- *Security*: This quality factor refers to the ability to prevent unauthorized access to the information used by the enterprise.

These quality attributes have been selected based on the needs of the *car rental* enterprise analyzed in our case study. However, it is true that some rental companies may consider a different set of quality attributes. For this reason, the determination of the quality attribute is a customer-based decision. Quality factors (represented as cloud figures) must also be modeled and refined in our goal diagram.

Fig. 3 illustrates a fragment of the goal diagram for the *employee* actor. In this example, the goal *manage car rentals* of the *employee* actor is refined into two alternative subgoals: 1) *carry out reservations directly in the branch*, and 2) *carry out reservations using alternative ways* (such as internet or phone reservations). The goal *carry out reservations directly in the branch* is refined into three subgoals using *And* decomposition: *analyze customer, analyze car availability*, and *formalize the reservation*. The goal refinement process ends when plans (represented as hexagons) to fulfill the goals are identified and represented in the internal goal refinement tree for the analyzed actor.

Once a goal model has been represented and the quality factors for the specific enterprise have been identified and decomposed, the next step focuses on the analysis of contributions between the elicited plans and the selected quality factors.

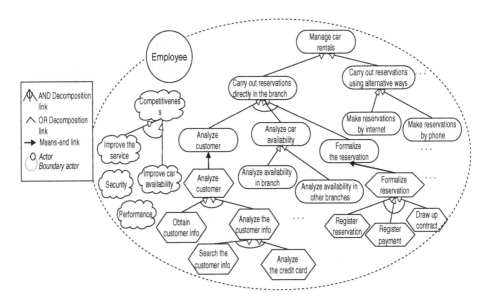

Fig. 3. Fragment of the goal diagram for the car rental case study

Phase 2: Analysis of contributions to the quality factors

In this phase, we associate elicited plans with the quality factors in order to determine what plans need to be automated through the system-to-be.

The first step of this process consists in propagating each *final plan* (those business plans that are not decomposed into other subgoals or into subplans) into two alternative categories: manual or automatic execution. By automatic execution we mean the execution of the plan by the system-to-be.

The second step consists of associating plans with selected quality factors. Here, we have to determine positive or negative contributions of manual/automatic plan execution with respect to quality attributes. An account of the meaning of goal contributions is given in [11]: "The intuitive meaning of the positive (+ and ++) and negative (– and – –) contributions, is that the satisfaction of a goal G contributes positively (negatively) to the satisfaction (denial) of another goal G'''". The measure of positive/negative degree of contribution is expressed in qualitative terms +,++,-,++. If a goal G_1 contributes to the goal G_2 with a ++ contribution, then if G_2 is satisfied, so is G_1. In the goal G_1 contributes to the goal G_2 with a + contribution, then if G_2 is satisfied, G_1 is partially satisfied.

Finally, the third step consists in selecting the plans that best fulfill the quality factors relevant for the enterprise.

Regarding the *car rental* case study, Fig. 4 presents a fragment of the model of quality factors contributions for the *employee* actor. The plans *search customer info* and *analyze credit card* have been propagated in two subplans to represent the manual and automatic execution of these plans. For each propagated plan, contribution links are created to associate the plans with the quality factors. This is done in order to identify the influence of the plans on quality attributes. For example, the manual execution of the plan *analyze credit card* has a negative contribution with *performance* attribute. We consider that the selection of the correct plan to be automated is not always a trivial task. This is because the contribution analysis can lead to contradictions among the alternatives to satisfy the quality factors.

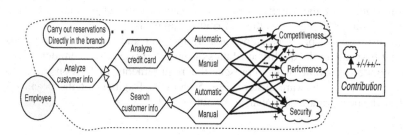

Fig. 4. The contribution of plans to quality factors

In order to deal with contradictory cases, it is necessary to compare the contributions of the propagated plans (manual or automatic options) with the selected quality factors and take decisions based on priorities defined by the enterprise. For example, in the case of the automatic execution of the plan *search customer info*, it positively contributes to the quality factor *Performance*; however, this plan has a negative contribution to the quality factor *Security*. If the enterprise wants to improve the security of the system over the performance of the plans, then, the option that seems to be more convenient is the manual execution of the plan.

Table 1 shows the relation among the alternatives to satisfy the business plans and the proposed quality attributes for the running example. The table also shows the plans selected to be automated according to their positive contribution to the quality factors.

Table 1. Matrix of plans and contributions for the *car rental* case study

Plans	Competitiveness	Performance	Security	
Obtain customer info (Manual)	-	-	-	
Obtain customer info (Automatic)	+	+	+	*To be automated
Search customer info (Manual)	-	--	+	
Search customer info (Automatic)	++	++	-	*To be automated
Analyze credit card (Manual)	+	+	+	
Analyze credit card (Automatic)	+	-	-	
Obtain reservation info (Manual)	-	-	+	
Obtain reservation info (Automatic)	++	++	+	*To be automated
Search car availability (Manual)	-	-	+	
Search car availability (Automatic)	++	++	+	*To be automated
Register reservation (Manual)	-	-	+	
Register reservation (Automatic)	++	++	+	*To be automated
Register payment (Manual)	-	-	+	
Register payment (Automatic)	+	+	-	*To be automated

This table is intended to support plan selection. To use it, the designer must decide what the priority of the quality attributes is, and then select its mode of execution (manual or automatic) based on the contribution analysis.

As a result of the previous steps (goal refinement and contribution analysis) the plans that best satisfy the quality attributes of the enterprise have been identified.

The elicited relevant plans represent the requirements to be considered in the construction of the software system. Fig. 5 shows a fragment of the organizational model, with special marks for plans to be automated.

4   Late Requirements Generation Process

The next step in our proposed method consists of inserting the software system actor (SSA) as another actor in the organizational model with the objective of determining the type of interaction of other actors with the SSA. This way, we identify the functionality expected for the system-to-be.

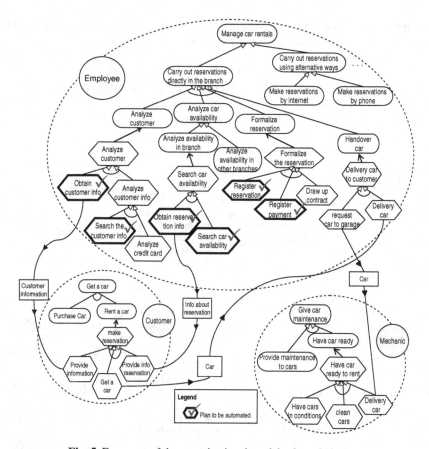

Fig. 5. Fragment of the organizational model selected plans

Four basic steps must be carried out to insert the software system as an actor in the organizational model:

Step 1. Insert the system actor in the organizational model.

Step 2. Delegate business elements that need to be automated from the business actors to the system actor. This indicates that the SSA is now responsible for performing particular actions within the context of business plans.

Step 3. There are plans that require information from the business actors when these plans are transferred to the SSA. In this case, it is necessary to create new resource dependencies between the system actor and the business actors.

Step 4. When resource dependencies are created, it is necessary to generate new plans for sending and receiving resources inside the business actors.

In order to make the application of these guidelines systematic, we have defined a set of patterns that permits us to delegate business plans and goals toward the SSA. The proposed pattern language considers all possibilities to delegate business elements from the business actor towards the SSA. As result of the application of the pattern language, a new organizational model that contains all the relevant information for constructing a software system that gives solutions to the problems detected in the goal reduction process is created.

Table 2 shows a brief description of the proposed pattern language called "FELRE" (From Early Requirements to Late Requirements).

In the following, a brief explanation of the proposed patterns is presented. The pattern explanation includes the definition of the specific problem that the pattern addresses and the proposed solution by the application of the pattern.

Table 2. A brief description of the FELRE patterns

Name of pattern	Use	☐ Element to be automated
The *atomic* plan delegation pattern	To be used when an *atomic* plan needs to be delegated to the SSA in order to automate its execution. The *atomic* plans are those elements that are not decomposed into other sub-elements	
The *composite* element delegation pattern	To be used when a *composite* element needs to be delegated to the SSA in order to automate its execution. The *composite* plans are those elements that are decomposed into other sub-elements.	
The *Depender-Dependee* element delegation pattern	To be used when all the elements of a dependency relationship (*depender-dependum-dependee*) need to be delegated to the SSA in order to automate its execution.	
The *Depender* element delegation pattern	To be used when only the element of the *depender* actor needs to be delegated to the SSA in order to automate its execution.	
The *Dependee* element delegation pattern	To be used when only the element of the *dependee* actor needs to be delegated to the SSA to automate its execution	

1) The *atomic* plan delegation pattern

This pattern concerns the delegation of an *atomic* plan to the SSA, which must fulfill the following conditions: (1) It is not decomposed into other subplans and (2) It is not associated with any dependency relationship (Table 2).

Solution: The process to delegate an *atomic* plan to the SSA is composed of four steps:

Step 1. Delegate the analyzed *atomic* plan to the SSA.

Step 2. Determine the roles that the business actor (who was responsible for this plan) will play after the plan is delegated to the SSA. These roles and their solutions are described in the following substeps:

Step 2.1. If the original plan owner will play the role of *provider* of information to perform the plan (once the plan has been delegated), then a resource dependency between the actor and SSA must be created in order to indicate the introduction of information to the software system from the business actor. The *depender* of this dependency will be the SSA and the *dependee* will be the original plan owner.

Step 2.2. If the original plan owner will play the role of *requester* of information (once the plan has been delegated), then a resource dependency between the actor and SSA must be created. The *depender* of this dependency will be the original plan owner and the *dependee* will be the SSA. This new dependency indicates the delivery of information to the business actor.

Step 2.3. If the original plan owner does not have any interaction with the SSA to perform the plan, no dependencies must be created.

Step 3. Determine the role that the other business actors play in the delegated plan. If they want to obtain or to provide information for the plan, then new dependencies among these actors and the SSA must be created.

Step 4. Analyze the context of the *atomic* plan. In this step, the *atomic* plan must be analyzed in the context of its hierarchical structure in order to determine if its parent goal must be also automated. In this specific case, the *composite* plan delegation pattern must be used.

2) The *composite* element delegation pattern

This pattern concerns the delegation of a *composite* element to the SSA. It can be a plan or a goal, which must fulfill the following conditions: (1) If the *composite* element is a plan, then it must be decomposed into other subplans, (2) If the *composite* element is a goal, then it must be decomposed only by subplans through *means-end* links, and (3) At least one subplan of the *composite* element has been delegated to the SSA.

Solution: The process of delegating a *composite* plan to the SSA is influenced by the previous delegation of at least one child node to the SSA. The delegation process is composed of four steps:

Step 1. Analyze the *composite* element to determine if it can be delegated to the SSA. When the *composite* element is a plan, its nodes must be analyzed if at least one child node of the *composite* plan was delegated to the SSA. If this condition is satisfied, then the *composite* plan must be delegated to the SSA. When the *composite* element is a goal, several conditions must be taken into account to delegate the goal to the SSA. 1) the children nodes of the *composite* goal must be plans, and they must be linked by *means-end* links, and 2) at least one child node of this goal has been delegated previously to the SSA. If these two conditions are satisfied, then the goal can be delegated to the SSA.

Step 2. Associate the subplans of the *composite* plan/goal located in the SSA. The link used to associate these elements must be the same link that the *composite* plan/goal had before being delegated to the SSA.

Step 3. Analyze the influence of this delegation on the business actors.

Step 3.1. If a business actor provides information to the *composite* plan to execute the plan, a resource dependency between the actor and the SSA must be created. The *depender* of this dependency is the SSA. The new dependency indicates the reception of information from the business actor to the SSA.

Step 3.2. If an actor requires information from the *composite* plan, a resource dependency between the actor and the SSA must be created. The *depender* of this dependency is the business actor and the *dependee* is the SSA. The new dependency indicates the delivery of information to the business actor from the SSA.

Step 3.3. If the delegation of the *composite* element does not affect any actor because there is no direct interaction with the element, then no dependency relationship between the business actors and the delegated element is created.

Step 4. Determine whether the *composite* plan/goal to be delegated to the SSA is linked to it through a dependency relationship. In this case, it is necessary to determine if an associated pattern must be applied. The patterns that can be applied are: the *depender-dependee* element delegation pattern or the *depender* element delegation pattern.

3) The *Depender-Dependee* element delegation pattern

This pattern concerns the automation of the elements of the *depender* actor and the *dependee* actor, where the elements to be delegated are associated by a dependency relationship. To apply this pattern, the following conditions must be fulfilled: (1) The elements of the business actors associated by the dependency relationships need to be delegated to the SSA; these elements can be goals or plans. (2)The *dependum* object must be a resource or a plan .

Solution: The delegation of the elements of *depender* and *dependee* actors to the SSA focuses on the following issues: a) the roles played by the business actors, b) the type of the elements involved in the dependency relationship, and c) the type of the *dependum*. Therefore, the alternative solutions are classified depending on the elements to be delegated. 1) First alternative: Plan-Resource-Plan, 2) Second alternative: Plan-Plan-Plan, and 3) Third alternative: Goal-Plan- Plan.

The first element indicates the *depender* actor; the second element indicates the *dependum*, and the third element belongs to the *dependee* actor. Due to space limitations, this paper only details the first alternative.

a) First Alternative (Plan-Resource-Plan):

The first alternative is used when both the *depender* and the *dependee* plan must be delegated to the SSA, and the *dependum* object is a resource. This indicates the need to automate the sending and receiving of the resource. The first alternative of solution is done in third steps:

Step 1. Delegate both the *depender* actor plan as well as the *dependee* actor plan to the SSA, and place a composite plan (in the SSA) which associates these plans through an AND decomposition. Fig. 6 illustrates this situation.

Step 2. The original resource dependency between the business actors must be redefined. The *depender* actor of the new dependency will be the SSA, and, the plan associated with the dependency will be the plan which needs the resource to be performed. The selection of the *dependee* actor in the relationship will depend on which actor acts as *Provider* of information to perform the plan.

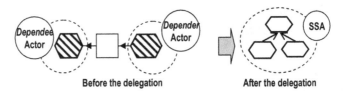

Before the delegation   After the delegation

Fig. 6. The delegation of plans of the *depender/dependee* actors to the SSA

Step 2.1. If the actor who acts as *depender* in the dependency relationship analyzed (that we called *O-Der*) will play the role of *Provider* of information to execute the plan, then the original dependency between the *O-Der* actor and original *dependee* actor (*O-Dee*) remains the same and a new dependency between the SSA and *O-Der* actor is created. These dependencies indicate that the SSA depends on the business actor to obtain the information required to execute the plan (Fig. 7).

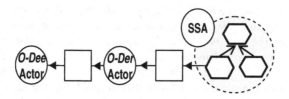

Fig. 7. Organizational model generated after applying step 2.1

Step 2.2. In contrast to step 2.1, if the original *dependee* actor (*O-Dee*) actor will play the role of *Provider* of information to execute the plan, then the original resource dependency is redefined between the SSA and the *O-Dee* actor. The SSA will act as *depender*. Fig. 8 shows the resource dependency where the *depender* actor is the SSA and the *dependee* actor is the same of the original dependency.

Step 2.3. If no actor has any interaction with the SSA to execute the delegated plans, no dependencies must be created.

Step 3. Analyze the influence of the delegation of the elements of the *depender and dependee* actors on the business actors. When other business actors must obtain or provide information from/to the delegated plans, new dependencies among these actors and the SSA must be created. If there is an interaction between the business actors (*O-Der* and *O-Dee*), a new dependency between the actors must be created.

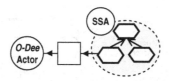

Fig. 8. Organizational model generated after applying step 2.2

4) The *Depender* element delegation pattern

This pattern concerns the automation of the element of the *depender* actor, where the analyzed element has associated a dependency relationship. Two conditions must be fulfilled in order to delegate the analyzed element: (1) An element of the *depender* actor needs to be delegated to the SSA; this element can be a goal or a plan, (2) The *dependum* object must be a resource or a plan.

Solution: The proposed solution for delegating only the *depender* actor element is guided by the *dependum* object. Therefore, when the *dependum* is a resource, it will indicate the need to automate the reception of the resource by the SSA. Otherwise, if the *dependum* is a plan, it will indicate the need for the execution of a plan by a business actor to fulfill the delegated plan or goal. This process is summarized in four steps:

Step 1. Delegate the *depender* actor element to the SSA.

Step 2. Analyze the *dependum* of the dependency; if the *dependum* is a resource, then the actor that will provide the resource to the SSA must be determined.

> **Step 2.1.** If the *O-Dee* will play the role of *Provider* of information to execute the plan, (i.e. if the *O-Dee* provides the resource directly to the SSA) then the original resource dependency is redefined between the SSA and *O-Dee* actor. The SSA will act as the *depender* actor. Fig. 9 shows a scenario of the pattern described in this section (on the left). Thus, the element to be delegated is a plan, and the object *dependum* is a resource. The model on the right shows the obtained solution before applying the step 2.1, where the resource dependency has been redefined between the SSA and the O-Dee actor to indicate that *dependee* actor will provide the resource to SSA directly.

Fig. 9. The application of step 2.1 to delegate a plan of the *depender* actor

> **Step 2.2.** In contrast to step 2.1, if the *O-Der* is the actor that will play the role of *Provider* of information to execute the plan, then the original resource dependency remains the same, and another resource dependency must be created between the SSA and the *O-Der* actor. The *depender* actor of this new dependency will be the SSA. Fig. 10 shows the representation of the solution for this substep.

Fig. 10. The application of the step 2.2 to delegate a plan of the *depender* actor

> **Step 2.3.** If no actor has any interaction with the SSA to execute the delegated plan, no dependencies must be created.

Step 3. If the *dependum* object is a plan, the business actor responsible to execute the plan dependency must be determined.

> **Step 3.1.** If the *O-Der* is the actor responsible for executing the plan dependency, the plan dependency must be redefined between the SSA and the *O-Der* actor. However, if the *O-Dee* actor is the one performing the plan

of the dependency, then it must be redefined between the SSA and the *O-Dee* actor. Fig. 11 shows the two scenarios where the *dependum* is a plan. The first scenario shows a *depender* actor plan which must be delegated to the SSA; after applying step 3.1, the plan dependency must be redefined among some actors involved in the dependence (the *O-Der* or the *O-Dee* actor) and the SSA. The *depender* actor is the SSA. On the other hand, the second scenario of the figure shows a goal associated with a plan (Fig. 11); after applying step 3.1, both business actors (the *dependee/depender*) can be responsible to execute the plan, in order to fulfill the delegated goal.

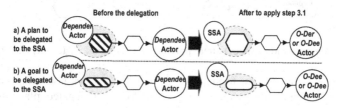

Fig. 11. Two examples where the *dependum* object is a plan and the delegated element is a goal or plan of the *depender* actor

Step 4. Analyze the influence of the delegation of the *depender* actor plan on the business actors. When other business actors must provide information to the delegated plan, a new resource dependency between the actor and SSA must be created. The *depender* of this dependency will be the SSA. When other business actors require obtain information about the delegated plan, then a new resource dependency between the actor and SSA must be created. The *dependee* actor will be the SSA.

5) The *Dependee* element delegation pattern
This pattern concerns the automation of the element of the *dependee* actor, which is associated by a dependency relationship. This pattern must fulfill the following conditions (1) One plan of the *dependee* actor joined by a dependency relationship needs to be delegated to the SSA, (2) The *dependum* must be a resource or a plan.
   Solution: The proposed solution for delegating only the *dependee* actor element is guided by the *dependum* object. Therefore, when the *dependum* is a resource, it will indicate the need to automate the generation of the resource. Otherwise, if the *dependum* is a plan, it will indicate a plan delegation from the *depender* actor to the *dependee* actor. This process is summarized in five steps:
   Step 1. Delegate the *dependee* actor plan to the SSA.
   Step 2. The *dependum* of the dependency relationship under study must be analyzed; if the *dependum* is a resource, it will be necessary to determine the actor that will provide the resource to the SSA.
      Step 2.1. If the *O-Der* actor will play the role of *Requester* of information to execute the plan, (i.e. if the *O-Der* provides the resource directly to the SSA) then the original resource dependency is redefined between the *O-Der* actor and the SSA. The SSA will act as the *dependee* actor. Fig. 12 shows a scenario of the pattern described in this section (on the left). Thus, the

element to be delegated is a plan, and the object *dependum* is a resource. The model on the right of the figure shows the solution obtained after applying step 2.1, i.e. when the *O-Der* actor can access the SSA directly in order to obtain the generated resource by the delegated plan. Thus, the original resource dependency is redirected from the *O-Der* actor to the SSA.

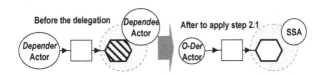

Fig. 12. Organizational model after applying step 2.1 to automate a *dependee* plan

Step 2.2. In contrast to step 2.1, if the *O-Der* does not have access to the SSA to obtain the resource generated by the delegated plan, the original resource dependency remains the same and another resource dependency must be created between the SSA and the *O-Dee*. The *dependee* actor of this new dependency will be the SSA. Fig. 13 shows the delegation of plan of the *dependee* actor. The plan has a resource dependency associate to it. Once the plan is delegated to the SSA, the dependency relationship remains the same between the business actors and a new resource dependency between the SSA and *O-Der* actor is created. In this case the SSA will act as *provider* of information of the delegated plan.

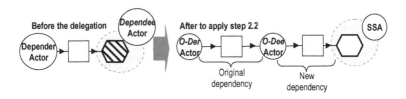

Fig. 13. Organizational model after applying step 2.2 to automate a *dependee* plan

Step 3. Analyze the *dependum* object in the dependency relationship under study; if the *dependum* is a plan, the dependency plan must be redirected between the *O-Der* actor and the SSA.

Step 4. Analyze the influence of this delegation in the business actors.

    Step 4.1. When a business actor provides information to a delegated plan to execute it, a resource dependency between the actor and the SSA must be created. The *depender* actor of this new dependency will be the SSA. The new dependency indicates the reception of information from the business actor to the SSA.

    Step 4.2. When an actor requires information from the delegated plan, a resource dependency between the actor and SSA must be created. The *depender* of this dependency will be the business actor. This new dependency indicates the delivery of information to the business actor from the SSA.

Step 5. If more than one dependency relationship is generated during the delegation of the *dependee* actor plan to the SSA, then they must be labeled with the same number in order to indicate their association.

In order to apply the proposed patterns, the following steps must be performed: (1) Identify the relevant plans to be automated. In this step, we use the plans selected in the goal analysis phase (Fig. 5). (2) Place the SSA into the new business model; also place all the actors that have plans, goals, or dependency relationships to be automated. (3) Transfer the plans or goals to be automated to the SSA. To perform this step, each goal decomposition tree in the business actor must be analyzed. Then the appropriate pattern to delegate the plans or goals to be automated to the SSA must be used.

Fig. 14 shows a partial view of the organizational model generated through the use of the pattern language. This model includes the SSA and the actors that interact with it. The new organizational model represents the final result of the application of the goal analysis and the pattern language. In this model, the software system is represented as an actor (*car rental* system). The specification of the internal elements of this actor represents all the functionalities that this actor must provide for fulfilling the business goals. The model also represents the interactions among the business actors and the software system.

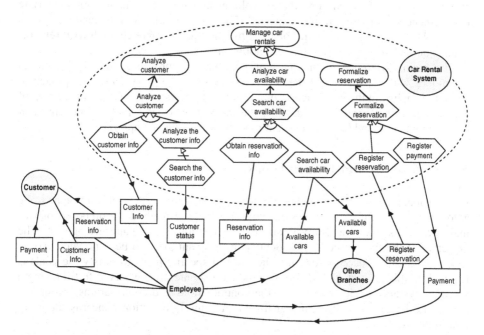

Fig. 14. Partial view of the organizational model which includes the software system actor

5 Related Work

Nowadays, several research efforts use goal mechanisms for supporting the requirements elicitation process. One of the most relevant works in this field is the KAOS approach [12][13][14]. KAOS provides formal rules for deriving requirements based on theories of formal specification languages. This method analyzes functional and non-functional requirements.

However, the use of this approach is restricted to analysts who are used with formal methods. KAOS also provides only partial support for goal reasoning about the alternatives to satisfy goals.

Another goal oriented method is GBRAM (Goal Based Requirements Analysis Method) [15][16], which is focused on the generation of operational requirements from high level goals. However, this method does not establish a clear distinction between the information used in the early and late requirements phase [17]. As a consequence, GBRAM does not offer full support of the development process. Another important research contribution is the NFR Framework proposed in [4]. This approach focused on analyzing the impact of non-functional requirements in the development process.

Regarding organizational modeling methods, at present, several research efforts have been made to accurately represent an organizational model (early requirements) [6][18][19]. In these works, conceptual primitives represent business goals, organizational actors and dependencies among these actors. There are also several research works focused on the development of requirements models (late requirements) to represent the expected functionality of the information system [2][20][21][22]. However, the problem of linking business models with requirements models in methodological way has still not been solved.

The main difference among current goal-based approaches and organizational techniques with our proposed method is the definition of a systematic approach to guide the analyst in the construction of an information system from the information of the organizational context. To do this, the method provides a pattern language that helps to join early and late requirement models in a systematic approach.

6 Conclusions and Future Work

In this paper, we propose a methodological approach to identify relevant plans to be automated by an information system is proposed. The method is composed of two main processes: the goal analysis and the application of the pattern language. The objective of the first process is to identify the relevant plans to be automated. To do this, the goals are decomposed until the level of specific plans to satisfy the goals is reached. In this process, the quality factors that the enterprise wants to fulfill (using a software system) are identified, and the contradictions and contributions among the plans and the quality factors are analyzed. All this information concerns the early requirements phase.

The objective of the second process is to delegate the relevant plans to be automated to a new business actor that represents the software system. This process is carried out through a pattern language which permits us to guide the construction of the new organizational model with the SSA. The new organizational model explicitly represents the interactions among software and business actors, and the organizational context in which the system will be used. In this way, the proposed pattern language will permit to join the early and late requirements phases in a systematic way.

As the reader may have noticed already, the proposed approach could be applied not only in agent-oriented software development environments, but also in traditional object-oriented software development methodologies. In particular, an object-oriented conceptual schema could be obtained from a precise agent-oriented system description, making more robust a model-based software production process.

Object-oriented development methods can be positively influenced by the kind of analysis performed in agent-oriented methods. The use of goals, *softgoals*, plans, dependencies, and intentional concepts can play a relevant role in correctly capturing the semantics of the enterprise, which will be the basis for determining the expected functionality of the information system. At present, object-oriented techniques are not well-equipped to represent, in the correct abstraction level, the social aspects that are fundamental to understand the organizational context before starting to determine the expected functionalities of the system-to-be. This is why we propose to merge agent-oriented techniques with object-oriented methodologies in order to provide a robust software production process.

The research work presented in this paper is part of a more general project proposed to include an organizational modeling phase in the OO-Method approach. This is a model-transformation method that automatically generates complete information systems from object-oriented conceptual models. Currently, we are working on the improvement of the rules to generate an object-oriented conceptual schema from the organization model generated in the proposed approach.

References

1. Bresciani, P., Perini, A., Giorgini, P., Giunchiglia, F., Mylopoulos, J.: TROPOS: an agent-oriented software development methodology. Journal of Autonomous Agents and Multiagent Systems 8(3), 203–236 (2004)
2. Pastor, O., Gómez, J., Infrán, E., Pelechano, V.: The OO-Method approach for information systems modeling: from object-oriented conceptual modeling to automated programming. Information Systems 26(7), 507–534 (2001)
3. Pastor, O., Ramos, I.: OASIS 2.1.1: A Class-Definition Language to Model Information Systems Using an Object-Oriented Approach, 3rd edn. Servicio de Publicaciones. Technical University of Valencia, Spain (1995)
4. Chung, L., Nixon, B., Yu, E., Mylopoulos, J.: Non-Functional Requirements in Software Engineering. Kluwer Academic Publishers, Dordrecht (2000)
5. Martinez, A., Pastor, O., Estrada, H.: A pattern language to join early and late requirements. Journal of Computer Science and Technology, special issue on Software Requirements Engineering 2(5), 64–70 (2005)
6. Kolp, M., Giorgini, P., Mylopoulos, J.: Organizational Patterns for Early Requirements Analysis. In: Eder, J., Missikoff, M. (eds.) CAiSE 2003. LNCS, vol. 2681, pp. 617–632. Springer, Heidelberg (2003)
7. Giorgini, P., Massacci, F., Mylopoulos, J., Zannone, N.: Modelling Social and Individual Trust in Requirements Engineering Methodologies. In: Herrmann, P., Issarny, V., Shiu, S.C.K. (eds.) iTrust 2005. LNCS, vol. 3477, pp. 161–176. Springer, Heidelberg (2005)

8. Yu, E.: Modelling Strategic Relationships for Process Reengineering. Published Doctoral dissertation, University of Toronto, Canada (1995)
9. Boehm, B., Brown, J.R., Kaspar, H., Lipow, M., McLeod, G., Merritt, M.: Characteristics of Software Quality. In: TRW Series of Software Technology, Amsterdam (1978)
10. International Standard ISO/IEC 9126: Quality Characteristics and Guide Lines for their use, Switzerland (2001)
11. Giorgini, P., Mylopoulos, J., Sebastiani, R.: Goal-Oriented Requirements Analysis and Reasoning in the Tropos Methodology. Engineering Applications of Artificial Intelligence 18, 159–171 (2005)
12. Dardenne, A., van Lamsweerde, A., Fickas, S.: Goal directed requirements acquisition. Science of Computer Programming 20(1-2), 3–50 (2003)
13. Lamsweerde, A.: Goal-Oriented Requirements Engineering: A Guided Tour. In: Invited minitutorial, Proceeding 5th IEEE International Symposium on Requirements Engineering, Canada, pp. 249–263 (2001)
14. Letier, E., van Lamsweerde, A.: Reasoning about Partial Goal Satisfaction for Requirements and Design Engineering. In: Roy, B., Meier, W. (eds.) FSE 2004. LNCS, vol. 3017, pp. 53–62. Springer, Heidelberg (2004)
15. Anton, A.: Goal Identification and Refinement in the Specification of Software-Based Information Systems. Ph.D. Thesis, Georgia Institute of Technology, Atlanta, USA (1997)
16. Potts, C., Takahashi, K., Anton, A.: Inquiry-Based Requirements Analysis. IEEE Software 11(2), 21–32 (1994)
17. Yu, E.: Towards Modeling and Reasoning support for Early-Phase Requirements Engineering. In: RE'97. Proceedings of the 3rd. IEEE International Symposium on Requirements Engineering, pp. 226–235. IEEE Computer Society, Los Alamitos (1997)
18. Bubenko, J.A.: Worlds in Requirements Acquisition and Modeling. In: Kangassalo, H., et al. (eds.) Information Modeling and Knowledge Bases VI, pp. 159–174. IOS Press, Amsterdam (1995)
19. Cesare, S., Lycett, M.: Business Modelling with UML, distilling directions for future research, Proceedings of the Information Systems Analysis and Specification. pp. 570-579. Spain (2002)
20. Cockburn, A.: Writing Effective Use Cases. Addison-Wesley, Reading (2001)
21. Kulak, D., Guiney, E.: Use Cases requirements in context. Addison-Wesley, Reading (2000)
22. Ralyté, J., Rolland, R., Plihon, V.: Method Enhancement with Scenario Based Techniques. In: Jarke, M., Oberweis, A. (eds.) CAiSE 1999. LNCS, vol. 1626, pp. 103–118. Springer, Heidelberg (1999)

A Formal Description Language for Multi-Agent Architectures

Stéphane Faulkner [1], Manuel Kolp [2], Yves Wautelet [2], and Youssef Achbany[2]

[1] Information Management Research Unit, University of Namur, 5000 Namur, Belgium
stephane.faulkner@fundp.ac.be
[2]ISYS- Information Systems Research Unit, IAG-Louvain School of Management,
Université catholique de Louvain, 1348 Louvain-la-Neuve, Belgium
{kolp,wautelet,achbany}@isys.ucl.ac.be

Abstract. Multi-Agent Systems (MAS) constitute a highly promising software architectural approach for modern application domains such as peer-to-peer and ubiquitous computing, information retrieval, semantic web services or e-business. Unfortunately, despite considerable work in software architecture during the last decade, few research efforts have aimed at truly defining languages for designing such architectures. This paper identifies the foundations for an architectural description language (ADL) to specify multi-agent system architectures. We propose a set of system design concepts based on the BDI (belief-desire-intention) agent model and existing classical ADLs. We conceptualize it with the Z specification language to capture a "core" model of structural and behavioural elements fundamental to an architecture description for BDI-MAS. We partially apply it on a data integration system example to illustrate our proposal.

1 Introduction

In the last few years, software applications have increased in complexity and stakeholders' expectations principally due to new Internet-centric application areas. These areas demand robust software that can operate within a wide range of environments and can evolve over time to cope with changing requirements. Moreover, such software has to be highly customizable to meet the needs of different kinds of users and sufficiently secure to protect personal data and other assets on behalf of its stakeholders.

Not surprisingly, researchers are looking for new software paradigms that cope with such requirements. One source of ideas that is gaining popularity for designing such software is the area of multi-agent systems (MAS) architectures. They appear to be more flexible, modular and robust than traditional architecture including object-oriented ones. They tend to be open and dynamic in the sense that they exist in a changing organizational and operational environment where new components can be added, modified or removed at any time. Research in this area has notably emphasized that an MAS architecture is conceived as a society of autonomous, collaborative, and goal-driven software components (agents), much like social organizations.

M. Kolp et al. (Eds.): AOIS 2006, LNAI 4898, pp. 143–163, 2008.
© Springer-Verlag Berlin Heidelberg 2008

Such architectures become rapidly complicated due to the ever-increasing complexity of these new business domains and their human or organizational actors. Practitioners have come to realize that getting a complex architecture right is a critical success factor for the system life-cycle. They have recognized the value of making explicit architectural descriptions and choices in the development of new software: a rigorous architectural design can help ensure that a system will satisfy key requirements in such areas as performance, reliability, portability, scalability and interoperability [27].

To this end, over the past decade, software architecture has received increasing attention as an important subfield of software engineering. A number of researches has proposed architectural description languages [1, 12, 18, 20, 26] for representing and analysing architectural designs. An *architectural description language* (ADL) provides a concrete syntax for specifying architectural abstractions in a descriptive notation. Architectural abstactions concern the structure of the system's components, their behaviour and their interrelationships.

Unfortunately, despite this progress, few research efforts have aimed at truly defining description languages for MAS architectures. This paper deals with this issue in defining a "core" set of structural and behavioural concepts, including relationships and constraints, that are fundamental to proposing an architectural description language. This language, called SKwyRL-ADL[1], is aimed at describing BDI multi-agent systems.

The paper is structured as follows. Section 2 overviews the notions of agent and MASs, identifies the main concepts of the BDI model we will use in our ADL and discusses the need for such a language at architectural design stage. The section also outlines research limitations. Section 3 models SKwyRL-ADL and details some elements using the Z specification language. Section 4 partially applies our ADL to characterize the architecture of a simple data integration system. Finally, Section 5 summarizes the contributions of the paper and discusses some possible extensions.

2   Context

This section presents the context of the research. In section 2.1, the agent-concept, multi-agent systems as well as the BDI model are briefly defined. Section 2.2 introduces SKwyRL-ADL and summarizes the overall software development process it is part of. Section 2.3 justifies the need for an architectural description languages while section 2.4 underlines research limitations and future works.

2.1   The BDI Model

An agent defines a system entity, situated in some environment, that is capable of flexible autonomous action in order to meet its design objective [20].

An agent can be useful as a stand-alone entity that delegates particular tasks on behalf of a user. However, in the overwhelming majority of cases, agents exist in an environment that contains other agents. Such environment is a *multi-agent system* that can be defined as an *organization* composed of autonomous and proactive agents that interact with each other to achieve common or private goals.

---

[1] Socio-Intentional ArChitecture for Knowledge Systems & Requirements ELicitation (www. isys.ucl.ac.be/ skwyrl)

In order to reason about themselves and act in an autonomous way, agents are usually built on rationale models and reasoning. An exhaustive evaluation of these models would be out of the scope of this paper. However, a simple yet powerful and mature model coming from cognitive science and philosophy that has received a great deal of attention, is the Belief-Desire-Intention (BDI) model [3, 5]. This approach has been intensively proposed as a keystone model in numerous agent-oriented development environments such as JACK or JADEX. The main concepts of the BDI agent model (in addition to the concept of agent itself) are:

> - *Beliefs* that represent the informational state of a BDI agent, that is, what it knows about itself and the world;
>
> - *Desires* (or goals) that are its motivational state, that is, what the agent is trying to achieve;
>
> - *Intentions* that represent the deliberative state of the agent, that is, which plans the agent has chosen for possible execution

2.2 SKwyRL-ADL: An Architecture-Centric Process for MAS Development

The idioms proposed in this paper take place in the architectural design discipline of the agent-oriented Tropos methodology [7] and is described here in the context of a broader methodology called I-Tropos [30] based on Tropos and driven by the i* framework and organized following an iterative software development life cycle. Due to lack of space, we only focus here on architectural design, the stage at which the ADL takes place. This discipline is presented in this section as a sequential workflow but the reader has to keep in mind that they are "small" parts of a broader highly iterative process.

The process description that follows uses the *SPEM* (*Software Process Engineering Metamodel*) notation. Using this formalization, a discipline is modeled as a workflow in which each ProcessRole performs a series of Activities. WorkProducts (Documents or Models) are inputs or outputs of those activities. Fig. 1 summarizes the SPEM concepts we use. A complete specification of the SPEM notation can be found in [23] while the SPEM description of the disciplines is described in [30].

SPEM, i* and NFR diagrams in this paper are all designed and drawn with the DesCARTES tool [16].

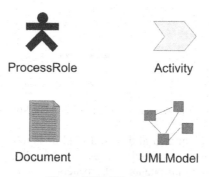

ProcessRole   Activity

Document   UMLModel

Fig. 1. SPEM Notation

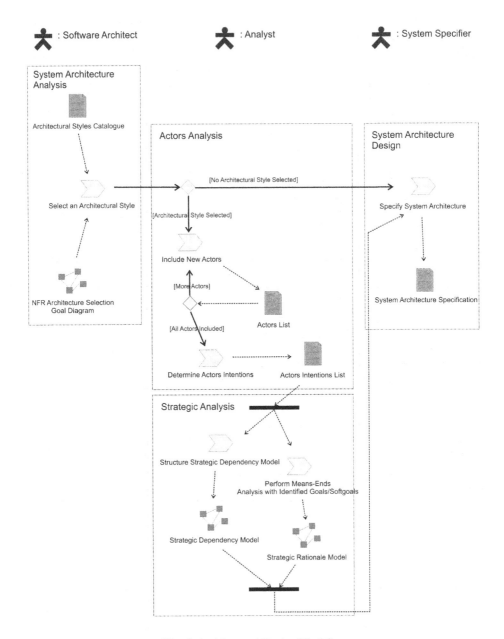

Fig. 2. Architectural Design Workflow

The objective of the architectural design discipline is to organize the dependencies between various subactors identified in previous disciplines in order to meet functional and nonfunctional requirements of the system.

Fig. 2 describes the Architectural Design discipline workflow. The Software Architect uses a non-functional requirements analysis to select the most appropriate

Architectural Style for the module to-be from the Architectural Styles Catalogue (see [11]). If such a style has been selected, new actors and their identified intentions are added to the Strategic Dependency and Strategic Rationale Models according to the semantics of the selected style. Finally, the System Architecture is formally specified with the ADL presented in this paper.

For a long time, the exploitation of software architectures and architectural styles was informal and ad hoc. Architectural configurations were typically described using informal box-line diagrams in design documentation, providing little information about the computations represented by boxes, the interface of the components, or the nature of their interactions. This lack of information severely limited the usefulness of these diagrams for reasoning and analyzing system architecture.

In recent years, there have been several proposals for providing a sounder basis for describing and reasoning about software architecture. In particular, modeling notations known as architecture description languages have emerged. Architectural description languages are formal languages that are used to specify the architecture of a system [27].

2.3 The Need for an Architectural Description Language

Fundamentally, there are five main benefits of formally specifying the architecture of a software system:

- *Understanding*: Architectural description helps us better comprehend large systems by presenting them at a level of abstraction at which a system high-level design can be easily understood [13, 25]. Moreover, at its best, architectural description exposes the high-level constraints on system design, as well as the rationale for making specific architectural choices;
- *Reuse*: Architectural description support reuse at multiple levels. Current work on reuse generally focuses on component libraries. Architectural design supports, in addition, both reuse of large components and also frameworks, and architectural design patterns has already begun to provide evidence for this [6, 21];
- *Construction*: An architectural description provides a partial blueprint for development by indicating the major components and dependencies between parts of a system's implementation, clearly identifying the major internal system interfaces, and constraining what parts of a system may rely in services provided by other parts;
- *Evolution*: By making explicit the "load-bearing walls" of a system, system maintainers can better understand the ramifications of changes, and thereby more accurately estimate costs of modifications. Moreover, architectural descriptions separate concerns about the functionality of a component from the ways in which that component is connected to (interacts with) other components, by clearly distinguishing between components and mechanisms that allow them to interact. This separation allows one to more easily change connection mechanisms to handle evolving concerns about performance interpretability, prototyping, and reuse;
- *Analysis*: Architectural descriptions provide new opportunities for analysis, including system consistency checking, conformance to constraints imposed

by an architectural style, conformance to quality attributes and, dependence analysis for architectures build in specific styles [8, 14].

2.4 Limitations

Much work remains to be done on improving MAS architecture design. Important directions for future developments include the following:

- Our research does not address automated support of consistency analysis and compatibility of SKwyRL-ADL specifications. Automating the analysis reduces the effort required to perform the analysis, and allows to find problems or properties that a human analyst would have missed. We should define a set of rules to perform most of the standard SKwyRL-ADL consistency that could be included in commercial verification tools such as PVS [24]. Once the architect has developed a candidate specification, he could run the tool on the specification which responds either with a guarantee that the consistency checks are satisfied or localization of the problem in the specification;
- We represent architectural specifications as isolated logical and textual formulations. Some authors propose to integrate a graphical representation of architectural aspects in structural and behavioural diagrams. The opportunity of expressing architectural aspects, for example within the UML representations, should be studied;
- Probably the most pressing short term need for research on our architectural framework is to gain experience with its use. In this paper we have applied it on only one two real-world case study. By doing so, we have explored the applicability of SKwyRL-ADL and shown how our framework can help the design of MAS architectures. However, it should be tested on larger cases, which perhaps require other organizational styles;
- A main motivation behind ADL is the possibility of reusing them during implementation. Numerous CASE tools such as Rational Rose include code generators for object-oriented design specification. According to the primitives the BDI agent programming languages, we could extend the design process of our framework with code generation capability. Then, we should propose a CASE tool to automatically generate the code skeleton of future multi-agent information system from their specifications with SKwyRL-ADL. This work is in progress within the DesCARTES tool [16].

3 SKwyRL-ADL

Fig. 1 introduces the main concepts and relationships of SKwyRL-ADL. Each of these entities has been identified from the generic features of current ADLs and the concepts defined through the theoretical BDI agent model.

The ADL is composed of two sub-models, a structural and a behavioural formalization. The *structural model* captures the primitive entities that support the construction of configurations. They represent the elements that are "instantiated" to form an architecture. The *behavioural model* captures the informational and motivational states that form the intentional behaviour of the agent.

The next sub-sections describe the models and detail some of their concepts using the Z specification language [29]. Z is widely used as a formal specification language in the field of software architecture and has been shown to be clear, concise and relatively easy to learn.

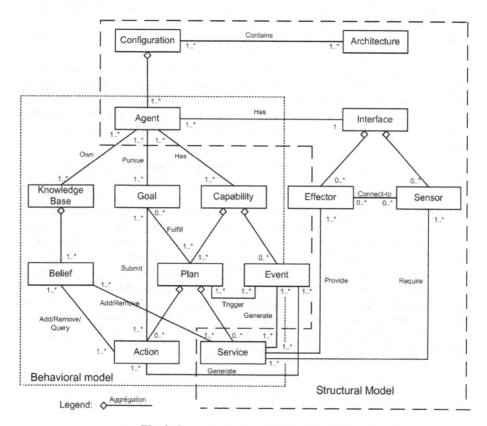

Fig. 3. Conceptualization of SKwyRL-ADL

3.1 The Behavioural Model

The behavioural model illustrated in Fig. 3 is composed of eight main design entities: agent, knowledge base, goal, capability, belief, plan, event, action and service.

An *agent* needs knowledge about its environment in order to make good decisions. Knowledge is contained in the agent in the form of one or many *knowledge bases* structuring its informational state.

A knowledge base consists of a set of *beliefs* the agent has about its environment. A belief represents a view of the current environment of an agent.

However, beliefs about the current state of the environment are not always enough to decide what to do. In other words, in addition to a current state description, the agent needs *goal* information. A goal describes an environment state that is (or is not) desirable. An agent pursues one or many goals that represent its motivational state.

The intentional behaviour of an agent is represented by its *capabilities* to react to *events*. A capability is a set of events that an agent can handle, post or send to its environment and a set of plans. An event is generated either by an *action* that modifies beliefs or adds new goals, or by *services* provided by another agent. Note that services also appear in the structural model because they involve interactions among agents that compose the MAS.

Interactions serve as basic elements to support the construction of configurations. An event may invoke (trigger) one or more *plans*; the agent is committed to executing one of them, that is, it becomes its intention. A plan defines the sequence of actions or services to be chosen by the agent to accomplish a task or fulfil a goal. An action can query, add or remove beliefs, generate new events or submit new goals.

Due to lack of space, we only detail and formalize below the belief, goal and plan aspects of the model. We refer the reader to [11] for a complete formalization of the model.

Belief. *A belief is a predicate describing a set of states about the current agent environment being either true or false.*

Beliefs describe the environment of the agent in terms of states of objects with individual identities and properties, and relations on objects as being either true or false. We use *predicate* symbols to specify a particular relation that holds (or fails to hold) between several objects, and *terms* to represent objects. Each term can be build from constant, variable or function symbols. An expression can also be required to refer to an object. In this case, a complex term can be formed by a function symbol followed by a parenthesized list of terms as arguments to the function symbol.

From the above primitives, we can define an *AtomicBelief*. The set of all predicate, function, constant and variable symbols are denoted by [*PredSymb*], [*Function*], [*Constant*], and [*Variable*], respectively. An *AtomicBelief* is formed from a predicate symbol followed by a sequence of terms.

[*PredSymb*]
[*Funtion*]
[*Constant*]
[*Variable*]
[*Term*]:= Function(Term,...) l Constant l Variable

AtomicBelief

head: *PredSymb*
terms: seq *Term*

head $\neq \varnothing \wedge$ terms $\neq \varnothing$

A *Belief* is specified either as an *AtomicBelief*, a negated *AtomicBelief*, a series of *AtomicBeliefs* connected using logic connectives, or an *AtomicBelief* characterized with a temporal pattern. The following temporal patterns are used in SKwyRL-ADL: $\circ$ (in the next state), $\bullet$ (in the previous state), $\Diamond$ (some time in the future), $\blacklozenge$

(some time in the past), □ (always in the future), ■ (always in the past), $\mathcal{W}$ (always in the future unless), and $\mathcal{U}$ (always in the future until).

[*Belief*]:= *AtomicBelief* | ¬*AtomicBelief* | Temp_Pattern *AtomicBelief*

   | *AtomicBelief* Connective *AtomicBelief*

[*Connective*] → ∧ | ∨ | ⇒

[*Temporal_Pattern*]:= ○ | ● | ◊ | ◆ | □ | ■ | $\mathcal{W}$ | $\mathcal{U}$

Goal. *A goal describes an environment state an agent wants to bring about.*

Beliefs about the current state of the environment are not always enough to decide what to do.

The goal information is an operational objective to be achieved by an agent. Operational means that the objective can be formulated in terms of appropriate state transitions under the control of one agent.

To this end, we consider goals according to the four following patterns [9]:

- *Achieve*: P ⇒ ◊Q
  ◊Q means "state Q holds in the current or in some future state"
- *Cease*: P ⇒ ◊¬Q
- *Maintain*: P ⇒ □Q
  □Q means "state Q holds in the current and in all future states"
- *Avoid*: P ⇒ □¬Q

With respect to beliefs, goals can be specified as follows:

[*GoalPattern*] := Achieve | Cease | Maintain | Avoid
[*GoalStatus*]:= Fulfilled | Unfulfilled

Goal
___

head: *GoalPattern*
state: *Belief*
status: *GoalStatus*

---

head ≠ ∅ ∧ state ≠ ∅

(∀ g: *Goal*) ∧ g.status = Fulfilled
⇒ (∃ blset = {bl$_1$,...,bl$_n$: *Belief*} ∧ g.state ⊆ blset)

State explicitly describes (in terms of beliefs) the environment in which the goal is fulfilled. The **status** indicates whether the goal has been fulfilled or not.

The goal patterns influence the set of possible agent behaviours: *achieve* and *cease* goals generate actions, plans or events, while *maintain* and *avoid* goals restrict them. When a goal is required, the agent identifies a set of plans to achieve or maintain it.

From then on, the agent chooses, according to its current beliefs, which of these plans will be executed.

Plan. *A plan defines a sequence of actions or/and services to accomplish a task or achieve a goal.*

Plans are selected by agents in the way we describe below. Selected plans constrain the agent behaviour and act as intentions. A plan consists of:

- an *invocation condition* detailing the circumstances, in terms of beliefs, events or goals, that cause the plan to be triggered;
- a *context* that defines the preconditions of the plan, i.e., what must be believed by the agent for a plan to be selected for execution;
- the plan *body*, which specifies either the sequence of formulae that the agent needs to perform, a formula being either an action or a service (i.e., action that involves interaction with other agents) to be executed;
- an *end state* that defines the postconditions under which the plan is succeeded;
- a set of services or actions that specify what happens when a plan *fails* or *succeeds*.
  A *Plan* can be specified as follows:

[*PlanName*]
[*AtomicPlan*]:= Action I Service
[Invocation]:= Belief I Goal I Event

Plan
_____

name: *PlanName*
invocation: ℙ *Invocation*
context: ℙ *Belief*
body: seq *AtomicPlan*
endState: ℙ *Belief*
succeed: seq *Atomicplan*
failure: seq *AtomicPlan*

_____

name ≠ ∅ ∧ invocation ≠ ∅ ∧ body ≠ ∅

A Plan is said to have succeeded when it reaches its end state, and to have failed when not in the end state and there are no available actions or services.

3.2 The Structural Model

As illustrated in Fig. 3, the structural model is composed of seven main design entities: agent, configuration, architecture, interface, effector, sensor and service. It describes the interaction among agents that compose the MAS.

Configurations are the central concept of architectural design, consisting of inter-connected sets of *agents*. The topology of a configuration is defined by a set of bind-ings between provided and required *services*.

An agent interacts with its environment through an *interface* composed of *sensors* and *effectors*. An effector provides a set of services to the environment. A sensor requires a set of services from the environment. A service is an operation performed by an agent that interacts by entering into a dialogue with one or several agents.

Finally, the whole MAS is specified with an *architecture* which is composed of a set of configurations. The concept of architecture allows representing agents by one or more detailed, lower-level configuration descriptions.

Due to lack of space, the rest of this section only details and specifies the con-figuration aspeect. We refer the reader to [11] for a complete formalization of the model.

Configuration. *A configuration is an interconnected set of agent instances.*

An MAS is represented as a configuration of instantiated agent components. The topology of the system is defined by a set of bindings between services provided by effector instances and services required by sensor instances.

The configuration separates the descriptions of composite structures from the ele-ments in those compositions. This allows reasoning about the composition as a whole and changing the composition without having to examine each of the individual com-ponents in a system.

Because there may be more than one use of a given agent in an MAS, we distin-guish the different instances of each agent type that appear in a configuration. To this end, we define the type *Instance* representing the name given to an agent instance that has been instantiated within a configuration:

[*IAgent*]

Instantiating an agent also has the secondary effect of instantiating the services that are defined by its interface. We define provided and required service instance type such as follows:

[*IRService*]
[*IPService*]

Once the instances have been declared, a configuration is specified by describing the collaborations. The collaborations define the topology of the configuration, show-ing which agent instance participates in which interactions. This is done by defining a one-to-many mapping relation between provided and required services.

A configuration can be then specified as follows:

[*AgentDescription*]
[*IAgent*]
[*Instance*] := IAgent | IPService | IRService

Configuration

---

description: $\mathbb{P}$ *AgentDescription*
instance: $\mathbb{P}$ *Instance*
collaboration: (*IAgent* X *IRService*) $\longmapsto$ (*IAgent* X *IPService*)

---

description $\neq$ $\varnothing$ $\wedge$ *instance* $\neq$ $\varnothing$ $\wedge$ *collaboration* $\neq$ $\varnothing$

---

4 A Data Integration Case Study

GOSIS (aGent-Oriented Source Integration System) provides an MAS architecture to support the integration of information coming from dynamic, distributed heterogeneous sources. Significant parts will be used illustrate the formal SKwyRL-ADL specification.

The architecture of GOSIS in Fig. 2 is modelled in $i*$ [32]. Each node represents an agent component and each link between two agents indicates that one agent depends on the other for some dependum. The type of the dependency describes the nature of the dependum. *Goal* dependencies represent delegation of responsibility for fulfilling a goal; *softgoal* dependencies are similar to goal dependencies, but the fulfilment of the softgoal cannot be defined precisely; task dependencies are used in situations where one agent is required to do a specific activity for the other agent; resource dependencies are used to model that one agent is required to provide a specific resource to the other agent.

As shown in Fig. 2, agents are represented as circles; dependums – goals, softgoals, tasks and resources – are respectively represented as ovals, clouds, hexagons and rectangles; dependencies have the form *depender* → *dependum* → *dependee*.

GOSIS can be described as follows. When a user wishes to send a data request, it contacts the broker agent, which serves as an intermediary to select one or more mediator(s) that can satisfy the user information needs. Then, the selected mediator(s) decompose(s) the user's query into one or more sub-queries regarding the appropriate information sources, eventually compiles and synthesizes results from the source and returns the final result to the broker.

When the mediator identifies repetitively the same user information needs, this information of interest is extracted from each source, merged with relevant information from the other sources and stored as knowledge by the mediator. Each stored knowledge constitutes a materialized view the mediator has to maintain up-to-date.

A wrapper and a monitor agents are connected to each information source. The wrapper ensures two roles. It has to translate the sub-query issued by the mediator into the native format of the source and translate the source response into the data model used by the mediator.

The monitor is responsible for detecting changes of interest (e.g., a change that affects a materialized view) in the information source and for reporting them to the mediator. Changes are then translated by the wrapper and sent to the mediator.

It may also be necessary for the mediator to obtain information concerning the localization of a source and its connected wrapper able to provide current or future relevant information. This kind of information is provided by the matchmaker agent, which lets the mediator directly interact with the correspondent wrapper. The matchmaker plays the role of a "yellow-page" agent. Each wrapper advertises its capabilities by subscribing to the yellow page agent.

Finally, the multi-criteria analyzer reformulates a sub-query (sent by a mediator to a wrapper) through a set of criteria in order to express the user preferences in a more detailed way, and then refines the possible domain of results.

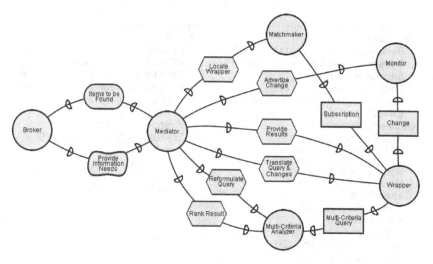

Fig. 4. The GOSIS Architecture

The architecture described in Fig. 4 can serve as a basis for understanding and discussing the assignment of system functionalities, but it is not enough to provide a precise specification of the system details.

An ADL will complement it with a concrete specification to formally detail the system architecture. In the following, we partially present the SKwyRL-ADL specification of some aspects of the two main components of GOSIS: the mediator and the wrapper. We illustrate some concepts detailed in Section 3 (belief, goal, plan and configuration) plus other concepts introduced in Fig. 3 (agent, knowledge base, service and capabilities). We refer the reader to [11] for a more complete specification of GOSIS.

Fig. 3 shows a high-level formal description of the mediator and the wrapper agents identified in Fig. 4.

Three aspects of each agent component are of concern: the interfaces representing interaction in which the agent will participate, the knowledge bases defining the agent knowledge capacity and the capabilities defining agent behaviours.

Interface. The agent interface consists of a number of effectors and sensors for the agent. Each effector provides a service that is available to other agents, and each sensor requires a service provided by another agent. The correspondence between a required and a provided service defines an interaction. For example, the Mediator needs the query_translation service that the Wrapper provides.

Such interface definition points out two aspects of an agent. Firstly, it indicates the expectations it has about the agents with which it interacts. Secondly, it reveals that the interaction relationships are a central issue of the architectural description. Such relationships are not only part of the specification of the agent behaviour but reflect the potential patterns of communication that characterize the ways the system reasons about itself.

```
Agent: { Mediator                          Agent: { Wrapper
  Interface:                                 Interface:
    Sensor[require(query_translation)]         Effector[provide(query_translation)]
    Sensor[require(query reformulation)]       Effector[provide(results)]
    Sensor[require(results)]                   Effector[provide(subscription_info)]
    Sensor[require(locate_wrapper)]            Sensor[require(multiCriteria_query)]
    Sensor[require(change_advertizings)]       Sensor[require(change)]
    Effector[provide(found_items)]           KnowledgeBase:
  KnowledgeBase:                                WrapperSubscription_KB
    Results_KB                                   Translation_Management_KB
    MatchMaker_Info_KB                         Capabilities:
    DataManagement_KB                            Translate_Query_CP
    Request_KB                                   ProvideResults_CP
    Notification_KB                              Subscription_CP }
  Capabilities:
    Handle_Request_CP
    Handle_Results_CP
    Materialized_Views_CP
    Wrapper_Localization_CP
    Handle_Change_CP }
```

Fig. 5. Mediator and Wrapper Structural Descriptions

The required **query translation** service is described in greater detail in Fig. 6. We can see that the mediator (**sender**) initiates the service by asking the wrapper (**receiver**) to translate a query. To this end, the mediator provides to the wrapper a set of **parameters** allowing the definition of the contents of this query. Such a mediator query is specified as a belief with the predicate **search** and the following terms:

$$\text{search}(RequestType, ProductType(+), FilteredKeyword(+))$$

Each term represents, respectively, the type of the request (normal request or advanced in the case of multi-criteria refinement), the type of product and one or many keywords that must be included in or excluded from the results.

```
Service:
  performative: Ask(query_translation)
  sender: Mediator
  parameters: rt: RequestType ∧ pt:ProductType ∧ fk(+):FilteredKeyword
  receiver: Wrapper
  Affect: Add(Translation_Management_KB, search(rt,pt,fk(+)))
```

Fig. 6. Query_Translation Service Description

The Affect indicates that a new search belief is added to the Translation _ Management knowledge base of the wrapper.

Knowledge Base. KBs structure the informational state of the agents. Fig. 7 shows the specification of the Translation_Management KB. The content of this KB concerns the specific information needed by the wrapper to translate a query. This information is represented by the following beliefs:

- source_resource, which defines which kind of data is available from the connected source;
- source_modelling, which describes how the information is structured;
- dictionary, which provides the term correspondence between the mediator and the source.

```
KnowledgeBase: {
    name: Translation_Management_KB
    composed-of:
            source_resource(InfoType(+))
            source_modelling(SourceType,Relation(+),Attributes(+))
            dictionary(MediatorTerm,SourceType,Correspondence)
    type: closed_world
                }
```

Fig. 7. Knowledge Base Descriptions

Capability. Capabilities formalize the behavioural elements of an agent. They are composed of plans and events that together define the agent's abilities. It can also be composed of subcapabilities that can be combined to provide complex behaviour. As shown in Fig. 5, the mediator specification presents five capabilities:

- Handle_Request decomposes a user query into one or more subqueries and sends them to adequate wrappers;
- Handle_Results synthesizes the source answers and returns the answers to the broker;
- Materialized_Views manages the storage, updates, queries and results related to a set of materialized views;
- Wrapper_Localization manages the information (provided by the matchmaker) concerning the localization of a source and its connected wrapper;
- Handle_Change executes the materialized view updates when a monitor detects changes from its source.

Each capability is specified with a name and a body (composed-of) containing the plans that the capability can execute and the events that it can post to itself (handled by one of these plans) or send to other agents. For example, the Handle_Request is specified as follows:

The DecompNmlRq and the DecompMCRq plans deal with the decomposition of normal and multi-criteria (expressing the user preferences) requests.

Capability: {
    name: Handle_Request_CP
    composed-of:
        Plan: DecompNmlRq
        Plan: DecompMCRq
        SendEvent: FaillUserRq
        SendEvent: FailDecompMCRq
        PostEvent: ReadyToHandleRst
    availability: available
    }

Fig. 8. Capability Description

The DecompNmlRq plan, as illustrated in Fig. 9, is triggered each time a new user_keyword belief is added to the Request KB. The argument values of the user_keyword belief are required by the Ask(*user_info-needs*) service that the mediator initiates. However, the plan is only executed if a materialized_view belief which has the same argument values as the invocation user_keyword belief does not exist. A materialized_view belief represents a repetitive user information need whose content is extracted from each source, merged with relevant information from other sources and stored as a belief by the mediator.

The complementary condition on the existence of a materialized_view belief is specified by the context. The context helps for the selection of the most appropriate plan in a given situation.

As soon as the invocation condition and the context are true, the sequence of actions or services specified in the plan body is executed. The plan body of the DecompNmlRq plan is composed by the sequence of an action and a service. The mediator selects from their wrapper beliefs one or many wrappers (wp(+)) capable of translating the decomposed subqueries. Then, a translation service (Ask(query_translation) is asked from the selected wrappers.

The plan will only succeed if the statement described by the endstate is successful. Moreover, SKwyRL-ADL also allows specifying what happens when a plan reaches its endstate or fails, by considering further courses of action or service. For example, the succeed specification of the DecompNmlRq plan counts the number of occurrences of the current subquery in order to identify a possible new materialized view, while the fail specification returns to the execution of the DecompMCRq plan.

Configuration. To describe the complete topology of the system architecture, the agents of an architectural description are combined into a SKwyRL configuration.

Instances of each agent or service that appear in the configuration must be identified with an explicit and unique name. Once the instances have been declared, a configuration is completed by describing the collaborations. The collaborations define the topology of the configuration by showing which agent participates in which interaction. This is done by defining a one-to-many mapping between provided and required service instances.Part of the GOSIS configuration with instance declarations and collaborations is given in Fig. 10. "(min)...(max)" indicates the smallest acceptable integer, as well as the largest one. An omitted cardinality (as is the case with (*max)* in the broker, mediator and wrapper agents), means no limitation to dynamic and evolving structures which can change at runtime.

Plan: {
  name: DecompNmlRq
  invocation: Add(Request_KB, user_keyword(pt(+),kw(+)))
              /* **with** pt:ProductType From
                 Mediator.Ask(*user_info-needs*).reply_with
              /* **with** kw:Keyword From
                 Mediator.Ask(*user_info-needs*).reply_with
  context: ¬ materialized_view(*ProductType* = pt(+),*Keyword* = kw(+))
  body: ∀ pt : ProducType ∈ user_keyword(pt(+),kw(+)) **Do**
          Action: select_wrapper
                          (wrapper (*WrapLocalization,TranslationService*(+))
          as wp(+): Wrapper
          Service:
              performative: Ask(query_translation)
              sender: Mediator
              parameters: rt:*RequestType* ∧ pt:*ProductType*
                          ∧ kw(+):*Keyword*
              receiver: wp(+): Wrapper
          Affect: Add(Translation_Management_KB, search(rt,pt,kw(+)))
        End-Do
  endstate: ∀ pt : ProducType ∈ user_keyword(pt(+),kw(+)) **Do**
              Add(Translation_Management_KB, search(rt,pt,fk(+)))
          End-Do
  suceed: **Action:** count(search(rt,pt,kw(+)))
              Affect: Add(Request_Kb, old_user_keyword(pt,kw(+)))
  failure: **Plan:** DecompMCRq
    }

Fig. 9. A Plan Specification

Such a configuration allows for dynamic reconfiguration and architecture resolvability at run-time. Configurations separate the description of composite structures from the description of the elements that form those compositions. This permits reasoning about the composition as a whole and its reconfiguration without having to examine each component.

5 Related Work

Over the past decade, the field of software architecture has received increasing attention as an important subfield of software engineering. Practitioners have come to realize that getting an architecture "right" is a critical success factor for system design and development. They have begun to recognize the value of making explicit architectural descriptions and choices in the development of new products. In this context, a number of researches have proposed architectural description languages for representing and analysing architectural designs. An *Architectural Description Language* (ADL) provides a concrete syntax for specifying architectural abstractions in a descriptive notation. Architectural abstractions concern the structure of the system's components, their behaviour, and their interrelationships.

Configuration GOSIS
    Description
        Agent Broker[*nb: 1...*]   **Agent** Mediator[*nm: 1...*]
        Agent Wrapper[*nw: 1...nS*]
           /***with** nS = number of information sources
        Agent Monitor[*nmo: 1...nS*]   **Agent** Matchmaker
        Agent Multi-Critria-analyzer
        Service Tell(*query_translation*)   **Service** Ask(*query_translation*)
        Service Achieve(*result*)   **Service** Do(*result*)
        Service Tell(*subscription_info*)   **Service** Ask(*subscription_info*)
        ...
    Instance
        BR$_{nb}$: Broker   ME$_{nm}$: Mediator
        WR$_{nw}$: Wrapper   MO$_{nmo}$: Monitor
        MA: Matchmaker   MCA: Multi-Criteria-Analyzer
        Tellquerytrans: Tell(*query_translation*)
        Askquerytrans: Ask(*query_translation*)
        Achres: Achieve(*result*)   Dores: Do(*result*)
        Tellsubs: Tell(*subscription_info*)   Asksubs: Ask(*subscription_info*)
        ...
    Collaborations
    ME$_{nm}$.Askquerytrans --- Tellquerytrans.WR$_{nw}$;
    ME$_{nm}$.Achres --- Tellres.WR$_{nw}$;   ME$_{nm}$.Asksubs --- Tellsubs.MA;
    ...
End GOSIS

Fig. 10. Configuration Description

We have a number of ADLs that vary widely in terms of the abstractions they support and analysis capabilities they provide. Bass et al. [4] defines the following set of requirements for a language to be an ADL. This section surveys the characteristics of ADLs in terms of the classes of systems they support, the inherent properties of the language themselves, and the process and technology support they provide to represent, refine, analyze, and build systems from an architecture. Some existing ADLs are described.

Recognizing that the *Unified Modeling Language 2.0* (*UML*) supports software architectural description [22, 28], C. Silva et al. [28] present an extension to the UML metamodel to capture the features of agency to support MAS modeling at the architectural level. In doing so, they define a notation to model MAS architectures. Tropos is a framework which offers an approach to guide the development of multi-agent systems (MAS). It relies on the i* notation to describe both requirements and architectural design. However, the use of i* as an ADL is not suitable, since it presents some limitations to capture all the information required for designing MAS architectures. Furthermore, they provide a set of heuristics to describe MAS using a UML-based notation derived from an architectural description using i*. They illustrate their approach by modeling a Conference Management System.

Rapide is an event-based, concurrent, object-oriented language specifically designed for prototyping system architectures [18]. *Rapide* allows architectural designs to be simulated, and has tools for analyzing the results of those simulations. The primary design criteria for *Rapide* are (i) to provide architecture constraints that permit system architectures to be expressed in an executable form for simulation before implementation decision are made, (ii) to adopt an execution model that captures distributed behaviour and timing as precisely as possible, (iii) to provide formal constraints and mappings to support constraint-based definition of reference architectures and testing of systems for conformance to architecture standards, and (iv) to address some of the issues of scalability involved in modelling large system architectures. *Rapide* consists of five sub-languages: (i) the *type language* describes the interfaces of components, (ii) the *architecture language* describes the flow of events between components, (iii) the *specification language* describes abstract constraints on the behaviour of components, (iv) the *executable language* specifies executable modules, and (v) the *pattern language* describes patterns of events.

Darwin [19] is a language for describing software structures that has been around, in various syntactic guises, since 1991. *Darwin* encourages a component- or object-based approach to program structuring in which the unit of structure (the component) hides its behaviour behind a well-defined interface. Programs are constructed by creating instances of component types and binding their interfaces together. *Darwin* considers such compositions also to be types and hence encourages hierarchical composition. The general form of a *Darwin* program is therefore a tree in which the root and all intermediate nodes are composite components; the leaves are primitive components encapsulating behavioural as opposed to structural aspects.

Wright supports the specification and analysis of interactions between architectural components [2]. The primary purpose of *Wright* is to analyze the interconnection behaviour. *Wright* uses a subset of CSP [15] to provide a formal basis for specifying the behaviour of components and connectors, as well as the protocols supported by their interface elements. In *Wright*, components are computation elements with multiple ports. A port is a logical point of interaction between component and its environment. A port defines the expectations of a component. The computation of a component describes the relationship between ports.

ACME [12] is developed as a joint effort of the software architecture research community as a common interchange format for architecture design tools. *ACME* provides a structural framework for characterizing architectures, together with annotation facilities for additional ADL-specific information. This scheme permits subsets of ADL tools to share architectural information that is jointly understood, while tolerating the presence of information that falls outside their common vocabulary.

UniCon (language for UNIversal CONnector support) [33] is an architecture description language (ADL) that describes software architectures in general. *UniCon* is organized around two symmetrical constructs: components and connectors. Components represent loci of computation and data in a software system. They are used to organize the computation and data into parts that have well-defined semantics and behaviours. Connectors represent classes of interactions among the components. They are used to mediate component interactions. Both components and connectors have a specification part and an implementation part. With proper set of primitive components, an architecture that is described in *UniCon* may be executable. *UniCon* supports external analysis tools. *UniCon* has a high-level compiler for architectural designs that support a mixture of heterogeneous component and connector types.

6 Conclusion

Software engineering for new applications domains such as Interned-based services is forced to create open architectures able to cope with distributed, heterogeneous and dynamic information issues. The area of multi-agent systems (MAS) looks promising for helping design such complex system. MASs provide an open and evolving architecture that can change at run-time to exploit the services of new agents, or replace existing ones.

Unfortunately, architectural design for MAS has not received sufficient attention. More specifically, very few efforts have been made to define architectural description languages (ADL). This paper has defined a set of system architectural concepts to propose such a language for BDI-MAS. This ADL allows the specification of each agent component (in terms of knowledge base, interface and capabilities), agent behaviour (in terms of belief, goal and plan) and agent interactions (in terms of service and configuration).

The research reported here calls for further work. We are currently working on:

- the development of a CASE tool to automatically generate code for the future multi-agent system from SKwyRL-ADL specifications;
- the definition of a set of rules to perform consistency analysis to be included in verification tools such as PVS;
- the identification of a suitable set of core abstractions, inspired by organizational metaphors, to be used during the design of the multi-agent system architecture.

References

1. Allen, R., Garlan, D.: Formal Connectors. Software Architecture Lab., Carnegie Mellon University, Pittsburgh, USA, Technical Report CMU-CS-94-115 (1994)
2. Allen, R., Garlan, D.: Beyond Definition/Use: Architectural Interconnection. In: Proceedings of ACM Workshop on Interface Definition Languages, Portland, Oregon, pp. 35–45 (January 1994)
3. Austin, J.L.: How to do things with worlds. Oxford University Press, New York (1962)
4. Bass, L., Clements, P., Kazman, R.: Software Architecture in Practice. Addison-Wesley, Reading (1998)
5. Bratman, M.: Intentions, Plans and Practical Reasoning, Harvard Univ (1988)
6. Buschmann, F., Meunier, R., Rohnert, H., Sommerlad, P., Stal, M.: Pattern Oriented Software Architecture: A System of Pattern. Wiley and Sons, Chichester (1996)
7. Castro, J., Kolp, M., Mylopoulos, J.: Towards requirements-driven information systems engineering: The Tropos Project. Information Systems 27(6), 365–389 (2002)
8. Coglianese, L.H., Szymanski, R.: DSSA ADAGE: An Environment for Architecture Based Avionics Development. In: AGARD 1993. Proc. Of the 4th Int. Conf. on: Aerospace Software Engineering for Advanced Systems Architecture, Paris, France, pp. 321–328 (1993)
9. Dardenne, A., van Lamsweerde, A., Fickas, S.: Goal-Directed Requirements Acquisition. Science of Computer Programming 20(1), 3–50 (1993)
10. Formo, D., Mendenlo, U.: A Multi-Agent Simulation Platform for Modeling Perfectly Rational and Bounded-Rational Agents in Organizations. Artificial Societies and Social Simulation 5(2), 166–177 (2001)
11. Faulkner, S.: An Architectural Framework for Describing BDI Multi-Agent Information Systems, Ph.D. thesis, Department of Management Science, University of Louvain, Belgium (May 2004)
12. Garlan, D., Monroe, R.: Acme: an architecture description interchange language. In: Proc. of the 7th Annual IBM Centre for Advanced Studies Conference, Toronto, Ontario, pp. 78–86 (1997)
13. Garlan, D., Shaw, M.: An Introduction to software architecture. In: Ambriola, V., Tortora, G. (eds.) Advances in Software Engineering and Knowledge Engineering, pp. 1–39. World Scientific Publishing, Singapore (1993)

14. Garlan, D., Allen, R., Ockerbloom, J.: Exploiting Style in Architectural Design Environment. In: SIGSOFT 1994. Proc. Of the 2th Int. Conf. on ACM Symposium on the Foundation of Software Engineering, New Orleans, Louisiana, pp. 175–188 (1994)
15. Hoare, A.R.: Communicating Sequential Processes. Prentice-Hall, Englewood Cliffs (1995)
16. Kolp, M., Wautelet, Y.: DesCARTES Architect: Design CASE Tool for Agent-Oriented Repositories, Techniques, Environments and Systems. In: Louvain School of Management, Université catholique de Louvain, Louvain-la-Neuve, Belgium (2007), http://www.sys.cl.ac.be/descartes
17. Luck, M., d'Inverno, M.: A formal framework for agency and autonomy. In: Proc. of the 1st Int. Conf. on Multi-Agent Systems, San Francisco, USA, pp. 254–260 (1995)
18. Luckham, C., Kenney, J.J., Augustin, L.M., Vera, J., Bryan, D., Mann, W.: Specification and Analysis of System Architecture Using Rapide. IEEE Transactions on Software Engineering 21(4), 336–355 (1995)
19. Magee, J., Dulay, N., Eisenbach, S., Kramer, J.: Specifying Distributed Software Architectures. In: Botella, P., Schäfer, W. (eds.) ESEC 1995. LNCS, vol. 989, pp. 137–153. Springer, Heidelberg (1995)
20. Magee, J., Kramer, J.: Dynamic Structure in Software Architectures. In: Proc. of the 4th Int. Conf. on the Foundations of Software Engineering, San Francisco, CA, USA, pp. 3–14 (1996)
21. Mettala, I., Graham, M.H.: The domain-specific software architecture program. Technical Report CMU/SEI-92-SR-9. Carnegie Mellon Univ (1992)
22. Mylopoulos, J., Kolp, M., Castro, J.: UML for Agent-Oriented Software Development: the Tropos Proposal. In: Gogolla, M., Kobryn, C. (eds.) Unified Modeling Language (UML). LNCS, vol. 2185, pp. 422–441. Springer, Heidelberg (2001)
23. Object Management Group, The Software Process Engineering Metamodel Specification. Version 1.1 (2007)
24. Owre, S., Rajan, S., Rushby, J.M., Shankar, N., Srivas, M.: PVS: Combining Specification Proof Checking and Model Checking. In: Alur, R., Henzinger, T.A. (eds.) CAV 1996. LNCS, vol. 1102, Springer, Heidelberg (1996)
25. Perry, D.E., Wolf, A.L.: Foundations for study of software architecture. In ACM SIGSOFT Software Engineering Notes 17(4), 40–52 (1992)
26. Shaw, M., DeLine, R., Klein, D.V., Ross, T.L., Young, D.M., Zelesnik, G.: Abstractions for Software Architecture and Tools to Support Them. IEEE Transactions on Software Engineering 21(4), 314–335 (1995)
27. Shaw, M., Garlan, D.: Software Architecture: Perspectives on an Emerging Discipline. Prentice Hall, Englewood Cliffs (1996)
28. Silva, C., Araújo, J., Moreira, A., Castro, J., Alencar, F., Ramos, R.: Modeling Multi-Agent Systems using UML. In: Proc. of the 20th Brazilian Symposium on Software Engineering (SBES), Florianópolis, Brazil (October 2006)
29. Spivey, J.M.: The Z Notation: A Reference Manual. Prentice-Hall, Englewood Cliffs (1992)
30. Wautelet, Y., Kolp, M., Achbany, A.: I-Tropos, An Iterative SPEM-Centric Software Project Management Process, Working Paper IAG Series 13/06, Louvain School of Management, ULouvain, Belgium (2006)
31. Wooldridge, M., Jennings, N.R.: Special Issue on Intelligent Agents and Multi-Agent Systems. Applied Artificial Int. Journal 9(4), 74–86 (1996)
32. Yu, E.: Modeling Strategic Relationships for Process Reengineering, Ph.D. thesis, Dpt. of Computer Science, University of Toronto, Canada (1995)
33. Zelesnik, Y.: The UniCon Language Reference Manual, May (1996), http://www.cs.cmu.edu/UniCon/reference-manual/ Reference Manual 1.html

Comparing Three Formal Analysis Approaches of the Tropos Family

Dominik Schmitz[1], Gerhard Lakemeyer[2], and Matthias Jarke[1,2]

[1] Fraunhofer FIT, Schloss Birlinghoven, 53754 Sankt Augustin, Germany
dominik.schmitz@fit.fraunhofer.de
[2] RWTH Aachen University, Informatik 5, Ahornstr. 55, 52056 Aachen, Germany
{lakemeyer,jarke}@cs.rwth-aachen.de

Abstract. Tropos is a software development methodology founded on concepts used to model early requirements, the i* framework. In addition to a methodological framework, research addresses also formal analysis support. In previous work, we proposed the prototype environment SNet based on the Trust-Confidence-Distrust (TCD) approach for the representation and dynamic evaluation of agent-based designs for inter-organizational networks. There are two major ingredients: i* for modeling the domain statically and ConGolog for analysing it dynamically via simulations. In this paper, we compare our approach with two other approaches that enrich i*/Tropos models to allow for more formal analyses, Formal Tropos and Secure Tropos. While the intended use of these is quite different from SNet, there are a number of commonalities, which will be highlighted as well as the differences that suggest a combined use, including complementary forms of analysis such as model checking versus simulation.

1 Introduction

Tropos [3] is an agent- and goal-oriented software development methodology. As opposed to methodologies that have been inspired by programming constructs (e.g. structured or object-oriented methodologies), Tropos is founded on concepts used to model early requirements. Consequently, a key feature of Tropos is to include the organizational environment of the system to be developed in the modeling. Thus, the i* organizational modeling framework [27] is at the center of this methodology.

In previous work, we proposed to apply Tropos also to support requirements engineering for strategic inter-organizational networks, which are comprised of human, organizational, and technological actors. The prototype environment SNet is the result of this research [10]. A crucial aspect of these networks are the interdependencies among the various actors, which result, for example, from the need to delegate certain activities, which in turn requires a certain level of trust between the (human) members of the network. The agent-based graphical modeling language i* has proven to be particularly suitable as a modeling means in this context because it explicitly deals with dependency relations, besides other

M. Kolp et al. (Eds.): AOIS 2006, LNAI 4898, pp. 164–182, 2008.

notions like actors, goals, resources, and tasks. To capture the dynamic aspects of agent networks, we [10] as well as Wang and Lespérance [25] independently proposed to amalgamate i* and the action formalism ConGolog [7]. To bridge the gap between the two formalisms we extended i* by features to describe task preconditions and effects. These extended i* diagrams are automatically translated into executable ConGolog programs, supported by the metadata manager ConceptBase [17]. With the help of simulations, the modeler can then evaluate different complex scenarios especially with regard to how trust relationships evolve, how to ensure that the network maintains its flexibility and innovative culture, or to decide how a particular network member should behave in some situation. This provides the foundation of a decision support tool to manage inter-organizational networks.

There exist several other approaches that try to enrich i*/Tropos in order to allow for more formal analyses. In this paper, we compare our approach with two of them. Formal Tropos (hereafter FT) [8] is intended to support the elicitation of early requirements by enriching the i* specification with additional constraints in linear time logic [21], e. g. on how to create or fulfill goals. On this elaborated specification and with the help of an intermediate language, model-checking techniques can be applied using NuSMV [5] a state-of-the-art model checker that they adapted to their needs. Thus, FT's main purpose is to check for the consistency of a specification.

Secure Tropos (hereafter ST) [15] is a derivative of Tropos and results from the observation that current approaches dealing with security requirements do not consider them as first class citizens. Giorgini et al. argue that security is not a technical problem alone but should be considered at the organizational level as well. In contrast to FT, ST's enrichments of i* focus on the modeling level only, especially on the refinement of dependencies. No additional extension concerning dynamics is added. Formal analysis is provided by a transformation to either a Datalog representation or to FT. Recently, support for the automatic generation and exploration of design alternatives was added [1].

There is a major basic difference between our approach and these two. While they are intended for agent-based requirements engineering preceding some kind of (security-aware) software development, our target is decision support for real-world inter-organizational networks (with a special focus on trust). Thus, differences are to be expected. Nevertheless, since we use a common starting point, it seems to be worth to analyse the similarities and differences in detail in order to identify potential opportunities of a combined use.

The paper is organized as follows. In Sect. 2, we shortly introduce the basics of SNet, i. e. our extended i* and the mapping to ConGolog. The example is adapted from [8] and thereby prepares already the detailed comparison with Formal Tropos that follows in Sect. 3. An example from the same domain is considered for the comparison with Secure Tropos that is presented in Sect. 4. In Sect. 5 we discuss ideas of a combined use in both domains, software requirements engineering as well as decision support for inter-organizational networks. We end with a short conclusion and an outlook on future work (Sect. 6).

2   SNet: A Combination of i* and ConGolog

We base our modeling and simulation environment SNet for inter-organizational networks on a combination of two formalisms: $i*$ – a graphical modeling language originally intended for describing early requirements – for statically modeling the network and *ConGolog* – a logic-based high-level programming language – for simulations so that dynamic aspects such as trust can be analyzed. We take an agent-oriented view in that each actor of an inter-organizational network is represented by a deliberative agent and provide an automated transformation of the i* model to ConGolog code.

2.1   An Extended Version of i*

The i* framework [27] is a graphical language and includes the *strategic dependency (SD)* model for describing the network of relationships among actors (refined into agents, roles, and positions) and the *strategic rationale (SR)* model, which, roughly, describes the internal structure of an actor in terms of tasks, goals, resources, and softgoals. Compared to Yu's original formulation we added a few new features to SR models such as preconditions and effects to tasks and goals, represented by an additional element and by sequence links. Resources are interpreted in a similar fashion as effects of task/goals that provide them and as preconditions to task/goals that want to consume them. Softgoals are used just as in the original i* to characterize other intentional elements like goals and tasks and they are given a quantitative interpretation. For details, see [11].

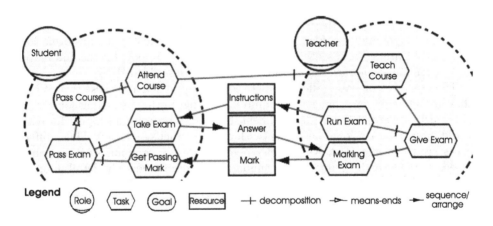

Fig. 1. SNet SR model for teacher-student management

Figure 1 shows a partial SR model of the course management example at a university adapted from [8]. A "Teacher" teaches a course and provides a corresponding exam, while a "Student" attends the course and aims at passing it. While our TCD approach as a whole makes use of i*'s *strategic dependency* *model*, the SNet tool currently can only cope with implicit dependencies resulting from the delegation of intentional elements. Since it is common practice in the combined use of SR and SD diagrams (and thus also here) to attach dependency relations to some internal activity of an agent, we have rewritten the example in [8]. Task or goal dependencies have become delegations, i. e. they interconnect task or goal elements of different actors via decomposition or means-ends links (see, for example, "Teach Course" of the "Teacher" and "Attend Course" of the "Student"). During simulations, a simple bidding protocol and the planning component figure out the details of a concrete delegation. Resources are used as constraints on the execution order of connected task/goal elements. Figure 1 shows the same resources as their picture in [8] except for using dependency links (and we had to adapt the sources/destinations to the simplified setting). Due to its origin, this example is not perfectly suited to present SNet's features, but well suited for the comparison with Formal Tropos in Sect. 3.

2.2   Mapping the i* Model to a ConGolog Program

ConGolog [7] is based on the situation calculus, an increasingly popular language for representing and reasoning about the preconditions and effects of actions [20]. It is a variant of first-order logic, enriched with special function and predicate symbols to describe and reason about dynamic domains. Relations and functions whose values vary from situation to situation are called *fluents*, and are denoted by predicate symbols taking a situation term as their last argument. There is also a special predicate $Poss(a, s)$ used to state that action a is executable in situation s.

ConGolog is a language for specifying complex actions (high-level plans). For this purpose, constructs like sequence, procedure, *if-then-else*, but also non-deterministic (e. g. *ndet*) and concurrency (e. g. *conc*) constructs are provided. Table 1 gives an overview of the available constructs. ConGolog comes equipped with an interpreter which maps these plans into sequences of atomic actions assuming a description of the initial state of the world, action precondition axioms (*poss*), and effect axioms where the latter describe the effects of actions on fluents. For details see [7].

The automated mapping of the i* elements results in a possibly non-deterministic ConGolog program. A complex task is transformed into a procedure whereby the body is derived from the sub-elements. The sequential relations between the sub-elements are reflected via the use of sequence and *conc*. Figure 2 shows the resulting procedure for "Give Exam" with the concurrent calls for "Run Exam" and "Marking Exam". *proc* introduces the definition of a procedure. Its body starts with the sequence construct (*[...]*). There are primitive actions preceding and following the body, so that the preconditions to and effects of this element can be reflected in the program.

Figure 3 shows the poss axioms of the finishing action of "Give Exam" and of the starting and finishing actions of "Marking Exam". The poss axiom of a starting action collects all incoming *sequence links* as well as links from *resource* and *precondition/effect* elements. Resources are treated as special preconditions

Table 1. Overview of available ConGolog constructs

α	primitive action
$\phi?$	test action
$[\sigma_1, \sigma_2, \ldots, \sigma_n]$	sequence
if ϕ then σ_1 else σ_2	conditional
while ϕ do σ	loop
$ndet(\sigma_1, \sigma_2)$	nondeterministic choice of actions
$pi(x, \sigma)$	nondeterministic choice of arguments
$star(\sigma)$	nondeterministic iteration
$conc(\sigma_1, \sigma_2)$	concurrent execution
$pconc(\sigma_1, \sigma_2)$	prioritized concurrent execution
$interrupt(\phi, \sigma)$	triggers σ whenever ϕ holds
$proc(\beta(\overrightarrow{x}), \sigma)$	procedure definition

```
proc(give_Exam(Agent, teacher, PID, T, Course),
    [give_Exam(pre, Agent, teacher, PID, _, Course),
    conc(run_Exam(Agent, teacher, PID, _, Course),
        marking_Exam(Agent, teacher, PID, _, Course)),
    give_Exam(post, Agent, teacher, PID, _, Course)])).
```

Fig. 2. Fragment of ConGolog code resulting from transformation of "Give Exam"

in that the current owner is checked. Accordingly they have to be mapped to fluents to capture that the owner might change over time. The precondition/effect element finally provides means to define arbitrary additional conditions referring to any fluent that exists in the system (e. g. fluents related to trust) via a *formula* attribute (not needed here). Similarly, its *fluent* and *function* attributes are used to describe arbitrary effects of the connected task/goal element associated with its finishing primitive action. For resources, an effect axiom sets the new owner.

```
poss(give_Exam(post, Agent, teacher, PID, T, Course),
    and(executed(run_Exam(post, Agent, teacher, PID, _, Course)),
        executed(marking_Exam(post, Agent, teacher, PID, _, Course)))))
poss(marking_Exam(pre, Agent, teacher, PID, T, Course),
    owner(answer(PID, Course)) = Agent)
poss(marking_Exam(post, Agent, PID, T, Course),
    and(executed(marking_Exam(pre, Agent, PID, TO, Course)),
        time = TO + dur))
```

Fig. 3. Examples for *poss axioms* in SNet

To clarify the relationship between (i*) tasks and (ConGolog) primitive actions, it is worth to mention that we map even primitive tasks, i. e. tasks that are not decomposed any further such as "Marking Exam", to a procedure. In this case, the body consists only of the starting primitive action and the finishing primitive action, following Reiter's suggestion [22] to model activities with a duration via processes with instantaneous starting and finishing actions.

In i*, goals can be viewed in two ways. One view is forward-directed, with goals representing the post-conditions of the tasks that fulfill them. The other is backward-directed or intentional, that is, starting from a goal, one asks what would be the best way of achieving this goal, given a number of possible alternatives. The original i* framework did not commit to a reading direction. But in order to make the model description executable and to resolve ambiguities, we commit to the second, goal-driven reading direction. Thus, goals and their fulfilling tasks are also mapped onto procedures but the different alternatives for achieving the goal are combined using the nondeterministic choice operator *ndet* so that the agents can deliberate about this decision at run-time using the decision-theoretic planning component introduced in [11]. It allows for reasoning about the different alternatives not only according to their contributions to the criteria specified via softgoals but also according to the evolution of trust relationships and/or gain. To be able to collect the various contributions (over time), softgoals are represented by fluents.

```
proc(pass_Course(Agent, student, PID, T, Course),
     [pass_Course(pre, Agent, student, PID, _, Course),
      pass_Exam(Agent, student, PID, _, Course),
      pass_Course(post, Agent, student, PID, _, Course)])).
```

Fig. 4. Fragment of ConGolog code resulting from transformation of "Pass Course"

Figure 4 shows an excerpt of the transformation into ConGolog of the goal "Pass Course" from Fig. 1. Since there is only one alternative to achieve this goal, the *ndet* that would enclose the call to "Pass Exam" has been omitted.

2.3   The SNet Environment

The current SNet environment supports the modeling of generic relationships within inter-organizational networks. The user can establish a concrete scenario by specifying agents that play the generic roles. This instantiation includes information such as the agent-specific durations of primitive tasks and numerical contributions to softgoals. Other details concern intial trust values the agents exhibit to each other, experiences, gain, and general characteristics concerning risk attitude and trust orientation. All the information is compiled as described above via ConceptBase to ConGolog code that can be executed within the simulation environment. The simulation environment does not only provide the decision-theoretic planning component to reason about which alternative to choose at run-time, but also the communication facilities to implement a delegation protocol and the possibility to initiate proactivities of agents via so called exogenous actions. The latter are the means for influencing a concrete simulation run. The user creates a particular setting by initiating different agents' activities, thereby possibly generating competing requests and thus conflicts, that can be analysed especially with regard to how trust is involved and effects the outcome. Conclusions derived by the user might lead to modifications of the model or of scenario conditions which provide the basis for new simulation runs.

3   Comparison with Formal Tropos (FT)

The key idea of FT is to enrich the i* specification of early requirements with additional constraints in linear time logic. These details enable formal analyses, especially of dynamic issues. For example, it can be checked whether regarding some particular setting, a goal is fulfillable (in the future). The main aim of these analyses is to ensure the consistency of the specification. As mentioned, we base our comparison with FT on the example in [8] that has already been introduced in the previous section (see Fig. 1). Figure 5 shows a partial FT representation of the example that can be derived from the graphical i*/Tropos representation similarly to SNet automatically by applying some heuristics. The subsequent comparison is separated into a comparison concerning the modeling means distinguishing static and dynamic aspects and concerning the analysis/simulation. Table 2 gives an overview of the results.

Entity **Course**
Entity **Exam**
   Attribute constant **c:Course**
Actor **Student**
Goal **PassCourse**
   Mode achieve
   Actor **Student**
   Attribute constant **co:Course**
   Fulfillment definition
      $\forall$ **e:Exam** (**e.c=co** $\rightarrow$ $\exists$**p:PassExam**
      (**p.ex=e** $\wedge$ **p.pc=**self $\wedge$ Fulfilled(**p**)))
Task **PassExam**
   Mode achieve
   Actor **Student**
   Attribute constant **pc:PassCourse**
        constant **ex:Exam**
   Creation condition $\neg$ Fulfilled(**pc**)
   Invariant **pc.actor=actor** $\wedge$ **pc.co=e.c**

Actor **Teacher**
Task **GiveExam**
   Mode achieve
   Actor **Teacher**
   Attribute constant **exam:Exam**
Resource Dependency **Answer**
   Mode achieve
   Depender **Teacher**
   Dependee **Student**
   Attribute constant **exam:Exam**
Resource Dependency **Mark**
   Mode achieve
   Depender **Student**
   Dependee **Teacher**
   Attribute constant **ex:Exam**
              passed:boolean
Invariant
   Fulfilled(self)$\rightarrow$
          (**passed**$\leftrightarrow$ X**passed**)

Fig. 5. Partial FT model of the course management example (taken from [8])

3.1   Similarities and Differences Concerning Static Modeling

FT distinguishes an outer layer and an inner layer. The *outer layer* resembles a class declaration and defines the structure of instances together with their attributes. The *inner layer* on the other hand concerns constraints on the lifetime

Table 2. Concepts in FT vs. SNet

	Formal Tropos	**SNet**
static modeling	dependencies	[only implicitly]
	cardinality constraints	[only some]
	attributes, entities	parameters, precondition/effect
	mode	utility computation, planning
	[not considered]	agent, role, position
dynamic modeling	prior-to links	sequence links
	creation/fullfilment	*poss* of starting/finishing prim. actions
	invariant	procedural scope, fluents
	temporal operators	[restricted, less expressive]
	trigger, condition, definition	definition only
analysis	debugging via model-checking	experiments via simulations
	finite domain	no restrictions

of objects in the linear-time temporal logic mentioned before. Finally, global properties on the whole domain complete a FT specification.

But before we consider the details of FT's textual representation, we have a short look at the extensions and differences at the graphical modeling level. FT introduces *cardinality constraints* to define the number of instances of an element that can exist in a system. SNet does not consider such constraints on links yet, but assumes a 1-to-1 relationship concerning execution. But similarly to Wang and Lespérance [25], we also discussed to allow for annotating that a subtask or -goal can be iterated several times, but this is not yet fully integrated [18]. Furthermore concerning delegations, connections between roles already now implicitly describe a 1-to-many relationship in the sense that each agent playing the source role can choose one of the agents playing the destination role at run-time. The absence of the distinction between the *actor* subtypes role, position, and agent in FT seems less important.

The main differences on FT's *outer layer* (structure of the elements in the domain) result from the addition of *entities* and *attributes*. One main purpose of these is to set up the context of elements, for example, that in Fig. 5 the same "Course" is referenced by "Pass Course" and "Pass Exam". Our transformation into ConGolog programs ensures that a subtask or goal can only be considered from within the super task or goal, i. e. the super task or goal sets the scope (or context) for the subtasks/-goals. For example, the only call to "Pass Exam" is made from the body of the procedure resulting from "Pass Course" (see Fig. 4). In addition, similar to attributes in FT, SNet allows the user to specify arbitrary *parameters* of task and goal elements and they are passed through within such procedures. A default parameter is "PID" which separates different calls to the same task/goal within one simulation. We can also use a parameter "Course" to allow for different courses without the need to model each course separately. And finally, we can specify with the help of *precondition/effect elements* arbitrary fluents that can be referred to from within preconditions and effects of completely different modeling elements. Thus altogether, we have similar constructs available, except for the strong typing and additional *facets* FT provides.

In the outer layer FT introduces also a distinction between different *modes* of intentional elements, i. e. *achieve, maintain*, the combination of the two, and *avoid*. In SNet a goal has always to be achieved, a task completed, a resource provided, and softgoals are supposed to be fulfilled as much as possible. Additionally, the latter ones are used in order to capture how well a goal was achieved or a task was completed via a utility computation. In SNet this becomes much more important since a goal or task can be instantiated (and thus also achieved) several times within one simulation. For example, a "Student" can take several courses with the same or other "Teachers". Thus implicitly, task and goal elements in SNet have a mode between *achieve* (once) and *maintain*.

Furthermore with the help of precondition/effect elements and fluents, we can describe objects that exist longer than one instantiation. Especially our representation of trust is also realized that way. Since the agents in SNet have the implicit goal of achieving high utilities, maintain good trust relationships and/or earn much gain, these measures thus affect each of the instantiations differently. This is dealt with by our deliberative planning component at simulation runtime. And since the activity of an agent is triggered externally (either by a user interaction or a resulting delegation from another agent), it is not up to the agent to *avoid* behavior (except for paths of behavior with low utility or gain).

3.2   Similarities and Differences Concerning Modeling Dynamics

A graphical modeling extension that affects FT's inner layer are *prior-to* links. They allow to capture the temporal order of intentional elements and have the same meaning as our *sequence* links, except that FT allows them between a larger set of intentional elements.

The *inner layer* expresses detailed constraints on the dynamics of objects in LTL. FT distinguishes three modalities. A formula is a *constraint* if it is respected while building-up the model-checking automaton (thus, ensured!). If a formula describes only a desired behavior, *assertion* declares that the formula should hold for all valid scenarios, whereas *possibility* denotes that one valid scenario suffices. Such formulas can be assigned globally to the system as a whole or to individual (intentional) elements as conditions on *creation* (supposed to hold at the time of creation), *invariant* (throughout the lifetime of all class instances), and *fulfillment* (whenever a goal/softgoal is achieved, a task completed, or a resource made available). An additional modifier describes whether the stated condition is sufficient (*trigger*), necessary (*condition*), or both (*definition*).

Many formulas associated with individual elements follow immediately from the i*/Tropos graphical model. For example, the fulfillment condition of "Pass Course" enforces that "Pass Exam" is completed. Similarly, the creation condition for "Pass Exam" explicitly refers to the (non-fulfillment of the) super element. Invariants mostly ensure that some referred objects/instances within an element fit together (e. g. belong to the same course or student). Both FT and SNet are capable of encoding this kind of constraints automatically during transformation. SNet reflects such conditions via *poss* (precondition) and *effect axioms* of primitive starting and finishing actions resulting from the transformation of tasks and goals (see pass_Course(pre, ...) and pass_Course(post, ...) in Fig. 4). These conditions are necessary and sufficient. Consequently, the poss axiom of a primitive starting action relates to FT's creation constraint whereas the precondition of the finishing action relates to the fulfillment constraint. Invariants are not considered in SNet. In return, FT does not provide means to explicitly specify what changes are caused by a modeling element (see SNet's effect axioms).

Similarly to FT, conditions are evaluated according to the current simulation situation (state in FT). But SNet does not allow for referring to the future or the past explicitly as it is possible in FT via the corresponding LTL operators. In SNet, this is possible only indirectly via fluents. For example, the duration dur of a primitive task is respected in SNet by mapping it to the poss axiom of the corresponding finishing action of this task (see Fig. 3). The fluent executed(marking_Exam(pre,...)) (true if the action has already been executed, false otherwise) provides the means to determine the time T0 at which the corresponding starting action was executed. If T0 increased by the specified duration equals to the current time (again a fluent!) the finishing action has to be executed. If the condition of a poss axiom does not evaluate to *true*, the corresponding primitive action is not possible in the current situation. It will be re-checked again at a later date. Thus, while the operators of LTL in FT provide much more general means to cope with past and future states, SNet is also capable of coping with conditions that were true some time in the past or will be true some time in the future.

3.3 Similarities and Differences Concerning Analysis

While FT and SNet both use constraints to restrict the resulting model that is analysed (simulated) afterwards, FT's (mostly global) assertion and possibility modalities describe already parts of the analysis. This brings us also to the point that we need to consider the differences concerning the different aims of the two formalisms. FT aims at elaborating and completing a requirements specification. For this purpose, FT and the corresponding T-Tool provide means for checking consistency as well as testing the above mentioned assertions and possibilities. In their example, they identified, for example, the need to ensure that a "Mark" does not change its value once produced. Thus, the major focus is on detecting bugs and missing details in the specification and iterating this process until the specification seems to be complete.

SNet expects its model to be correct and functioning. Its main purpose is not to help the user arrive at a correct representation, although it might be the case that a modeler runs several simulations and makes updates to the model until the simulation adheres to what is happening in the real world. Instead, once such a calibrated model exists, the main purpose of SNet is to enable the user to play around with it: What happens, when I change this modeling aspect (e. g. a network rule)? How does this affect the network as a whole, each agent individually, or the trust relationships between agents? Or what happens if my view on a trust relationship is incorrect? What damages can I incur? The modeler tries out different alternatives that are too costly to experiment with in the real world. Thus, similar to FT we aim at an explorative analysis of the network.

A key difference that results from SNet's strong connection to the real world is that we need to be able to cope with much more instances than FT can cope with (due to its reliance on finite model-checking). Consider, for example, the unlimited number of instances of tasks and goals that can occur within one simulation (distinguished by the parameter "PID"). This is possible due to the fact that SNet relies on simulations backed up by progression, thus after proceeding the simulation we can throw away the history about what has happened before as long as the effects of it are captured. For analysis purpose it is of course possible to store the whole trace of a simulation (from which all intermediate results can be recovered). On the other hand, this approach allows only statements about the single setting that has been investigated and not about a variety of situations as it is possible with a model-checking based approach.

Furthermore, FT does not have an explicit notion of actions with pre- and postconditions. Hence FT does not support deliberation about different courses of actions, which is an essential feature of SNet. It allows the agents to decide on their internal goals (i.e. choice points) on their own but according to rules that reflect the real world (utility-based).

4   Comparison with Secure Tropos (ST)

For the comparison with ST, we stick to the university domain by using the example from [15]. It concerns information access in a setting that includes an administrative officer (Alice), a student IT system (Sam), and a student (Bob), see Fig. 6. Since ST does not have a particular dynamic view, we focus for the comparison on static modeling and analysis only (see overview in Table 3).

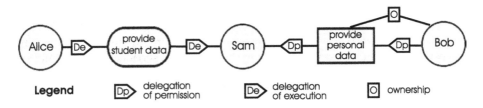

Fig. 6. ST model of university setting (based on [15])

4.1   Similarities and Differences Concerning Modeling

ST's main idea is to replace i*'s dependency model by a more fine-grained model. Similar to SNet, ST considers trust explicitly and thus separates a dependency into a *delegation* and a *trust* relationship to enable delegations without trust. In the example, Bob has to delegate to Sam the provisioning of his data although he might not be confident that it will not be misused.

Table 3. Concepts in ST vs. SNet

	Secure Tropos	**SNet**
static modeling	delegation: perm vs. exec	execution only
	trust: permission vs. execution	trust
	negative authorization	[not considered]
	[possible]	quantitative trust
	ownership vs. provisioning	[no distinction]
	social vs. individual trust	confidence vs. individual trust
analysis	detect static conflicts (Datalog)	focus on dynamics, evolution of trust
	exploring design alternatives	decision-theoretic planning component
	at modeling time	at simulation run-time

Additionally, ST distinguishes between *delegation of permission* and *delegation of execution*. The idea behind this is that, referring again to the example, the relationship between Alice and Sam differs from the one of Bob and Sam. While Alice relies on Sam for providing some service and Sam can at-least provide this service (execution), Bob relies on Sam for not misusing the provided data (permission), i.e. that the data is at-most used in the intended way (formal passage of authority). The flexible networks that SNet is concerned with avoid formal procedures and rely on trust instead. Thus, SNet does not consider the notion of permission. But in [16], Giorgini et al. explicitly mention that permission relates to resources whereas execution relates to tasks and goals. SNet also treats these modeling elements differently in that only tasks and goals can be delegated whereas resources are mapped to preconditions and effects.

Concerning trust, ST introduces also the difference between permission and execution. *Trust of execution* denotes the belief that the trustee is capable of providing the goal, task, etc. This corresponds to the notion of competence in the nomenclature of Castelfranchi & Falcone [2]. SNet takes this part of trust for granted since capabilities are modeled explicitly. *Trust of permission* reflects the belief that the permission will not be misused, i.e. the trustee does not overstep its authority. And similar to us, they also consider *distrust* separately, but only to allow for modeling negative authorization. SNet's understanding and use of these concepts is a little bit different. While we consider *trust* as a combination of Castelfranchi & Falcone's senses of disposition, dependence, and fulfillment, our *distrust* reflects the belief of misuse or opportunistic behavior. Negative authorization does not occur in SNet. This difference results from the different application domains. ST explicitly allows for specifying relationships that should not occur. In SNet we have to deal with all the relationships that are present in the real world and attribute always trust and distrust relationships to them. The actual level of trust (distrust, respectively) is reflected by a quantitative value that might evolve during simulation. Thus in addition, we do not have a binary view on trust. While in [14] the authors state that taking into account several degrees of trust would be easy, they do not present a quantitative model.

The use of the more detailed strategic rationale level in SNet makes the *owner* of a task or goal explicit during modeling. Currently, we do not allow to pass on such capabilities, thus, *ownership* and *provisioning* are coupled. But it occurs often that subtasks or -goals are delegated further. Additionally, we are currently considering *agent evolution* [12] which means that agents can acquire (or lose) roles during simulation. This relates to the provisioning and passage of authority and thus might enforce to incorporate these concepts in the future.

In [16], the authors distinguish also between social and individual levels. This distinction is also present in SNet since modeling concerns only roles and positions, which are then instantiated (agents) separately. In contrast to ST, SNet considers trust relationships on an individual level only. This results from the emphasis on the dynamics of trust, i. e. how trust evolves during a simulation, which ST does not consider at all. Consequently, in this regard the two approaches are not comparable. Furthermore, SNet supports the notion of *confidence* that captures trust into the whole mesh of dependencies (the network), whereas ST allows for checking a trust relationship on social level against the individual trust relationship on instantiated level. Altogether, these features seem complementary.

In [15], Giorgini et al. refer to our work for introducing *monitoring*, which they map on some pattern that can be applied at modeling time. Since they have again only a static view, they do not consider the dynamics of monitoring: What information can be monitored? How to evaluate monitoring results? How to react to the results? Furthermore, they forward monitoring in case of sub-delegations, i. e. if an actor that is monitored delegates a sub activity to a third actor, this is transparent to the original delegator. We [12] explicitly avoid this since it violates the autonomy of agents (network members, respectively). In such a setting, the monitoring agent needs to know too many details about the internals of the monitored agent.

4.2   Similarities and Differences Concerning Analysis

Concerning analysis, the ST-Tool provides means to create a Datalog representation as well as a FT representation. The latter seems to be an initial model that can be extended with LTL formulas as described in the previous section. The Datalog representation instead provides means to analyse specific ST issues such as trust and distrust. For this purpose, the authors give an axiomatization of intensional predicates. For example, they describe trust and distrust chains and specify how monitoring can overcome problems resulting from distrust relationships. Other axioms are used to establish the mapping from social to individual level, or to describe whether some actor can satisfy some task, goal, etc. or has the needed permissions. With the help of the ST-Tool, the modeler can then check for the consistency of her model. Are the established trust, distrust, and monitoring relationships sufficient to enable the execution of a service by some particular role or agent? Are there any conflicts regarding trust on social level or between social and individual level? SNet currently does not provide any means to analyse trust relationships any further.

In recent work [1], an enrichment of the tool support for requirements engineering (and Secure Tropos in particular) is proposed that supports the automatic generation and exploration of alternative options. Given a set of actors and goals as the input, a planner generates design alternatives by generating alternative multi-agent plans to fulfill all given goals. By using the "standard" planning language PDDL [13], a suitable off-the-shelf planner can be used.

While both ST and SNet utilize planning approaches, the use is quite different. ST uses the planner to generate and evaluate alternatives at modeling-time, whereas the decision-theoretic planning component in SNet is used at simulation run-time. Furthermore in ST, the designer is intended to remain in the loop in that the suggestions that are generated by the planner need "to be refined, amended, and approved" [1]. Also the solutions that are proposed by the planner are not expected to be optimal. In contrast to this, the agents in SNet are supposed to reflect real-world behavior without requiring user interaction in regard to choosing from alternatives. Consequently, they also strive for an optimal solution. The criteria according to which the optimum is searched combine general aspects such as gain and trust considerations with domain-dependent issues that are modeled with the help of softgoals relying on their quantitative interpretation.

Due to the different purposes the planners serve in ST and SNet, also the actions that are considered are different. In ST, generic domain-independent actions concerning delegation, satisfaction, refinement as well as special actions in regard to the absence of trust are defined. In SNet, the actions result from the domain. Delegations are dealt with in that the delegator agent can choose from all agents that play the role to which a task or goal is delegated as if they have been defined as non-deterministic alternatives [12]. The actions that are proposed in ST to cope with the absence of trust — negotiate, contract, delegate execution under suspicion, fulfill, and evaluate – remind of the definition of speech acts [26]. In recent work [24], we proposed a transformation of individual speech act-based business processes to i*'s strategic rationale level and thus we have similar actions available.

Unsurprisingly, the main differences regarding analysis result from the fact, that ST does not itself concern dynamic aspects. Neither the dynamics of delegation nor of trust or monitoring are considered. For example, the chains of trust are based on the specified trust relationships that are assumed to be fixed even when the planner is applied. Thus, different trust settings have to be considered separately. Unfortunately, history knows several examples, e. g. equilibrium analysis for a chemical plant, where such steady-state simulations showed beautiful results but the desired steady state could never be reached. Therefore, SNet takes the evolution of trust into account. Similarly, ST assumes that monitoring ensures the fulfillment of a service, but that might not be true. Monitoring is nonetheless useful because it allows to detect problems early and to initiate appropriate counter measures. In regard to planning, ST might profit from extending the set of actions to domain-dependent actions. Considerations on how to integrate the ConGolog approach that is used in SNet and the planning definition language PDDL are already on the way [6].

5 Ideas on a Combined Use

While a comparison with the two other formalisms is in itself already helpful, a combined use of the three formalisms might be even more valuable. Thus, in the following the potentials and limits of such a combined use are discussed in regard to the two different application areas the formalisms originate in, software requirements engineering and decision support for inter-organizational networks.

5.1 Application to Software Requirements Engineering

In an original FT setting, SNet's simulations might be helpful simply due to the possibility to cope with more instances. As it has been shown in [8], the model-checker currently used puts severe restrictions on the number of instances per class for the given example setting. While SNet due to its reliance on simulations is not able to answer questions about fullfillment of assertions, possibilities can easily be generated and tested without any restrictions on the number of instances as we have experienced so far.

The Speech-Act perspective [26] of our multi-perspective modeling methodology, while not elaborated here, is intended to refine the plans that result from strategic rational considerations in regard to strategic depencencies that are involved. Speech-Acts are also used to analyse the interaction of business partners in regard to completeness [23]. This fits nicely with FT's view on completing a specification and ST's consideration of planning actions in the absence of trust. Furthermore, the mapping from the speech act perspective onto the strategic rationale perspective as described in [24] alleviates to apply FT analysis to such models.

Applied to a requirements engineering setting, SNet's simulations via Con-Golog can be interpreted (or utilized) in the view of Christie [4]. He recommended to make use of simulations more extensively during the whole software engineering process, also during requirements elicitation. In contrast to rapid prototyping technologies, in SNet's simulations the user does not interact directly with the "system-to-be" but investigates the scenario from a third person's view. Thus, both — users and developers — can see how things are supposed to run once the intended system is in place. This emphasises nicely the environment of the intended system and thus picks up on the stress the original i*/Tropos approach puts on modeling the environment. Such high-level simulations might provide a suitable means to help predict how a new or altered system will change the environment especially the processes therein, thereby revealing misconfigurations (also in regard to security) or opportunities for further improvements. The findings can be fed back into the formal models, be analyzed with FT and ST means, and provide a new starting point for another set of simulations.

Another nice feature of ConGolog that encourages this approach is the free choice of granularity. As detailed out in Sect. 2.2, the simulations build on a basic action theory that has to be specified by the modeler. While this might seem tedious at a first glance (though automated support is provided), it now is a major advantage. The modeler is free to decide about what is "primitive" in her world. Consequently, she can always choose the most appropriate level of granularity for the analysis and simulations. Thus, the preciseness of the simulations follow strictly the refinements of the model. If a model is improved and detailed out, renewed simulations might reveal different, new issues. This allows to make use of ConGolog simulations not only in the requirements elicitation phase but also at the design and detailed design phases.

An example where such a high-level simulation could be helpful concerns the other major point of SNet, the consideration of the dynamics of trust (see ST discussion in Sect. 4.2). SNet could be used to project how the "system-to-be" can earn the trust of its users. This can lead, for example, to a gradual realization of a system leaving the users enough time to gain confidence into it.

5.2   Application to Support Inter-organizational Networks

In Sect. 3.3, the difference between FT and SNet regarding the aim of the analysis was clarified. While FT tries to analyse the specification in regard to completeness and inconsistency, SNet takes these things for granted. Consequently, the most obvious combination is to support the capturing and construction of SNet models and their instantiation. Next to time-independent consistency issues (e. g. unique names, goal and task decomposition analysis), FT allows to address timedependent issues that have to be respected in all simulations. For example, the specified preconditions can partly be checked for whether at least one possible trace of execution exists (possibility). Furthermore, the maximum/minimum duration of complex tasks can be computed to estimate the complexity and duration of batch simulations.

Another application area of such kind of pre-analysis concerns the evaluation of sets of network rules [24]. Network rules are defined on an organisational level (e. g. a delegation protocol or the admittance procedure for entering a network) and are intended to support the growth of trust relationships. On the other hand, too many network rules let the network degenerate to a normal organization [9]. Thus, a suitable set of network rules needs to be chosen. While many simulations are needed to evaluate such sets, a dynamic FT analysis of their technical interaction could avoid wasteful and costly constructed simulations that fail simply due to design errors. Especially, since we support to model such network rules separately, interference problems are likely to occur.

Regarding the combination with ST, up to now there is no support for further analysis of the outcomes of simulations. The user has to interpret the outcome by comparing trust values and by interpreting the events in the simulation (such as re-delegations due to conflicts) manually. Thus, high-level analyses means are the next step in the development of the SNet tool. Again this can be a field where an integration of the two other formal approaches could help. The examples below illustrate this.

– ST can be used to analyse and compare the initial, any intermediate, or the final situation in regard to the trust setting. Has the created situation the intended effect, i. e. are planned delegation relationships a result of the specified trust setting? What trust chains have evolved in the current situation?

- Since SNet is dedicated to an explorative use, it is very likely that the user wants to make minor adjustments to an intermediate or final simulation situation. FT and ST can help to ensure that the created scenario is still consistent.
- Also the SNet approach has to struggle with complexity issues. While the current implementation takes care of long simulation traces by using progression [22], the number of fluents considerably influences the complexity. Thus, it might be possible that the modeler decides to omit the tracking of some particular properties, in order to make the simulations faster (and thus more interactive). After running several of such complex simulations, it might be possible to adapt FT to work on logs of such simulations in order to check for some specific dynamic property that might have been violated inbetween. Due to the model-checking characteristic, potentially the check can be performed for a whole set of simulation traces at the same time by generalising their specifics.

6   Conclusion

In this paper, we presented a comparison of the TCD/SNet approach with two other formalisms based on i*, Formal Tropos and Secure Tropos. While Secure Tropos just as SNet considers trust issues, it focuses solely on static aspects. Also the use of planning is different in the two formalisms: for one in regard to when it is applied (modeling versus simulation run-time) and for another in regard to how much user interaction is required. Nevertheless, both have many concepts in common such as the separation of delegation and trust and the incorporation of distrust and monitoring. ST's model is even more detailed regarding the difference between permission and execution as well as the considerations about ownership and provisioning. Thus, it needs to be investigated further whether some of these details should also be incorporated in SNet. On the other hand, SNet simulations could enrich the trust investigations of ST. While static analyses of these issues can be seen as a first step, we emphasized the need to take also the dynamics of trust into account.

FT provides more sophisticated means to express rich temporal constraints than SNet. But many, more technical issues like entities and attributes are covered in SNet as well. Furthermore, although in general a formal approach like model-checking is to be preferred over simulations, SNet does not have the restrictions of a finite domain while still being amenable to formal analysis at least of the dedicated simulation trace. Another commonality concerns the use. Both tools support the user to interactively explore the domain in order to find parts that can be corrected (FT) or improved (SNet, see network rule adaptation).

Additionally, we discussed potentials of a combined use of these formalisms. From SNet's perspective, especially for initial, intermediate, or final situations, i.e. snapshots from the dynamic simulations, both formalisms, Formal Tropos and Secure Tropos, seem to provide helpful feedback that enriches the not yet well established analysis features of TCD/SNet. The user can be supported in evaluating the outcome of simulations and in regard to how to change the setting to investigate the scenario in more detail. From FT's and ST's perspective, the main advantage of a combination results from SNet's simulation capability. Especially, the clarification of how the "system-to-be" will interact with its environment, also in regard to trust issues, seems to be valuable in order to smoothly put the new or adapted system at work.

Thus, future work concerns investigating the combined uses in more detail. Furthermore, comparisons with other i* based approaches can be considered as for example the combination of i* and CASL [19], as well as the original work of Wang and Lespérance [25].

Acknowledgment. This work was supported in part by the Deutsche Forschungsgemeinschaft in its Priority Program on Socionics, and its Graduate School 643 "Software for Mobile Communication Systems".

References

1. Bryl, V., Massacci, F., Mylopoulos, J., Zannone, N.: Designing security requirements models through planning. In: Dubois, E., Pohl, K. (eds.) CAiSE 2006. LNCS, vol. 4001, pp. 33–47. Springer, Heidelberg (2006)
2. Castelfranchi, C., Falcone, R.: Trust and Deception in Virtual Societies, chapter Social Trust: A Cognitive Approach. Kluwer, Dordrecht (2001)
3. Castro, J., Kolp, M., Mylopoulos, J.: Towards requirements-driven information systems engineering: The Tropos project. Information Systems 27(6), 365–389 (2002)
4. Alan, M.: Christie. Simulation – An enabling technology in software engineering [Accessed: 2007-11-20] (April 1999), http://www.sei.cmu.edu/publications/articles/christie-apr1999/christie-apr1999.html
5. Cimatti, A., Clarke, E.M., Giunchiglia, E., Giunchiglia, F., Pistore, M., Roveri, M., Sebastiani, R., Tacchella, A.: NuSMV 2: An opensource tool for symbolic model checking. In: Brinksma, E., Larsen, K.G. (eds.) CAV 2002. LNCS, vol. 2404, Springer, Heidelberg (2002)
6. Claßen, J., Eyerich, P., Lakemeyer, G., Nebel, B.: Towards an integration of Golog and planning. In: Veloso, M.M. (ed.) IJCAI, pp. 1846–1851 (2007)
7. de Giacomo, G., Lespérance, Y., Levesque, H.J.: ConGolog, a concurrent programming language based on the situation calculus: language and implementation. Artificial Intelligence 121(1-2), 109–169 (2000)
8. Fuxman, A., Liu, L., Pistore, M., Roveri, M., Mylopoulos, J.: Specifying and analyzing early requirements in Tropos. Requirements Engineering Journal 9(2), 132–150 (2004)
9. Gans, G., Jarke, M., Kethers, S., Lakemeyer, G.: Continuous requirements management for organization networks: A (dis)trust-based approach. Requirements Engineering Journal 8(1), 4–22 (2003)
10. Gans, G., Jarke, M., Kethers, S., Lakemeyer, G., Ellrich, L., Funken, C., Meister, M.: Requirements modeling for organization networks: A (dis-)trust-based approach. In: Proc. 5th IEEE Int. Symposium on Requirements Engineering (2001)
11. Gans, G., Jarke, M., Lakemeyer, G., Schmitz, D.: Deliberation in a metadata-based modeling and simulation environment for inter-organizational networks. Information Systems 30(7), 587–607 (2005)

12. Gans, G., Schmitz, D., Arzdorf, T., Jarke, M., Lakemeyer, G.: SNet reloaded: Roles, monitoring, and agent evolution. In: Bresciani, P., Giorgini, P., Henderson-Sellers, B., Low, G., Winikoff, M. (eds.) AOIS 2004. LNCS (LNAI), vol. 3508, pp. 68–84. Springer, Heidelberg (2005)

13. Ghallab, M., Howe, A., Knoblock, C., McDermott, D., Ram, A., Veloso, M., Weld, D., Wilkins, D.: PDDL – the planning domain definition language. In: AIPS 1998 Planning Committee (1998)

14. Giorgini, P., Massacci, F., Mylopoulos, J., Zannone, N.: Requirements engineering meets trust management: Model, methodology, and reasoning. In: Proc. of the 2nd Int. Conf. on Trust Management (iTrust) (2004)

15. Giorgini, P., Massacci, F., Mylopoulos, J., Zannone, N.: Modeling security requirements through ownership, permission and delegation. In: RE 2005. Proc. of the 13th IEEE Int. Requirements Engineering Conf (2005)

16. Giorgini, P., Massacci, F., Mylopoulos, J., Zannone, N.: Modeling social and individual trust in requirements engineering methodologies. In: Proc. of the 3rd Int. Conf. on Trust Management (iTrust) (2005)

17. Jarke, M., Eherer, S., Gallersdörfer, R., Jeusfeld, M.A., Staudt, M.: ConceptBase – a deductive object base for meta data management. Journal of Intelligent Information Systems 4(2), 167–192 (1995)

18. Kethers, S., Gans, G., Schmitz, D., Sier, D.: Modelling trust relationships in a healthcare network: Experiences with the TCD framework. In: Proc. of the 13th European Conf. on Information Systems (ECIS) (2005)

19. Lapouchnian, A., Lespérance, Y.: Modeling mental states in agent-oriented requirements engineering. In: Dubois, E., Pohl, K. (eds.) CAiSE 2006. LNCS, vol. 4001, pp. 480–494. Springer, Heidelberg (2006)

20. McCarthy, J.: Situations, actions and causal laws. Technical report, Stanford, Reprinted 1968 in Minsky, M.(ed.) Semantic Information Processing, MIT Press (1963)

21. Pnueli, A.: The temporal logic of programs. In: Proc. of the 18th IEEE Symposium on Foundation of Computer Science (1977)

22. Reiter, R.: Knowledge in Action: Logical Foundations for Specifying and Implementing Dynamical Systems. MIT Press, Cambridge (2001)

23. Schael, T. (ed.): Workflow Management Systems for Process Organisations, 2nd edn. LNCS, vol. 1096. Springer, Heidelberg (1996)

24. Schmitz, D., Lakemeyer, G., Jarke, M., Karanfil, H.: How to model inter-organisational networks to enable dynamic analyses via simulations. In: Proc. 17th Workshop on Agent-Oriented Information Systems (AOIS), pp. 697–711 (2007)

25. Wang, X., Lespérance, Y.: Agent-oriented requirements engineering using Con-Golog and i*. In: Working Notes of the AOIS Workshop (2001)

26. Winograd, T., Flores, C.F.: Understanding computers and cognition - a new foundation for design. Ablex Publishing Corporation, Greenwich (1986)

27. Yu, E.: Modelling Strategic Relationships for Process Reengineering. PhD thesis, University of Toronto (1995)

Integration of Aspects with i* Models

Fernanda Alencar[1], Jaelson Castro[1], Ana Moreira[2], João Araújo[2],
Carla Silva[1], Ricardo Ramos[1], and John Mylopoulos[3]

[1] Universidade Federal de Pernambuco, Brasil
fmra@ufpe.br, {jbc,ctlls,rar2}@cin.ufpe.br
[2] Universidade Nova de Lisboa, Portugal
{amm,ja}@di.fct.unl.pt
[3] University of Toronto, Canada
jm@cs.toronto.edu

Abstract. The i* framework has been widely adopted for agent-oriented modeling, as it offers a notation that provides a description in terms of dependency relationships among agents. However, the resulting models may be large and complex, with scattered concerns within the same, or among several models. These crosscutting concerns are not handled explicitly in i* models, affecting several other elements in the same model. In this paper we investigate if the Early Aspects, as promoted by the Aspect-Oriented Software Development community, can help to deal with the complexity which may arise when i* is used to develop large multi-agent systems. To achieve this we identify crosscutting concerns, keeping them in separate models. The consequence is a reduction in complexity and size of the original model. Composition rules are defined simultaneously, to keep a record of these modularized crosscutting elements. Thus, these rules work as transformations in model-driven engineering allowing us to recover the original, more refined model.

Keywords: Agent-Oriented Modeling, Aspect-Oriented Requirements Engineering, Early-Aspects.

1 Introduction

The incremental evolution of paradigms allows software engineering to become increasingly capable of managing the growing complexity of software applications. Agent-oriented techniques appear as another approach for analyzing, designing and implementing complex software systems. Although agent orientation is beginning to be used in commercial and industrial applications [17], this paradigm cannot become a mainstream approach unless a development process for engineering agent oriented software systems is provided. In the last few years some techniques appeared to address this, such as Tropos [8, 13], a framework which supports multi-agent systems engineering. Tropos is based on the requirements engineering framework, i* [24]. It supports the initial phases of software development lifecycle aiming at building software that operates within a dynamic environment.

M. Kolp et al. (Eds.): AOIS 2006, LNAI 4898, pp. 183–201, 2008.

The i* framework provides a graphical description to specify dependencies between actors in a system, emphasizing their intentions, responsibilities and vulnerabilities. Since we are dealing with complex systems, the i* models can become very large, hard to read and understand. This is largely due to the difficulty of modularizing certain properties, or keeping crosscutting relationships localized. Existing software development paradigms do not handle the aforementioned problems well, decreasing the system reusability and maintainability.

Crosscutting concerns naturally cut across the boundaries of other concerns [16], producing scattered and tangled representations (specifications and implementations) that are hard to understand and maintain. Aspect-Oriented Software Development (AOSD) aims at proposing techniques and mechanisms to modularize crosscutting concerns in separate modules called aspects [3] and later compose them back. In the last few years, several existing requirements engineering approaches (e.g. use case driven, goal oriented and viewpoint centered) have been complemented to integrate the advantages offered by aspect-orientation [4, 7, 21, 23, 15].

Aspect oriented requirements engineering [6] permits modularization and composition of crosscutting concerns which cannot be encapsulated using artifacts provided by both traditional approaches (e.g., use cases and view points) [21] and i* models. Thus, we are investigating the principles of aspect orientation to incorporate them in the development of i* models to reduce their complexity and to improve their reusability and understandability.

This paper proposes a systematic approach to identify crosscutting concerns present in the i* models and to compose these concerns with the remaining elements in the model. The resulting models are simpler, therefore easier to understand, maintain and evolve.

The rest of the paper is organized as follows. Section 2 presents an overview of Aspect-Orientation and a short introduction to i* modeling framework. Section 3 introduces the Meeting Schedule example [24], which will be used to illustrate our approach. In Section 4, we present our main contribution, a proposal for the identification of crosscutting concerns in i* models as well as the definition of the composition rules. Section 5 discusses some related work. Finally, Section 6 summarizes our work and points out open research issues.

2 Background

This section presents aspect-oriented software development concepts and the modeling technique used for the definition of the requirements in the context of agent-oriented software development.

2.1 An Overview of Aspect-Orientation

Aspect-Oriented Software Development (AOSD) [3] focuses on the modularization, encapsulation and composition of crosscutting concerns. The term "crosscutting concerns" refers to properties of software (concerns) that cannot be effectively modularized using traditional software development techniques, such as object-oriented methods. Notice that "crosscutting" is a relationship between concerns.

When we say that a concern is crosscutting we are implicitly acknowledging some *dominant* decomposition that offers the base over which the crosscutting concern cuts across. This relationship highly depends on the representation chosen to model, specify, or implement concerns. This means that what is crosscutting in requirements may not be crosscutting in design, for example, or what is crosscutting in an object-oriented representation may not be crosscutting in a functional representation, and vice-versa[1]. Typical examples of crosscutting concerns are non-functional requirements, such as security, fault tolerance, persistency. However, crosscutting concerns can also be functional requirements, such as auditing, or validation [5, 6, 7, 9].

Crosscutting concerns are encapsulated in separate modules, known as *aspects*, and composition mechanisms are later used to weave them back with other core modules, at loading time, compilation time, or run-time. However, aspects, as well as their compositions, also have an important role to play before the implementation activity. Aspects allow the modularization of crosscutting concerns that cannot be encapsulated by a single use case [14], for example, and are typically spread across several of them. Composition, on the other hand, apart from allowing the developers to picture a broader part of the system, allows them to identify conflicting situations whenever a concern contributes negatively to others. This offers the opportunity to establish critical trade-offs before the architecture design is derived, supporting the necessary negotiations among the stakeholders [21, 18].

AOSD aims at addressing such crosscutting concerns at the various levels of the software development process, by providing means for their systematic identification, separation, representation and composition.

2.2 The i* Framework

When developing systems, we usually need to have a broad understanding of the organizational environment and goals. The i* technique [24] provides understanding of the "why" by modeling organizational relationships that underlie systems requirements. i* offers a modeling framework that focuses on strategic actor relationships. It can be used to: (i) obtain a better understanding of the organizational relationships among the various organizational agents; (ii) understand the rationale of the decisions taken; and (iii) illustrate the various characteristics found in the early phases of requirements specification. The participants of the organizational setting are actors with intentional properties, such as, goals, beliefs, abilities and compromises. These actors depend upon each other in order to fulfill their objectives and have their tasks performed. The i* technique offers two models: Strategic Dependency (SD) model, and Strategic Rationale (SR) model. To guarantee consistency among models, all SD dependencies are preserved in the SR model.

Strategic Dependency Model. The SD model consists of a set of nodes and links connecting them, where nodes represent actors and each link indicates a dependency between two actors (see Fig. 1). The depending actor is called *depender*, and the actor who is depended upon is called the *dependee*. Hence, an SD model consists of a network of actors, capturing the motivation and the rationale of activities.

---

[1] The interested reader can consult, for example, aosd.net and [5].

i* distinguishes four types of dependencies. Three of these are related to existing intentions – goal dependency, resource dependency and task dependency, while the fourth is associated with the notion of non-functional requirements, the so called softgoal dependency. In i* we can also model different degrees of dependency commitment on the part of the relevant actors (e.g. open, committed, or critical). We can also classify actors into agents, roles and positions. An agent is an actor with concrete physical manifestations (a person or a system). A role is an abstract characterization of the behaviour of a social actor within some specialized context, domain or endeavor. A position is a set of roles typically played by one agent. Finally, i* supports the analysis of opportunities and vulnerabilities for different actors [24].

Strategic Rational Model. The SR model provides a more detailed level of modeling by looking "inside" actors to model internal intentional relationships (see Fig. 2). It is used to: (i) describe the interests, concerns and motivations of participant process; (ii) enable the assessment of the possible alternatives in the definition of the process; and (iii) provide the rationale behind the dependencies between the various actors. Nodes and links also compose this model. It includes the previous four types of nodes (present in the SD model, Fig. 1): goal, task, resource and soft-goal. However, three new types of relationship are incorporated: (i) means-end that suggests that there could be other means of achieving the objective (alternatives), (ii) task-decomposition that describes what should be done in order to perform a certain task and (iii) the means-end contributing for softgoals links (not identified on Fig. 2) that will represent a partial contributions of a means (task ou softgoal) to an end (softgoal).

Tasks are partially ordered sequences of steps intended to accomplish some (soft)goal. Tasks can be decomposed into goals and/or subtasks, whose collective fulfilment completes the task.

3   Case Study

The case study we have chosen to illustrate our ideas is an extension of the Meeting Schedule system [24]. The aim of the Meeting Schedule system is to support the organization of meetings. For each meeting request, the meeting scheduler should try to determine and broadcast a meeting date and location so that most of the intended participants will participate effectively. The system finds dates and locations that are as convenient as possible. The meeting initiator asks potential participants for information about their availability to meet during a date range, based on their personal agendas, as well as, an exclusion set of dates. The meeting scheduler comes up with a proposed date. The date to be chosen must be an available date, and should ideally belong to as many preference sets as possible. Participants would agree to a meeting date once an acceptable date has been found. The example has been extended to guarantee confidentiality for dates and location of the meeting, as well as for participants' data. When the meeting date is agreed, it should be announced to all interested parties. Fig. 1 illustrates the i* Strategic Dependency Model for this example.

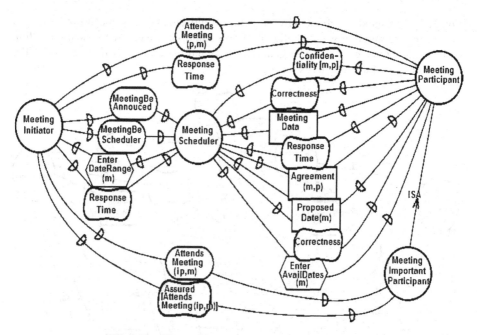

Fig.1. The SD model for the Meeting Schedule system

The meeting initiator depends on participants to attend the meeting. S/he delegates most of the work to the meeting scheduler. This determines what are the acceptable dates, given the available information (task dependency *EnterAvailDates(m)*). Note that the meeting scheduler depends on the meeting initiator to provide a date range (task dependency *EnterDateRange(m)*) for the scheduling. The meeting initiator does not care how the scheduler does this, as long as the acceptable dates are found. This is reflected in the goal dependency *MeetingBeScheduled* from the initiator to the scheduler. Also, it does not care how the scheduler does the meeting announcements. After finding a meeting date, it will broadcast the meeting date to all participants. A participant requires confidentiality of the meeting and personal information (softgoal dependency *Confidentiality [m, p]*). Also, to find a consensual date, participants depend on the meeting scheduler for date proposals (resource dependency *ProposedDate(m)*). Once proposed, the scheduler depends on the participants to indicate whether they agree with the date or not (resource dependency *Agreement(m,p)*). For key participants, the meeting initiator depends critically on their attendance, and thus also on their assurance that they will attend (softgoal dependency *Assured(Attends-Meeting(ip.m))*).

Fig. 2 shows the strategic rationale model for the Meeting Scheduler actor. This model provides a more detailed level of modelling by looking "inside" the actor to model internal intentional relationships. In the SR model, task-decomposition (like Schedule Meeting that is decomposed in a sub-goal, *Find Agreeable Slot*, and three sub-tasks: *Handle Response Time, Obtain AvailDates, Obtain Agreement*) provides a hierarchical description on intentional elements. Each element or sub-element in a task is needed for the success of this task. The means-end link in the SR model provides understanding about why an actor would engage in some tasks, pursue a goal, need a resource or want a softgoal. In this example, we can see a means-end link between the *Find Agreeable Slot* goal (the end) and the *Merge Avail Dates* task (the means through which the end is reached).

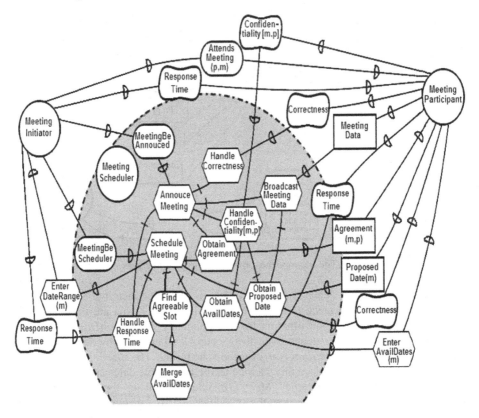

Fig. 2. The Meeting Schedule system partial SR model

4 Handling Crosscutting Concerns in i* Models

A general approach for handling crosscutting concerns in i* models is illustrated in Fig. 3. It takes as input the i* models and consists of four steps: (1) identification and representation of candidates aspects; (2) identification of the relationship among candidate aspects; (3) composition; and (4) trade-offs analysis, which can initiate a new iteration. The first and second phases are performed in parallel.

The first activity of our approach, namely the identification and representation of crosscutting concerns, is described in Section 4.1. The second activity, identification of relationships among aspects, is outlined in Section 4.2. The third activity, composition, is considered in Section 4.3finally, the fourth activity, trade-off analysis, will be explored in future work, having as basis the previous results in [21].

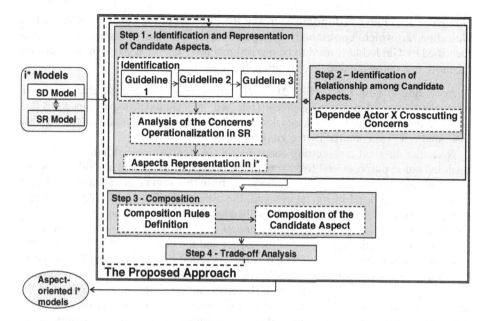

Fig. 3. Proposed approach

4.1 Identification and Representation of Candidate Aspects

A crosscutting concern can be seen as a model element that is required by several other model elements. In [1, 2] we proposed three guidelines to detect crosscutting concerns in the SD and SR model, as well as to eliminate redundancies. These guidelines are as follows:

Guideline 1 (**in the SD model**): If the same dependum is provided by at least two dependee actors, then the operationalization corresponding to that dependum is a candidate crosscutting concern.

For example, the *Meeting Initiator* actor (Fig. 1) depends to the *Meeting Participant* (dependee actor) to satisfy a *Response Time* softgoal dependency. On the other hand, the *Meeting Participant* actor is related with the *Meeting Scheduler* (dependee actor) through the same dependency. The two distinct dependee actors operationalize the same dependum element (*Response Time*), then its operationalization will be a candidate crosscutting concern.

Guideline 2 (**in the SR model**): If a task, that is directly or indirectly related to an external dependency, is required by (i.e. is a decomposition element of) two or more tasks (which are also related to other external dependencies), then that task is a candidate crosscutting concern. Notice that a task is indirectly related to an external dependency if, in the hierarchy where it belongs, at least one of its parents is connected to an external dependency.

For example (Fig. 2), the *Obtain Proposed Date* task is simultaneously required by the *Broadcast Meeting Data* and *Schedule Meeting* tasks. Hence, the first task is a candidate crosscutting concern.

Guideline 3 (**remove redundancies**): The list of crosscutting concerns identified by Guideline 2, which corresponds to operationalizations of crosscutting concerns identified by Guideline 1, need to be merged together. The final crosscutting concerns are those that correspond to the operationalizations.

According to guideline 2 (Fig. 2) the *Handle Response Time* task, that operationalizes the softgoal dependum *Response Time*, will be a candidate aspect since this task is simultaneously required by the task *Schedule Meeting* and *Announce Meeting*. But this same task was captured by the guideline 1.

Note that the final crosscutting concerns are, in fact, particular kinds of tasks. For modularization purposes and following the principles of AOSD we should externalize and modularize these tasks, taking them away from the original actors, and place each of them in a new kind of model element, the aspect (see Fig.4). Initially the dependency between the depender and the dependee actors involved in the crosscutting concern (Fig. 4a) is replaced by an aspect that modularizes the crosscutting concern. A *"Crosscuts"* relationship between the aspect and the element at the dependee actor it affects is defined (Fig 4b.). The type of the original link is indicated by the labels TD (Task-Decomposition link), or ME (Means-Ends link). The direction indicated by the triangles suggests the composition direction, meaning that the behaviour of the source element needs to be transferred to the behaviour of the target elements. The relationship between the depender and the dependum is specified by the compositions rules (see Fig. 4b). The candidate aspect is represented by a star (see *Response Time* in Fig. 4c) which includes an aspectual task (eg. *Handle Response Time*) that operationalizes its behaviour and a set of composition rules (e.g. *Response Time Composition Rules*) that specifies the way in which the aspectual task is weaved with (or affects) the model elements that it originally was related to.

We consider an intentional element (external or internal in i* models) which appears at least twice as a candidate crosscutting concern. However, we recognize that we need to perform further analysis to ensure that this element is an aspect in posterior development phase. For example, let us consider security as a concern which is represented as a softgoal in i* models. This softgoal is captured by the guideline 1 or guideline 2, and it will be modeled as an aspect at the requirements level. However, in a later stage we may conclude that this concern may not be an aspect because security may be related with a physical feature or a logical feature. Therefore, the full assurance that a candidate crosscutting concern will become an aspect depends on the abstraction level where this concern is specified.

Applying Guidelines to Meeting Schedule Example. By applying Guideline 1 to the SD model (Fig. 1), we obtain the following candidate crosscutting concerns: *Handle Correctness* and *Handle Response Time* tasks which operationalize Correctness and *Response Time* softgoals, respectively. On the other hand, by applying Guideline 2, the crosscutting candidates are *Obtain Agreement, Obtain Proposed Date, Handle Correctness, Handle Response Time* and *Handle Confidentiality* tasks.

Finally, with guideline 3, the operationalizations of some of the crosscutting concerns identified by guideline 1 are kept, while the corresponding ones given by guideline 2 are eliminated. This can be easily seen in the SR model (Fig. 2), where *Correctness, Response Time* and *Confidentiality* are operationalized by *Handle*

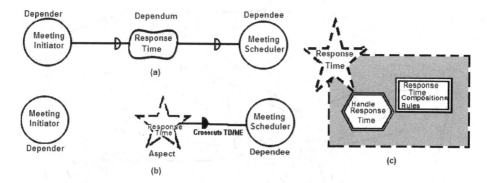

Fig. 4. An aspect element

Correctness, Handle Response Time and *Handle Confidentiality*. Therefore, the final list of crosscutting concerns is: *Handle Response Time, Handle Correctness, Handle Confidentiality, Obtain Agreement* and *Obtain Propose Date.*

4.1.1 Representing Aspects in i*

Since crosscutting concerns or aspects are scattered concepts that appear repeatedly in a representation (in this case i* models), their externalization and modularization will simplify the original representation. This can be seen in Fig. 5 where an aspectual SR model is shown. Aspects are represented by stars with its aspectual tasks and the composition rules as specified in section 4.3. The crosscutting relationships between each aspect and other model elements are shown as arcs, with a dark semi-circle. The direction indicated by the semi-circle suggests the direction of the composition, meaning that the source element's behaviour needs to be "injected" into the target elements' behaviours. Note that a label is placed on a crosscut link to indicate if the internal link is a task-decomposition (label TD) or a means-ends link (label ME) of the i* models, which will be recovered through the composition rules. When the actor's behaviour is expanded, the aspects can crosscut goals, softgoals, or tasks (e.g., the aspect *Response Time* crosscuts *Announce Meeting* and *Scheduling Meeting* tasks in the Meeting Scheduler actor, see Fig. 5). However, when the actor is contracted we can not show the intentional element affected by the aspect (e.g., the aspect *Response Time* crosscuts the *Meeting Participant* actor).

4.2 Identification of Relationship Among Candidate Aspects

From both i* models (e.g., Fig. 1 and Fig. 2) and the three guidelines proposed (Section 4.1) we relate in a table (Table 1) the candidate crosscutting concerns (columns) with the respective actors which are responsible for their operationalization (lines). Each cell in Table 1 contains information about which dependum is going to be operationalized by the task (candidate to become a crosscutting concern) and which are the depender actors on this relationship. In such way, this matrix facilitates the identification of scattered concerns through several dependee actors and its

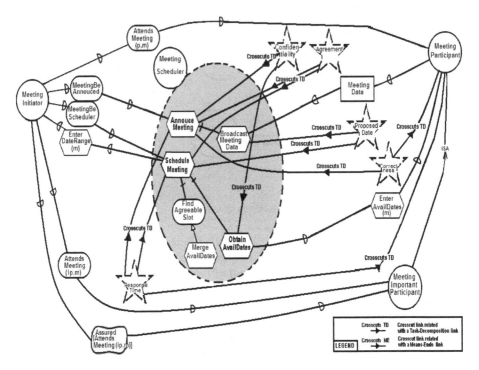

Fig. 5. An aspectual SR model

Table 1. Crosscutting concerns and its dependum. RT: Response Time; C: Correctness; Co: Confidentiality; PD: Proposed Date; MP: Meeting Participant; MS: Meeting Scheduler; MI: Meeting Initiator

Dependee Actor	Candidate Crosscuting Concerns				
	Handle Response Time	Handle Correctness	Handle Confidentiality	Obtain Agreement	Obtain Proposed Date
Meeting Participant	MI/RT	MS/C			
Meeting Scheduler	MP/RT, (MI/RT)	MP/C	MP/Co	MS/-	MP/PD

dependent actors, becoming useful for defining composition rules. For the Meeting Scheduler example (see Table 1), the first cell in the first line (MI/RT) specifies that *Response Time* (RT) will be operationalized by the dependee actor *Meeting Participant* (MP) which has the *Meeting Initiator* as its depender actor through the task *Handle Response Time*. In the first cell at the second line the same *Response Time* is being operationalized by dependee *Meeting Scheduler* (MS) which has two depender actors *Meeting Participant* and *Meeting Initiator*. Hence, in the set of composition rules for this concern, there is a rule indicating the actors that need (depend on) this concern as well as the actors (dependees) that will operationalize it

(MP and MS). For simplicity, in this paper we only expand the actor Meeting Scheduler (Fig.2).

In Table 1, the cell corresponding to column Obtain Agreement and line Meeting Scheduler (MS/-), specifies that the task *Obtain Agreement* is a candidate concern and is an internal task in the depender actor *Meeting Scheduler* which dependee actor is *Meeting Scheduler*. This task was captured by guideline 2.

4.3 Composition

The composition rules define "where" and "how" a crosscutting concern affects other concerns in a system. Hence, before performing a composition, it is necessary to identify, in the SR model, which elements are related with the crosscutting concerns and, in the SD model, which actors depend on the operationalization of these concerns (see Table 2). The next step defines a set of rules and operators to help us to simplify the i* models and, if needed, also to recover the original one.

Table 2. Identification of the crosscutting concerns in the SR model. AM: Announce Meeting; SM: Schedule Meeting; OPD: Obtain Proposed Date; OAD: Obtain Avail Dates; BMD: Broadcast Meeting Data.

Dependee Adtor	Candidate Crosscutting Concerns				
	Handle Response Time	Handle Correctness	Handle Confidentiality	Obtain Agreement	Obtain Proposed Date
Meeting Scheduler	AM, SM	AM	AM, OAD, OPD	AM, SM	SM, BMD

As we highlight in the identification rules, the crosscutting concerns can be goals, softgoals or tasks in the SR model, but in this paper we are only considering tasks. In the SR model, tasks either (i) are going to be decomposed into sub-elements (which can be any type of dependum, including another task); or (ii) are going to be the means to achieve an end (means-end link), where we consider that the most common situation is that the end is a goal or a softgoal. We call parent (task) the task that is being decomposed (decomposition task link in the SR model). Hence, in Table 2, for each of the identified crosscutting concern (column), for each of the dependee actors (line), it is informed which elements are related to the crosscutting concern. In case the crosscutting concern is the parent task itself, we associate the dependee actor name to it. To fill in Table 2, we use as reference the model depicted in Fig. 1, Fig. 2 and Table 1. Once more, note that for our example, we just expand the actor Meeting Scheduler. For example, let us consider the candidate concern *Handle Response Time*, in the SR model (Fig. 2) and in first column in Table 1. As we can see (Table 2), the first cell (AM, SM) specifies that *Handle Response Time* is a sub-task, in the task-decomposition link, which has *Announce Meeting* (AM) and *Schedule Meeting* (SM) as main tasks. Both tasks need *Handle Response Time* to be satisfied.

To fully complete Table 2, it is necessary to expand all the dependee actors into their corresponding SR models. The information presented in Table 2 is the base to help define composition rules.

Defining Composition Rules. In the SD model, it is important to preserve the dependum type that is involved with a dependency relationship (goal, task, softgoal or resource), as well as the actors who depend on the dependency relationship (depender actors). Hence, we propose: (i) an operator **is the type of**; and (ii) an operator **has depender … with dependee**. Table 3 presents the general form of the rules that preserve the links in the SD model. The symbol "|" is a separator between rules variation. Elements in a list are separated using ",".

Table 3. Rules to the dependencies links in the SD model

Rules for dependency links				
Aspect<name>	**is of type**	<dependum type >		
Aspect<name>	**has depender**	<depender name> | <list of depender name>	**with dependee**	<dependee name>

Let us consider the crosscutting concern *Response Time* (Fig. 1 and Table 1). The first rule shows the dependum type involved in the crosscutting relationship (Aspect *Response Time* is the type of a *softgoal*). The second one defines, which are the depender and dependee actors related to a given dependency. Hence, we end up with the following example:

Aspect *Response Time* **is of type** softgoal*;*

Aspect *Response Time* **has depender** Meeting Initiator **with dependee** Meeting Participant;

Aspect *Response Time* **has depender** Meeting Participant **with dependee** Meeting Scheduler.

Let us now focus on the SR model since when we externalize a crosscutting concern, all the links from this element with internal components of the SR model must be kept in the new aspectual element (e.g., in a task decomposition, all links with its sub-elements must be kept). For the *Response Time* aspect operationalized by *Meeting Scheduler* we need to define rules to keep the task-decomposition link between the *Handle Response Time* and the *Schedule Meeting* and *Announce Meeting* (Fig. 2). Thus, we define the rule for a task decomposition, in which the incorporated aspectual task (*Handle Response Time*) is a sub-element of the decomposition. The operator **is sub-task of** indicates the parent task which includes the aspectual task. If that task belongs to more than one decomposition tree then a list of parent tasks is established. We also need to keep the information about which is the actor responsible for the operationalization. Hence, we also define an operator **in** which informs the *dependee* actor. Therefore, we have the following rule expressed in Table 4.

Table 4. Rule for a sub-task in a task decomposition link in the SR model

Aspect <name>. <aspectual task>	**is a sub-task of**	<task name> | <list of tasks name> | Aspect.<task name> | Aspect.<list of tasks name> | <list of Aspect.<task name> | <list of Aspect.<list of tasks name>	**in**	<dependee name>

For the Response Time element in Fig. 2, we have:

Aspect *Response Time.Handle Response Time* **is a sub-task of** (*Announce Meeting, Schedule Meeting*) **in** *Meeting Scheduler.*

This means that the externalized *Handle Response Time* task is a sub-task of the *Announce Meeting* and *Schedule Meeting* tasks which belongs to the Meeting *Scheduler dependee* actor. However, if we observe the Table 2 that any of the parents tasks is also a candidate aspect (it is not the case in our example), then we must change the rule to:

Aspect *DependumName.OperationalTask* **is a sub-task of** (**Aspect**. OperationalTask$_A$) **in Dependee** Actor

A second case to be analyzed is related to the means-end links. We propose the operator **is the means of** which defines that the aspectual task is a way of satisfying a given type dependum. In our case study we do not have any. The general rule is defined in Table 5.

Table 5. Rules for a means-end link in the SR model

Aspect\<name>. \<aspectual task>	is the means of	\<end name> | \<list of end name> | Aspect.\<end name> | Aspect.\<list of end name> | \<list of Aspect.\<end name> | \<list of Aspect.\<list of end name>	in	\<dependee name>

In this case we are considering that the end element can be a goal or a softgoal, although it can be any type of dependum.

The third rule type is related to links which must be recovered when the aspectual task is the root element in a task decomposition link. In this case, all the links and children must be re-established through the composition rule. In Table 6 we present the general rules.

Table 6. Rules for the root of a task decomposition link

Aspect\<name>. \<aspectual task>	is the root of	\<sub-element name> | \<list of sub-element name> | Aspect.\<sub-element name> | Aspect.\<list of sub-element name> | \<list of Aspect.\<sub-element name> | \<list of Aspect.\<list of sub-element name>	in	\<dependee name>
Aspect\<name>. \<aspectual task>	is root in	\<dependee name>		

In this table, the second rule expresses the situation in which the aspectual task is the root of a whole decomposition tree in the dependee actor under analysis. We do not have this case in our example.

Finally, Table 7 summarizes all the operators proposed in the decomposition rules.

Table 7. Operators used in the composition rules

Operator	Description
with dependee	It defines the actor which operationalizes the crosscutting concern.
is of type	It defines the type of dependency that was included by the aspect.
has depender	It restores the link among the dependence element included by the aspect and the depender actor.
Aspect	It defines the object as an aspect.
<name>	It represents the name of dependum or element.
in <dependee name>	It informs in which dependee actor the action is being executed.
is root	It defines that the aspectual task is the root of the whole decomposition tree.
is sub-task of	It defines the decomposition link between the aspectual task and its "father" task.
is the means of	It restores the means-end link between the aspectual task and its end.
is the root of	It informs that the aspectual task is being decomposed and restores the link with its parts.
<list of...>	It represents a group of elements separated by ","

The proposed composition rules constitute an initial exercise to define a fully fledged language which ensures that all i* links in the original model are preserved. These rules are being improved. Thus, with these rules we can know which intentional element is considered as a crosscutting concern (in particular, we are dealing with tasks). Composition rules define how and when a crosscutting concern affects other concerns in a system. The "how" dimension is graphically captured by adding a label to the crosscuts link. This label indicates if the crosscutting concern is weaved with the other concerns of the system through a task-decomposition link (TD label) or a means-ends link (ME label) (see Fig. 5). Although the original i* framework only represents structural features of the desired system we add temporal feature through two new constructors: **is inserted** *after*, and **is inserted** *before* (likewise the reserved word of the AOP). These constructors capture the "when" dimension of the composition rules.

Let us consider the *Response Time* candidate aspect (Fig. 1, Fig. 2, Table 1 and Table 2). The set of composition rules which is inside the respective aspect will be as follows:

Aspect *Response Time* **is of type** *softgoal;*

Aspect *Response Time* **has depender** Meeting Initiator **with dependee** Meeting Participant;

Aspect *Response Time* **has depender** Meeting Participant **with dependee** Meeting Scheduler;

Aspect *Response Time.Handle Response Time* **is a sub-task of** (*Announce Meeting,Schedule Meeting*) **in** *Meeting Scheduler.*

Aspect *Response Time.Handle Response Time* **is a sub-task of** *Participant Be inMeeting* **in** *Meeting Participant* [2]

Aspect *Response Time.Handle Response Time is inserted after* **Aspect** *Confidentiality*

Now let us considerer another candidate aspect: Confidentiality. The set of the composition rules is as follow:

Aspect *Confidentiality* **is of type** *softgoal;*

Aspect *Confidentiality* **has depender** Meeting Participant **with dependee** Meeting Scheduler;

Aspect *ConfidentialityHandle Confidentiality* **is a sub-task of** (*Announce Meeting,Obtain Avail Dates*, **Aspect.***Obtain Proposed Date*) **in** *Meeting Scheduler.*[3]

Aspect *ConfidentialityHandle Confidentiality is inserted* before **Aspect** *Response Time*

Finally we have to do the same with all candidates presented in the Tables 1 and 2. Furthermore, all actors need to be expanded in SR model.

5 Related Work

In [23] we identify aspects in the requirements engineering level. This work has been made for the approach presented in [7], while this new approach in more generic. In [21] we identified aspects at early-requirements engineering level. We called them "candidate aspects", since at this early stage we are not sure if they will be handled as aspects during later stages of the software development process. We also based our approach in the i* framework [24] and tried to integrate the results within the requirements engineering model proposed before. The goal was to propose a set of guidelines to help identifying concerns and describe each one using a proposed template, but not directly using the i* models. In [7] one have an extension of this work, proposing a new process to compose the concerns in which it is introduced the notion of match point, dominate concerns and operators based on LOTOS to define composition rules.

In [27] the authors claim that satisfying OR-decomposed subgoals in the KAOS [10] model typically leads to tangled implementations, and agents responsible for multiple OR-refined goals should be implemented in the aspect-oriented manner. Instead of proposing requirement engineering (RE) treatments directly mapped to

---

[2] This case is not represented in Fig. 2 since this is a simplified version of the real case.

[3] The task Handle Confidentiality (Table 2) is a sub-task of the task Obtain Proposed Date that is a candidate aspect.

aspects, they examined existing well-established RE models and identified patterns in these models that could be better designed and implemented using aspect-oriented programming. They started from the code level and, through the technique of aspect mining, identified application features existing in a crosscutting fashion. In next step, they performed a consolidated modeling of the application requirements in terms of KAOS concepts. Then they compared the goal decomposition and the actual code decomposition, trying to identify the connection patterns in the goal decomposition graph which would give rise to aspects.

In [11] the authors advocate that the available agent- and goal-based approaches lack the ability to turn soft issues into precisely defined, agreed-upon, and "implementable" solutions. They describe a structured, goal-oriented, agent-based Requirements Engineering Framework (REF), where quality modelling is adopted and explicitly devised to support the requirements engineering process for complex socio-technical systems. They also attempt to deal with crosscutting concerns but REF emphasizes the operational role that soft goals can play in deriving the requirements of a new system. Our approach aims at identifying non-functional and functional requirements as candidate crosscutting concerns and improve the original i* model complexity [24].

In our previous work [26] we show that aspects can be discovered during goal-oriented requirements analysis. The proposal includes a systematic process for discovering aspects from relationships between functional and non-functional goals. The process presents a systematic way for the refinement of a V-graph. During each step of the process, the goal analysis tool is used to detect conflicts and deteriorations. The process ends when all the root goals and softgoals are satisfied. At this stage, we are able to identify candidate aspects by identifying tasks that have a high fan-in. The resulting graph can be further refined if candidate aspects are grouped into what we called goal aspects.

Multi-agent systems (MAS) are characterized by agency properties such as autonomy, adaptation and interaction, which are potentially crosscutting [12]. In this paper aspect-oriented mechanisms are used to modularize agency concerns (such as, interaction, adaptation, autonomy, learning, mobility and collaboration). Thus considering that agent concerns can be modeled through a set of intentional elements in i* models, we argue that those features can be captured as crosscutting concerns by our approach. In [20] the authors proposed to integrate i*, scenarios and AspectT in the context of MAS. In particular, the authors consider only softgoals as crosscutting concerns in i* models. These softgoals are implemented as aspects, as well as agency properties have been implemented in [12] as aspects. In our paper any intentional element of i* framework (goal, softgoal and task) can be considered as a crosscutting concern and may be implemented as an aspect too, but at this moment we are only focusin on tasks.

Our approach, outlined in Section 4, identifies the crosscutting concerns directly from the organizational model and does not need to use auxiliary RE techniques to achieve the purpose. The proposed composition rules ensure that all the links between the elements in the original models are re-established.

6 Conclusions and Future Work

In this paper we have introduced an approach to support early aspects identification in agent-oriented software development. In particular, we propose a set of guidelines to help the identification and representation of crosscutting concerns from the i* models which is the basis for Tropos. In particular, in the i* models, each actor can be autonomous as it is quoted by agent-oriented software technologies [25], and it has agency concerns which are associated with any intentional element in the i*models. In fact, the SD and SR models were extended to represent aspectual concepts and have its graphical complexity reduced.

By addressing crosscutting concerns earlier on agent-oriented software development, we will avoid tangled and scattered software artefacts. These crosscutting concerns are responsible for producing tangled representations that are difficult to understand and maintain. The identification and specification of crosscutting concerns in early phases will result in better support for modularization. This, in turn, helps us to reduce the complexity of the i* models, promoting understandability, and to modularize the requirements that are scattered and tangled in the system specification, which supports requirements change and its impact on other requirements.

The validation of these ideas has been achieved in two ways: we applied the rules to the YKeyK case study [23], and used the guidelines in [22] to transform i* model into UML models and then identify, in these models, the potential crosscutting concerns [1]. In both cases the results obtained were similar.

Our research is still in its infancy, but the idea is to identify graphics' features, e.g. high fan-in, that give us some evidence about requirements that are scattered or tangled over the model specification. These requirements will be identified as candidate crosscutting concerns. Crosscutting concerns at the requirements level are candidate aspects [21]. The candidate aspects can be mapped onto design aspects, functions or architecture decisions. In architectural design, the next step beyond the aspects identification is their specification and integration with other architectural components. Our future work will consider how these mapping will take place.

In this paper we have dealt explicitly with task and task-decomposition links when identifying and separating crosscutting concerns. However, we emphasize that a crosscutting concern can belong to any intentional element type (goal, softgoal or task). Moreover, the relationship involved in the weaving can be a means-ends link besides task-decomposition links. Typical crosscutting concerns are non-functional requirements although a crosscutting concern can also be a functional requirement represented as a set of intentional elements in i* models. Currently, these issues are being addressed.

As future work we also intend to (i) apply our approach to more case studies; (ii) support aspectual concepts in i* modeling support tools (e.g. OME); (iii) develop a metamodel for our approach; iv) improve the guidelines to capture routines [24] in i* models; (v) formalize the approach through the Software Process Engineering Metamodel (SPEM) [19] notation or other appropriate formalism. Some of these additional works are already being carried on.

Acknowledgements

This work was supported by several research grants: CAPES/ GRICES Proc. 129/05, and SOFTAS Project, POSC/EIA/60189/2004.

References

1. Alencar, F., Silva, C., Moreira, A., Araújo, J., Castro, J., Mylopoulos, J.: Using Aspects to Simplify i*Models. In: RE 2006. Poster in: 14th International Requirements Engineering Conference, Minnesota-USA (September 11-15, 2006)
2. Alencar, F., Moreira, A., Araújo, J., Castro, J., Silva, C., Mylopoulos, J.: Towards an Approach to Integrate i* with Aspects. In: Dubois, E., Pohl, K. (eds.) CAiSE 2006. LNCS, vol. 4001, Springer, Heidelberg (2006)
3. AOSD portal, http://aosd.net
4. Araújo, J., Moreira, A., Brito, I., Rashid, A.: Aspect-Oriented Requirements with UML. In: Jézéquel, J.-M., Hussmann, H., Cook, S. (eds.) UML 2002 - The Unified Modeling Language. Model Engineering, Concepts, and Tools. LNCS, vol. 2460, Springer, Heidelberg (2002)
5. Baniassad, E., Clements, P., Araújo, J., Moreira, A., Rashid, A., Tekinerdogan, B.: Discovering Early Aspects. IEEE Software, Special Issue on Aspect-Oriented Programming (January/ February 2006)
6. Berg, K., Conejero, J.M.: A Conceptual Formalization of Crosscutting in AOSD. In: Workshop on AOSD, in JISBD 2005, Granada (September 2005)
7. Brito, I., Moreira, A.: Integrating the NFR framework in a RE model. In: Workshop on Early Aspects, AOSD 2004, Lancaster, UK, pp. 22–26 (March 2004)
8. Castro, J., Kolp, M., Mylopoulos, J.: Towards Requirements-Driven Information Systems Engineering: The Tropos Project. In: Information Systems Journal, vol. 27, pp. 365–389. Elsevier, Amsterdam (2002)
9. Clarke, S., Baniassad, E.: Aspect-Oriented Analysis and Design: The Theme Approach. Addison-Wesley, Reading (2005)
10. Dardenne, A., van Lamsweerde, A., Fickas, S.: Goal-directed requirements acquisition. In: Science of Computer Programming, North Holland, vol. 20, pp. 3–50 (1993)
11. Donzelli, P., Bresciani, P.: Improving Requirements Engineering by Quality Modeling– A quality-based requirements engineering framework. Journal of Research and Practice in Information Technology (JRPIT) 36(4), 277–294 (November 2004)
12. Garcia, A.F.: From Objects to Agents: An Aspect-Oriented Approach. PhD thesis, PUCRio (2004)
13. Giorgini, P., Kolp, M., Mylopoulos, J., Castro, J.: Tropos: a Requirements-Driven Methodology for Agent-Oriented Software. In: Book Chapter in Agent-Oriented Methodologies, pp. 20–45. Idea Group, USA (2005)
14. Jacobson, I.: Object-Oriented Software Engineering - A Use Case Driven Approach. ACM Press, New York (1992)
15. Jacobson, I., Pan-Wei, N.: Aspect-Oriented Software Development with Use Cases. Addison-Wesley, Reading (2005)
16. Kiczales, G., Lamping, J., Mendhekar, A., Maeda, C., Lopes, C., Loingtier, J., Irwin, J.: Aspect-Oriented Programming. In: Aksit, M., Matsuoka, S. (eds.) ECOOP 1997. LNCS, vol. 1241, Springer, Heidelberg (1997)

17. Luck, M., McBurney, P., Preist, C.: Agent technology roadmap: Enabling next generation computing. AgentLink report (2003), http://www.agentlink.org/roadmap
18. Moreira, A., Rashid, A., Araújo, J.: Multi-Dimensional Separation of Concerns in Requirements Engineering. In: RE 2005. The 13th International Conference on Requirements Engineering, IEEE Computer Society, Los Alamitos (2005)
19. Object Manage Group: Software Process Engineering Metamodel (SPEM) Especification. Report, V. 1.1. Jan. 2005, Last access (September 2007), http://www.omg.org/docs/formal/05-01-06.pdf.
20. Oliveira, A.P.A., Cysneiros, L.M., Leite, J.C.S.P., Figueiredo, E.M.L., Lucena, C.J.P.: Integrating scenarios, i*, and AspectT. In the Context of Multi-Agent Systems. In: CASCON 2006 - The 16th Annual International Conference on Computer Science and Software Engineering, Toronto, Canada (2006)
21. Rashid, A., Moreira, A., Araújo, J.: Modularization and Composition of Aspectual Requirements. In: AOSD 2003. Proceedings of the International Conference on Aspect-Oriented Software Development, USA (2003)
22. Santander, V.F.A., Castro, J.: Deriving Use Cases from Organizational Modeling. In: RE 2002. Proceedings of the International Conference on, Germany (2002)
23. Spies, E., Rüger, J., Moreira, A.: Using I* to Identify Candidate Aspects. In: Baar, T., Strohmeier, A., Moreira, A., Mellor, S.J. (eds.) UML 2004. LNCS, vol. 3273, Springer, Heidelberg (2004)
24. Yu, E.: Modeling Strategic Relationships for Process Reengineering. Ph.D. thesis, Department of Computer Science, University of Toronto, Canada (1995)
25. Yu, E.: Agent-Oriented Modeling: Software Versus the World In Agent-Oriented Software Engineering. In: Wooldridge, M.J., Weiß, G., Ciancarini, P. (eds.) AOSE 2001. LNCS, vol. 2222, Springer, Heidelberg (2002)
26. Yu, Y., Leite, J.C.S.P., Mylopoulos, J.: From goals to aspects: Discovering aspects from requirements goal models. In: Proceedings of the International Conference on RE 2004, pp. 38–47. IEEE Computer Society, Los Alamitos (September 2004)
27. Zhang, C., Jacobsen, H., Yu, Y.: Linking Goals to Aspect. In: Proceedings of the Conference on RE 2005, IEEE Computer Society, Los Alamitos (September 2005)

Enhancing Information Sharing Through Agents

Marco Mari, Agostino Poggi, Michele Tomaiuolo, and Paola Turci

Dipartimento di Ingegneria dell'Informazione
Università degli Studi di Parma
Viale delle Scienze, 181A – 43100 – Parma
{mari,poggi,tomamic,turci}@ce.unipr.it

Abstract. This paper presents RAIS, a peer-to-peer multi-agent system for information sharing among a community of users connected through the Internet. RAIS offers a similar search power of Web search engines, but avoids the burden of publishing information on the Web and guarantees a controlled and dynamic access to information. The use of agent technologies has made straightforward the realization of three of the main features of the system: i) filtering of information coming from different users, on the basis of the previous experience of the local user, ii) pushing of new information that can be of interest for a user, and iii) delegation of access capabilities, on the basis of a reputation network, built by the agents of the system on the community of its users.

Keywords: Information sharing, multi-agent systems, peer-to-peer.

1 Introduction

The storage capability of hard disks is constantly growing, while the newly available space is quickly filled with a large amount of data in different and heterogeneous formats. The ordering of such data is a time wasting and often boring task: the result is that more and more files, containing important information, are lost or forgotten on hard drives. The classical file searching tools (e.g., Windows search function) are not effective: for each request they analyse the whole drive, and they support only few file formats. In last months, the providers of the main Web search engines (Google, Microsoft with MSN and Yahoo!) have released desktop search tools that make a research on a local drive as easy and fast as a Web search. These tools run in the background (when CPU load is low) and index the content of a wide range of file formats (e.g.: Office, PDF, e-mail, HTML, …) in a way similar to a Web crawler. Moreover, Google has released an SDK [1] for its desktop search software [2]. The SDK empowers developers to write plug-ins thanks to a set of APIs using COM and HTML/XML.

Besides a local drive, the better place to find files and, more in general, information is the Internet. The most used tools to share contents and information, avoiding the burden of exporting them on the Web, are peer-to-peer systems. The exchange of multimedia files with a peer-to-peer system is highly effective because their contents can be easily categorized by the title. On the other hand, files holding

M. Kolp et al. (Eds.): AOIS 2006, LNAI 4898, pp. 202–211, 2008.
© Springer-Verlag Berlin Heidelberg 2008

more information (e.g., documents, e-mails, etc.) could be effectively shared only if the categorization takes into account the whole content.

Finally, there is evidence from several research studies [3][4][5][6] that agents represent one of the most suitable technologies which can be used to meet the performance needs for the realization of effective information sharing systems.

This paper presents a system, called RAIS, that tries to combine the features of peer-to-peer information sharing systems and the Web. The next section introduces the main features and the behaviour of the RAIS system. Section three describes how this system has been designed and implemented by using some well-known technologies and software tools. Finally, section four gives some concluding remarks and presents our future research directions.

2 RAIS System

RAIS (Remote Assistant for Information Sharing) is a peer-to-peer and multi-agent system composed of different agent platforms connected through the internet. Each agent platform acts as a "peer" of the system and is based on three agents: a personal assistant, an information finder and a directory facilitator. A further agent, called personal proxy assistant (PPA), allows a user to remotely access her/his agent platform. Figure 1 shows the RAIS multi-agent system architecture.

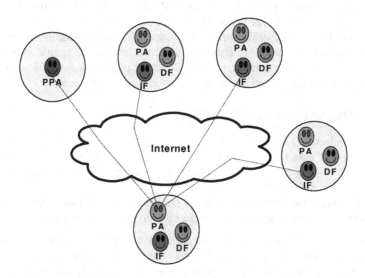

Fig. 1. The RAIS multi-agent system

A *Personal Assistant (PA)* is an agent that allows the interaction between the RAIS system and the user. This agent receives the user's queries, forwards them to the available information finders and presents the results to the user. Moreover, a PA allows the user to subscribe her/him to be notified about new documents and information on some topics in which she/he is interested. Finally, a PA maintains a profile of its user preferences. In our system, the management of user profiles is performed in two different phases: an initialization phase and an updating phase.

Profiles are represented by vectors of weighted terms whose value are related to the rate expressed by the user. The user, in fact, can rate the quality of the information coming from other users for each search keyword (the utility of this profile will be clear after the presentation of the system behaviour).

An *Information Finder (IF)* is an agent that searches information on the repository contained into the computer where it lives and provides this information both to its user and to other users of the RAIS system. An IF receives users' queries, finds appropriate results and filter them on the basis of its user's policies (e.g.: results from non-public folders are not sent to other users). Furthermore, an IF monitors the changes in the local repository and pushes the new information to a PA when such information matches the interests subscribed by that PA.

A *Personal Proxy Assistant (PPA)* is an agent that represents a point of access to the system for users that are not working on their own personal computer. A PPA is intended to run on a pluggable device (e.g., a USB key) on which the PPA agent is stored together with the RAIS binary and configuration files. Therefore, when the user starts the RAIS system from the pluggable device, her/his PPA connects to the user's PA and provides the user with all the functionalities of her/his PA. For security reasons, only a PA can create the corresponding PPA and can generate the authentication key that is shared with the PPA to support their communication. Therefore, for a successful connection, the PPA has to send the authentication key, and then the user must provide his username and password.

Finally, the *Directory Facilitator (DF)* is responsible to register the agent platform in the RAIS network. The DF is also responsible to inform the agents of its platform about the address of the agents that live in the other platforms available on the RAIS network (e.g., a PA can ask about the address of the active IF agents).

2.1 Searching and Pushing Information

In order to understand the system behaviour, we can present two practical scenarios. In the first, a user asks her/his PA to search for some information, while in the second the user asks to subscribe her/his interest about a topic. In both cases the system provides the user with a set of related information.

In the first scenario, the system activity can be divided in four steps: i) search, ii) result filtering, iii) results sending and presentation, and iv) retrieval.

Search: The user requests a search to her/his PA indicating a set of keywords and the maximum number of results. The PA asks the DF for the addresses of available IF agents and sends the keywords to such agents. The information finders apply the search to their repositories only if the querying user has the access to at least a part of the information stored into its repositories.

Results filtering: Each IF filters the searching results on the basis of the querying user access permissions.

Results sending and presentation: Each IF sends the filtered list of results to the querying PA. The PA orders the various results as soon as it receives them, omitting duplicate results and presents them to its user.

Retrieval: After the examination of the results list, the user can ask her/his PA for retrieving the information corresponding to an element of the list. Therefore, the PA forwards the request to the appropriate IF, waits for its answer and presents the information to the user.

In the second scenario, the system activity can be divided in five steps: i) subscription, ii) monitoring and results filtering, iii) results sending and user notification, iv) results presentation and v) retrieval.

Subscription: The user requests a subscription to her/his PA indicating a set of keywords describing the topic in which she/he is interested. The PA asks the DF for the addresses of available IF agents and sends the keywords to such agents. Each IF registers the subscription if the querying user has the access to at least a part of the information stored into its repository.

Monitoring and result filtering: Each IF periodically checks if there are some new information satisfying its subscriptions. If it happens, the IF filters its searching results on the basis of the access permissions of the querying user.

Results sending and user notification: Each IF sends the filtered list of results to the querying PA. The PA orders the various results as soon as it receives them, omitting duplicate results and stores them in its memory. Moreover, it notifies its user about the new available information sending her/him an email.

Results presentation: The first time the user logs into the RAIS system, the PA presents her/him the new results.

Retrieval: In the same way of the previous search scenario, the user can retrieve some of the information indicated in the list of the results.

As introduced above, a PA receives from the user a constraint on the number of results to provide (Nr) and uses it to limit the results asked to each IF agent. The number of results that each IF agent can send is neither Nr nor Nr divided to the number of IF agents (Nr/Nif), but a number (between Nr and Nr/Nif) for which the PA is quite sure to provide at least Nr results to its user without the risk of receiving a burden of unnecessary data. Moreover, each IF, before sending the list of results, creates a digest[1] of each result and sends them together with the list. Therefore, the PA causes the digests to omit duplicate results coming from different IF agents.

After the reception of results and the filtering of duplications, the PA has the duty of selecting Nr results to send to its user (if they are more than Nr) and order them. Of course, each IF orders the results before sending them to the PA, but the PA has not the information on how to order results from different IF agents. Therefore, the PA uses two more simpler solution on the basis of its user request: i) the results are fairly divided among the different sources of information, ii) the results are divided among the different sources of information on the basis of the user preferences. User preferences are represented by triples of the form <source, keyword, rate> where: source indicates an IF, keyword a term used for searching information, and rate a number representing the quality of information (related to the keyword) coming from that IF. Each time a user gets a result, she/he can give a rate to the

---

[1] A digest is a compact representation given in the form of a single string of digits that has the property to be different for data that are different [12]. A digest is usually used to compare remote files without the need of moving the files.

quality of the result and, as consequence, the PA can update her/his preferences in the user profile that the PA maintains.

The information stored into the different repositories of a RAIS network is not accessible to all the users of the system in the same way. In fact, it's important to avoid the access to private documents and personal files, but also to files reserved to a restricted group of users (e.g.: the participants of a project). The RAIS system takes care of users' privacy allowing the access to the information on the basis of the identity, the roles and the attributes of the querying user defined into a local knowledge base of trusted users. In this case, it is the user that defines who and in which way can access to her/his information, but the user can also allow the access to unknown users enabling a certificate based delegation built on a reputation network of the users registered into the RAIS community. For instance, if the user U_i enables the delegation and grants to the user U_j the access to its repository with capabilities C_0 and U_j grants to the user U_k the access to its repository with the same capabilities C_0, then U_k can access U_i's repository with the same capabilities of U_j. The trust delegation can be useful when the system is used by open and distributed communities, e.g. to share documents among the members of an Open Source project.

2.2 Security

The information stored into the different repositories of a RAIS network is not accessible to all the users of the system in the same way because it's important to avoid the access to private documents and personal files. The RAIS system takes care of users' privacy allowing the access to the information on the basis of the identity, the roles and the attributes of the querying user.

Of course, different levels of privacy can be assigned to the information stored into the same repository. Various models exist to deal with the authorization problem [7].

The best known is the *Discretionary Access Control (DAC)* model. It is the traditional model, based on *Access Control Lists*. In this model, each user is associated with a list of granted access rights. On the basis of this list of permissions, he will be allowed or denied access to a particular resource. A resource administrator is responsible for editing the Access Control Lists.

Another popular model is the *Mandatory Access Control (MAC)*, used to implement *Multilevel Secure (MLS)* systems. In these systems, each resource is labeled according to a security classification. Correspondingly, each principal is assigned a clearance, which is associated with a classification list. This list contains all the types of resources the principal should be allowed to access, depending on their classification. The multilevel security is particularly popular in the military field, and in inherently hierarchical organizations.

Another interesting model is the *Role Based Access Control (RBAC)* model. This model is centered around a set of roles. Each role can be granted a set of permissions, and each user can be assigned to one or more roles. A many to many relationship binds principals and the roles they're assigned to. In the same way, a many to many relationship binds permissions and the roles they're granted to, thus creating a level of indirection between a principal and his access rights. This also leads to a better separation of duties (between the assignment of principals to roles and the definition of role permissions), to implement privilege inheritance schemes among superior and subordinate roles and to permit temporary delegations of some of the assigned roles towards other principals.

Following the RBAC model, each resource manager of our system (i.e. each node in the peer-to-peer network) has to deal with three main concepts: principals (i.e. authenticable entities which act as users of resources and services), permissions (i.e. rights to access resources or use services) and roles. The fundamental principle here is that each node is in charge of defining its own roles, and of assigning principals to them.

In RAIS, authentication and authorization are performed on the basis of the local knowledge base of trusted users, though they can be delegated to external entities through an explicit, certificate based, delegation [8]. In this sense, the system completely adheres the principles of trust management. The definition of roles and attributes is also made in a local namespace, and the whole system is, in this regard, completely distributed. Local names are distinguished by prefixing them with the principal defining them, i.e. an hash of the public key associated with the local runtime. Links among different local namespace, again, can be explicitly defined by issuing appropriate certificates.

In this sense, local names are the distributed counterpart of roles in Role Based Access Control frameworks [9]. Like roles, local names can be used as a level of indirection between principals and permissions. Both a local name and role represent at the same time a set of principals, as well as a set of permissions granted to those principals. But, while roles are usually defined in a centralized fashion by a system administrator, local names, instead, are fully decentralized. This way, they better scale to internet-wide, peer-to-peer applications, without loosening in any way the principles of trust management.

In RAIS, the user can not only provide the permission to access his own files, but by defining appropriate XACML policies [10] he can also assign the permission to upload a new version of one or more existing files. In this case the PA informs his/her user about the updated files the first time he/she logs in. This functionality can be useful for the members of a workgroup involved in common projects or activities. Basic versioning capabilities are planned to be added to the Distribute Desktop Search system in the near future.

2.3 Mobile User Support

People travelling for work may often be in need of access from a remote system their own computer. In this situation, a solution could be to install a VNC server on the desktop computer and to find a system with a VNC client while travelling. This solution has the advantage that the user gains the complete control on his remote PC, but it has also two main drawbacks: it's not easy to find computers with VNC clients available and the VNC connects only to one computer, not to the whole set of files and information of a workgroup.

For users that don't require a complete control over a remote computer, but need to search and access a distributed set of documents, we have included in our system a remote search feature. The user can ask his/her PA to create a PPA on a pluggable device, e.g., an USB key or a removable hard disk. The PA copies on the device the RAIS run-time, the RPA and the authentication key shared by the PPA and the PA itself. When the user inserts the pluggable device on another computer, he can immediately launch his PPA and connect to its corresponding PA.

Therefore, the way of using the RAIS system is analogous to the situation in which the user works on her/his own computer, except for the interactions between the RPA and the PA, that, however, are transparent to the user. In fact, at the initialization, the PPA sends an authentication key to the PA. If the key matches those of the PA, the user can provide his/her username and password and enter the system (step that must be done by the user when she/he uses the RAIS system from her/his own computer too). After these two steps, the PPA acts as a simple proxy of the remote PA.

3 RAIS Development Components

The RAIS system has been designed and implemented taking advantage of agent, peer-to-peer, information retrieval and security management technologies and, in particular, of three main software components: JADE [11], JXTA [12][13] and Google Desktop Search [2].

RAIS agent platforms have been realized by using JADE: *JADE (Java Agent Development Framework)* [11] is probably the most known agent development environment enabling the integration of agents and both knowledge and Internet-oriented technologies. JADE allows to build agent systems for the management of networked information resources in compliance with the FIPA specification [14]. JADE provides a middleware for the development and execution of agent-based applications which can seamless work and interoperate both in wired and wireless environment. Moreover, JADE supports the development of multi-agent systems through the predefined programmable and extensible agent model and a set of management and testing tools. Currently, JADE is considered the reference implementation of the FIPA specifications and is one of the most used and promising agent development frameworks. In fact, is available under an LPGL open source license, it has a large user group, involving more than two thousands active members, it has been used to realize real systems in different application sectors, and its future development is guided by a governing board involving some important industrial companies.

The JADE development environment does not provide any support for the realization of real peer-to-peer systems because it only provides the possibility of federating different agent platforms through a hierarchical organization of the platform directory facilitators on the basis of a priori knowledge of the agent platforms addresses. Therefore, we extended the JADE directory facilitator to realize real peer-to-peer agent platforms networks thanks to the JXTA technology [13] and thanks to two preliminary FIPA specifications for the Agent Discovery Service [15] and for the JXTA Discovery Middleware [16].

JXTA technology [12][13] is a set of open, general-purpose protocols that allow any connected device on the network (from cell phones to laptops and servers) to communicate and collaborate in a peer-to-peer fashion. The project was originally started by Sun Microsystems, but its development was kept open from the very beginning. JXTA comprises six protocols allowing the discovery, organization, monitoring and communication between peers. These protocols are all implemented

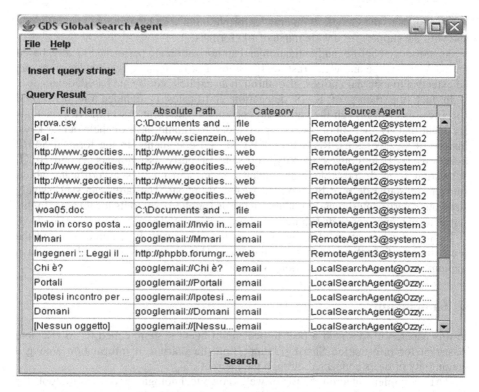

Fig. 2. RAIS search graphical user interface

on the basis of an underlying messaging layer, which binds the JXTA protocols to different network transports.

FIPA has acknowledged the growing importance of the JXTA protocols, and it has released some specifications for the interoperability of FIPA platforms connected to peer-to-peer networks. In particular, in [16] a Generic Discovery Service (GDS) is described, to discover agents and services deployed on FIPA platforms working together in a peer-to-peer network. RAIS integrates a JXTA-based Agent Discovery Service (ADS), which has been developed in the respect of relevant FIPA specifications to implement a GDS. This way, each RAIS platform connects to the Agent Peer Group, as well as to other system-specific peer groups. The Generic Discovery Protocol is finally used to advertise and discover df-agent-descriptions, wrapped in Generic Discovery Advertisements, in order to implement a DF service, which in the background is spanned over a whole peer group.

Different techniques and software tools can be used for searching information in a local repository. If the information is stored in form of files, the *Google desktop search* system [1] can be considered a suitable solution because Google provides an SDK for developing plug-ins based on its desktop search system. The API that comes with the SDK uses COM objects, so it's not directly available for JAVA development, but a bridge between the API and JAVA is provided by the Open Source project GDAPI [17]. Google desktop search indexes the content of the files of a local drive in a way similar to the Google Web crawler, providing a searching engine fast, effective and with the support for a wide range of file formats.

As introduced before, authentication and authorization are performed locally, based on local knowledge and local trust relationships. But local authorization decisions can be extended to external entities, also, through an explicit, certificate based, delegation.

In fact, the theory of RAIS delegation certificates is founded on *SPKI/SDSI* specifications [8], though the certificate encoding is different. As in SPKI, principals are identified by their public keys, or by a cryptographic hash of their public keys. Instead of s-expressions, RAIS uses XML signed documents, in the form of *SAML* assertions [18], to convey identity, role and property assignments. As in SPKI, delegation is made possible if the delegating principal issues a certificate whose subject is a name defined by another, trusted, principal. The latter can successively issue other certificates to assign other principals (public keys) to its local name. In this sense, local names act as distributed roles [9].

Finally, the extraction of a digest for each search result is required to avoid the presentation of duplicate results to the user. This feature is provided by a Java implementation of the hash functions MD5 or SHA-1 [19].

4 Conclusion

In this paper, we presented a peer-to-peer multi-agent system, called RAIS (Remote Assistant for Information Sharing), supporting the sharing of information among a community of users connected through the internet.

RAIS is implemented on the top of well known technologies and software tools for realizing: i) The agent platforms, i.e., JADE, ii) The peer-to-peer infrastructure, i.e., JXTA, iii) The searching of information into the local repository, i.e., Google Desktop Search, and iv) The authentication and authorization infrastructure, i.e., SPKI/SDSI specifications and the SAML assertions.

In our opinion, RAIS can be considered something more than a research prototype that couples the features of Web searching engines and of peer-to-peer systems for the sharing of information. Firstly, RAIS improves the security rules provided to check the access of the users to the information. Secondly, it offers a similar search power of Web search engines, but avoids the burden of publishing the information on the Web and guaranties a controlled and dynamic access to the information. Finally, an agent based implementation of the system makes quite straightforward but also effective the realization of three main features of the system: i) The filtering of the information coming from different users on the basis of the previous experience of the local user, ii) The pushing of the new information that can be of possible interest for a user, and iii) The delegation of authorization on the basis of a network of reputation built by the agents of the system on the community of its users.

A first prototype of the RAIS system has been developed, experimented and evaluated. The prototype includes all basic features; a graphical user interface simplifies the interaction between the user and the system (see figure 2). Practical tests on the first prototype were done installing the system in different labs and offices of our department asking some students and colleagues to use it for sharing and exchanging information. In a subsequent phase, we tested the system setting some computers of a Lab with different access policies and distributing information on their repositories in order to have different copies of the same information on different computers. The tests covered with success all system features: basic research, user defined policies, results filtering, duplicate results management and remote search through a proxy personal agent. The tests results were fully satisfactory and, in particular, the involved users were interested in continuing its use for supporting their work activities. The successful experimentation encouraged us in the further development of the system and we are currently working on studying the best way for introducing new types of information that can be managed (e.g., information stored into databases) and for including new techniques for the searching of such information (e.g., semantic Web techniques).

References

1. Google Desktop SDK, http://desktop.google.com/developer.html
2. Google Desktop Search, http://desktop.google.com
3. James, R., Chen, S.R., Wolfe, S.D.: A distributed multi-agent system for collaborative information management and sharing. In: Proc. of the 9th int. Conf. on Information and Knowledge Management, McLean, VA, pp. 382–388 (2000)
4. Babaoglu, O., Meling, H., Montresor, A.: A Framework for the Development of Agent-Based Peer-to-Peer Systems. In: ICDCS 2002. Proc. of the 22nd Int. Conf. on Distributed Computing Systems, Vienna, Austria, pp. 15–22 (2002)
5. Carter, J., Bitting, E., Ghorbani, A.: Reputation Formalization Within Information Sharing Multiagent Architectures. Computational Intelligence 2(5), 45–64 (2002)
6. Zhang, H., Croft, W.B., Levine, B., Lesser, V.: A Multi-agent Approach for Peer-to-Peer-based Information Retrieval Systems. In: Proc. of the Third Int. Joint Conf. on Autonomous Agents and Multiagent Systems, New York, pp. 456–463 (2004)
7. Sandhu, R., Samarati, P.: Access controls, principles and practice. IEEE Communications 32(9), 40–48 (1994)
8. Ellison, C., Frantz, B., Lampson, B., Rivest, R., Thomas, B., Ylonen, T.: SPKI: Certificate Theory. RFC 2693 (1999)
9. Li, N., Mitchell, J.M. RT: A Role-based Trust-management Framework. In: Proc. of the Third DARPA Information Survivability Conference and Exposition (DISCEX III), pp. 201-212, Washington, D.C (2003)
10. XACML - OASIS eXtensible Access Control Markup Language (XACML) TC, http://www.oasis-open.org/committees/xacml/
11. JADE software development framework, http://jade.tilab.com
12. Gong, L.: JXTA: A network programming environment. IEEE Internet Computing 5, 88–95 (2001)
13. JXTA technology, http://www.jxta.org
14. FIPA Specifications, http://www.fipa.org
15. FIPA Agent Discovery Service Specification, (2003), http://www.fipa.org/specs/fipa00095/PC00095.pdf
16. FIPA JXTA Discovery Middleware Specification (2003), http://www.fipa.org/specs/fipa00096/PC00096A.pdf
17. GDAPI, Google Desktop Search Java API, http://gdapi.sourceforge.net
18. SAML - Security Assertion Markup Language, http://xml.coverpages.org/ saml.html
19. Rivest, R.L.: The MD5 Message Digest Algorithm. Internet RFC 1321 (1992)

ToothAgent: A Multi-agent System for Virtual Communities Support

Volha Bryl[1], Paolo Giorgini[1], and Stefano Fante[2]

[1] University of Trento, DIT,
via Sommarive 14, Povo (TN) 38050, Italy
{volha.bryl,paolo.giorgini}@dit.unitn.it
[2] ArsLogica Lab, Mezzolombardo (TN), Italy
stefano.fante@arslogica.it

Abstract. People tend to form social networks within geographical areas. This can be explained by the fact that generally geographical localities correspond to common interests (e.g. students located in a university could be interested to buy or sell textbooks adopted for a specific course, to share notes, or just to meet together to play basketball). Cellular phones and more in general mobile devices are currently widely used and represent a big opportunity to support social communities. In this paper, we present a general architecture for multi-agent systems accessible via mobile devices (cellular phones and PDAs), where Bluetooth technology has been adopted to reflect users locality. We illustrate ToothAgent, an implemented prototype of the proposed architecture, and discuss the opportunities offered by the system.

1 Introduction

Being widespread and ubiquitous, cellular phones are recently used not only as means of traditional communication. They are also supposed to satisfy the information needs of their users, e.g. to support information search and filtering or electronic data exchange [15,1,17,12]. Users equipped with mobile devices, such as cellular phones or PDAs, can form so called mobile virtual communities [16], which makes possible the interaction and the information exchange between their geographically distributed members. Such communities are inherently open, new users can join and existing ones can leave anytime.

A number of multi-agent applications to mobile device environments have been proposed in literature. [12] presents a multi-agent system named KORE where a personal electronic museum guide provides to visitors (with Java-enabled mobile devices) information about artistic objects they are currently looking at. Information is filtered and adapted to the user profile. Bluetooth technology [2] is used to detect the user position. Bluetooth is a cheap and a widely used wireless communication technology able to connect Bluetooth-enabled devices located in a range of 100 meters. [17] proposes MobiAgent, an agent-based framework that allows users to access various types of services (from web search to remote applications control) directly from their cellular phones or PDAs. Once the user

M. Kolp et al. (Eds.): AOIS 2006, LNAI 4898, pp. 212–230, 2008.

sends a request for a specific service, an agent starts working on her behalf on a centralized server. The user can disconnect from the network and the agent will continue to work for her. When the request has been processed, the user is informed via Short Message Service and she can decide to reconnect the network and download the results. MIA information system [1] is another example that provides personalized and localized information to its users via mobile devices.

What is still missing in these systems is the interaction between the members of the virtual community. Just few proposals in literature introduce domain-specific environments where interacting agents act on the behalf of their users. For instance, [13] describes a context-aware multi-agent system for agenda management where scheduling agents can execute on PCs or PDAs and assist their users in building the meeting agenda by negotiating with the other agents. ADOMO [14] is an agent-based system where agents running on mobile devices sell the space on the device screen to commercial agents for their advertisements. Agents on behalf of their users negotiate and establish contracts with neighbors via Bluetooth.

There exist a number of multi-agent platforms that can be used on mobile devices. However, taking into account the limited computational and memory resources, it could be very problematic to run a multi-agent platform on such mobile devices as cellular phones. A possible solution is either to avoid running multi-agent platform on mobile devices, as for example in [14], or to use portal multi-agent platforms [15] where agents are executed not on the device itself but on the external host.

In this paper we present a general architecture based on this last option. The architecture proposes independent servers where multi-agent platforms can be installed and where agents can act on behalf of their users. Each server proposes one or more specific services related to the geographical area in which it is located (e.g. a server inside the university could offer the service of selling and buying textbooks, renting an apartment, etc.), and users can contact their personal agents using their Bluetooth-enabled mobile phones or PDAs.

The main advantage of the proposed framework with respect to the above described architectures is that the system is domain independent (it does not depend on the specific services offered by the servers) and independent from the multi-agent technology adopted (we can use different technologies on each server). The use of multi-agent approach is crucial for the framework, as it allows designing and implementing a virtual community of autonomous and proactive representatives of users on a platform, i.e. user personal agents. Moreover, platforms on a server are based on the Implicit Culture framework [11], which specifically aims at improving the agent performance.

The paper is organized as follows. Section 2 describes a motivating example for our system. The general architecture of the system is introduced in Section 3, while Section 4 provides some architectural details and describes ToothAgent, the implemented prototype. It also overviews the Andiamo project, an industrial extension of ToothAgent for the Rideshare scenario. Section 5 concludes the paper and provides some future work directions.

2   Motivating Example

Let us consider three places in a town: the university, the railway station and a bar. People spending some time at one of these places may have some common interests and needs. For instance, students at the university might want to buy or to sell secondhand textbooks, find a roommate or form study groups. People at the bar could be interested in the latest sport news (especially in Italian bars), or they could just be looking for someone to chat with. Passengers waiting at the railway station may want to know some details about the trip they are going to have — what cities their train goes through, or what the weather is like at the destination point. They may also want to find someone with common interests to chat with during the trip.

Let us suppose also that people cannot or do not want to spend their time on examining announcements on the bulletin boards, questioning people around them, or searching for the information office. They would prefer to ask their mobile phones and wait for the list of available proposals.

To support interests and needs of such groups of co-localized users, a server is placed at each of the three meeting points. Servers can provide a certain number of services to people equipped with mobile phones or PDAs (hereinafter referred as users). A user can have access to the services when she is close enough (depending on her Bluetooth device) to one of the three servers — at the bar, in the waiting room of the station, or at the main hall of the university.

Let us suppose that among the available services we have the following ones. At the university users can buy/sell their secondhand books and search for roommates. At the bar, users can access a sport news service or search for "interesting" people. Finally, at the railway station, users can receive information about their trips (including touristic information).

User interaction is often essential for the satisfaction of their needs. To sell a secondhand textbook, one should find a buyer and agree on the price. To find someone in the bar to chat with, one should look for the person with similar interests or preferences. Each server recreates the group of co-localized human users in a virtual community of personal agents (Figure 1) able to interact with one another. Users formulate their requests and forward them to their personal agents.

Personal agents interact with the other available agents (the interaction might include negotiation as in the case of selling or buying books), and produce results that will be sent back to the users. The main idea is to have a distributed system composed of a number of open virtual communities that evolve and act autonomously on the behalf of human communities.

3   System Architecture

In this section we describe the general architecture of the system. We start from the requirements and then we illustrate the various sub-components and their interaction.

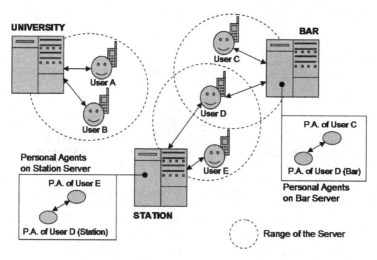

Fig. 1. Users, servers, and virtual communities of personal agents

3.1   System Requirements

We can summarize the requirements of the whole system in the following objectives.

- The system should allow the user to express her interests and choose the services she wants to access. It means that the user should be able to search for available servers and services by location, category, keywords, etc. The user should be provided with an interface to select services she is interested in and to customize them, i.e. to specify parameters of the requests to these services (e.g. book title and price for "buy/sell books" service). The system should allow the user view and edit customized requests, and transfer the list of requests to a mobile device.
- The system should provide access to the requested services when a mobile device and an appropriate server are co-localized (i.e. the Bluetooth connection is feasible). This means the system should be able to support the search for servers (and corresponding services) in the neighborhood of a mobile device, and the verification of the mobile device by a server. Then user's requests should be transferred to the server, where it should be possible to find correspondence between a user and her personal agent. The system should also support interaction among personal agents, store the results and let users access these results from their mobile devices.
- The system should allow its user to retrieve pending results. Results should be accessible both in case a user is still in the Bluetooth range of a server and when she is out of the range. In the second case the system should allow a user to access pending results from her mobile device by connecting to any server of the system, or from her PC via a dedicated interface. To do this, the system should support interaction between different servers and between a server and

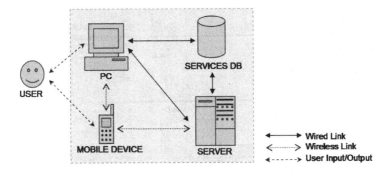

Fig. 2. Interaction of system components

a PC. The system should keep track of all servers visited by mobile devices and transfer these information to a PC or to a connected server.

3.2   System Components

The architecture of the system includes four main types of components: mobile device, PC, server and services database.

The *PC component* provides an interface for the user registration, retrieving and choosing available services, and building requests for the chosen services. Also the pending results can be retrieved via PC. The *mobile device* is used to send the user's requests to the servers and to get back the results. Each *server* within the system provides a list of predefined services. A server runs a multi-agent platform with personal agents representing single users, a database where results are archived, and an interface responsible for establishing connections with mobile devices and PCs, and for redirecting the users' requests to the corresponding personal agents. The central *services database*, accessible via web, contains information about all the servers and their properties, such as name, location, etc. The database also provides a description of available services on each server, and stores the information about users registered to the system.

Figure 2 illustrates the general architecture of the system and the interaction among its components. Connection between a mobile device and a PC, and between a mobile device and a server is established via Bluetooth wireless communication technology.

3.3   Getting Access to the Services

In the following we describe how the process of getting access to the services is organized (Figure 3).

The software running on a PC allows a user to search and discover servers and services, registered to the services database (steps 1–3). A user selects one or more services and provides information (i.e. requests) related to the use of such services (step 4). For example, using the service "Buy/sell secondhand books", a

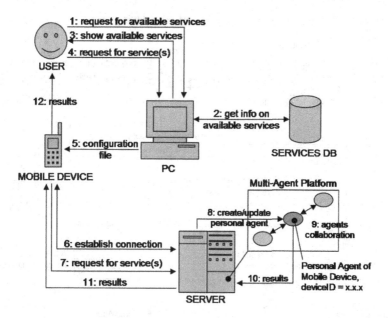

Fig. 3. Getting access to services

user could request to "Sell the copy of *Thinking in Java* by Bruce Eckel, printed in 1995, for the price not less than 20 euros". All the user's requests are stored in a configuration file, which is downloaded onto a mobile device via Bluetooth (step 5).

When a user with her mobile device approaches one of the servers, software on the device establishes a connection with the server (step 6) and sends requests related to the available services (step 7). Requests are built on the base of the configuration file of the mobile device. In other words, the mobile device checks in the configuration file if the user is interested in the services provided by the server and then builds and sends the requests to the server. The requests are processed on the server, and the results are sent back to the user (steps 8–12) The mobile device stores server address to keep track of the contacted servers. It stores the address even if there are no relevant services on the server. This allows the user to check later the list of all visited servers and associated services, and decide to update her preferences by including new servers/services in the configuration file.

3.4 Retrieving Pending Results

We describe now how the process of retrieving the pending results is organized (Figure 4).

A user has basically two options to get back the results of her requests. The first one is to receive them directly on her mobile device. However, this is not always possible. A user could leave the Bluetooth area or her mobile device may

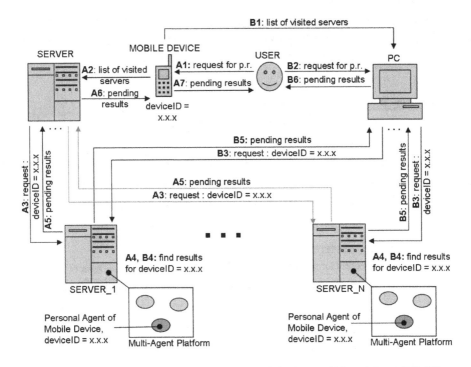

Fig. 4. Retrieving pending results from mobile device (A) and from PC (B)

not have enough memory or computational power to manage the answers (e.g. in the case the answers are a number of big files). Thus the second option is to get back the results later when the connection with the server they were requested from is closed.

Pending results can be retrieved both from a mobile device (steps A.x) and from a PC (steps B.x). In the first case a mobile device has to be configured to get the pending results and has to be in the Bluetooth range of some server. For example, if a student is going to spend a whole hour in the main hall of the university waiting for the next lecture, she will have enough time to download the results of her requests sent in the morning to the railway station server (where she bought her train ticket before going to the university). She switches on the option "get pending results" on her mobile phone (step A1), and waits for results. The mobile device sends to the university server the list of addresses of the servers its user has visited (step A2). The server establishes a connection with each server in the list, and sends the information that identifies the mobile device (e.g. its Bluetooth address) as a request for the pending results (step A3). The obtained information is sent back to the mobile device (steps A5–A6).

In the second case a user receives pending results through a PC. The student goes back home and runs the PC software that collects all the pending results obtained from the visited servers (steps B3–B5), after the list of the visited servers and their addresses is transferred from the mobile device to the PC (step B1).

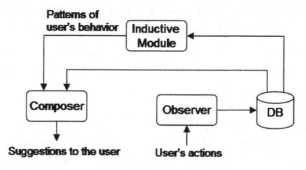

Fig. 5. General architecture of SICS

3.5 Agent Platform

Each server runs a multi-agent platform, where agents correspond to mobile devices and receive and process requests obtained from users. There is a one-to-one correspondence between agents and mobile devices (users). An agent is identified by a unique Bluetooth address of the corresponding mobile device. The same device can have many personal agents within different platforms on different servers.

When a server receives the request from a mobile device, it checks if the personal agent of this device exists within the platform. If not, a new personal agent is created. Each personal agent communicates and interacts with other agents in order to find "partners" which will satisfy its request. Interaction protocols are domain (services) dependent.

Multi-agent platforms on a server are based on the Implicit Culture [11] framework. In short, Implicit Culture allows new members of a community to behave in accordance with the culture of the community. For example, a new student may not know which textbooks can be helpful for the Programming Languages course and starts to search for *Textbook on Programming Languages*. The idea of the Implicit Culture framework is that the system suggests the student the items that are usually used by the other members of the community. So for example, the system could suggest the student to search for the book *Thinking in Java*.

Multi-agent systems with the Implicit Culture support are used for example for searching the web. See [10] for the description of Implicit, an agent-based recommendation system for web search, which improves the search for information for a community of users with similar interests. When a user submits a query, Implicit looks for the relevant information, exploiting observations of the behavior of other users when they have issued similar queries.

To follow the Implicit Culture concept an agent on the platform should contain System for Implicit Culture Support (SICS) [11]. SICS consists of three basic components (their interaction is illustrated in Figure 5):

- *Observer*, which stores in a database the information about user actions (observations).
- *Inductive module*, which analyzes the obtained observations and induces behavioral patterns of the community using Data Mining techniques.

– *Composer*, which produces suggestions on the base of the information from the Observer and Inductive module.

More details about the Implicit Culture framework are available at [3].

4   Implementation Issues

In this section we present the details of ToothAgent, an implemented prototype of the proposed architecture. Basically, the system is a first implementation of the architecture presented in Section 3 and focuses on a number of servers spread around the university campus (faculties, libraries, and departments). Each server offers only the service for selling and buying books.

We tested the system using Nokia 6260/6630/9500 and Sony Ericsson P910 cellular phones and PC/Server either equipped with Tecom or Billionton Bluetooth adapters, or having an integrated BT module. Bluetooth communication has been implemented using Blue Cove [4] which is an open source implementation of the JSR-82 Bluetooth API for Java.

4.1   Online Registration and Service Selection

To start working with the system, a user has to register. To do this she should fill the online registration form where she needs to put her personal information such as name, birth date, e-mail, Bluetooth address and phone number of her mobile device, and password. Registration, basically, allows the system to identify a user and a mobile device she is going to use. Password is used to access the information about servers and related services, and to upload/update user information (e.g. a user can decide to use different mobile device or just to change her data such as telephone number or e-mail address). Also a password is needed to access servers and their services via mobile device (for this purpose a user has to input a password while configuring an application on her mobile device). All the information about a user is stored in the services database. Registered users obtain the rights to download the software for PC and mobile device components (which are two jar files), and the XML file containing information about all available servers with corresponding services.

After the registration (or login), a user can start selecting services to use. Using the Java GUI interface shown in Figure 6, she can explore all the available services using filtering criteria such as server location (e.g. we can have servers located in different cities or in different places in the same city), type or category of the service (e.g. buy/sell books, exchange course notes, or meet people), and keywords (e.g. books, course, etc.). The list of the selected services is managed by the PC component that allows its user to customize these services with the specific requests (e.g. title of the book to buy or to sell, the desired price, minimal or maximal price).

The list of customized services (with related servers addresses) is stored in an XML configuration file, which is uploaded via Bluetooth in the mobile device. Figure 7 shows an example for the "sell/buy books" service. Note that

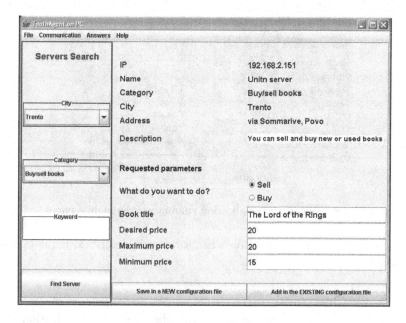

Fig. 6. Request input form

```
<server>
  <ip>       192.168.2.151                </ip>
  <name>     UnitnServer                  </name>
  <location> Trento, via Sommarive, Povo </location>
  <service>
    <description> Buy/sell new and used books </description>
    <parameters>
      <param>
        <paramname>  Book title         </paramname>
        <paramtype>  String             </paramtype>
        <paramvalue> Lord of the Rings  </paramvalue>
      </param>
      <param>
        <paramname>  Desired price </paramname>
        <paramtype>  int           </paramtype>
        <paramvalue> 15            </paramvalue>
      </param>
      <param>
        <paramname>  Maximum price </paramname>
        <paramtype>  int           </paramtype>
        <paramvalue> 20            </paramvalue>
      </param>
    </parameters>
  </service>
</server>
```

Fig. 7. Configuration file

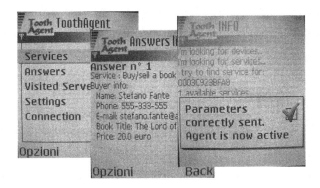

Fig. 8. ToothAgent application running on the mobile phone

the file format does not depend on what services it describes, i.e. it is domain independent.

4.2   Accessing the Services

To access the services, a user needs to run the Bluetooth application on her mobile device (Figure 8). The application is written in Java and uses JSR-82 [5], which is Bluetooth API for Java. The application starts a continuous search for Bluetooth-enabled devices in the neighborhood, and whenever it finds a server with the services specified in the configuration file, the mobile device sends the user requests to this server. Figure 9 shows the protocol we use for the interaction among the different components.

A specific communication module on a server is responsible for managing the interaction with a mobile device. It receives the Bluetooth address and the encrypted password from a mobile device (steps 1 and 3) and checks whether in the platform running on the server a personal agent assigned to that mobile device already exists (step 4), the Bluetooth address is used to map a mobile device with its personal agent. If there is no personal agent for a user, the communication module connects to the central services database and verify whether this user is registered to the system (steps 5–6) by matching the Bluetooth address of her device and the password. Only in case of a positive answer, it creates a new agent and assigns it to the mobile device user (step 8). Then, the mobile device sends the configuration file to the communication module (step 9), which forwards all the user requests to the personal agent (step 10).

Now, a personal agent starts interacting with other agents on the platform trying to satisfy all the user requests (step 12). In our example a personal agent receives one or more requests for buying and/or selling books (with specified title, desired price, maximum and minimum prices, etc.). If the agent reaches an agreement with another agent about their users requests it stores the results locally in the server database (step 13). Later the results could be sent back to

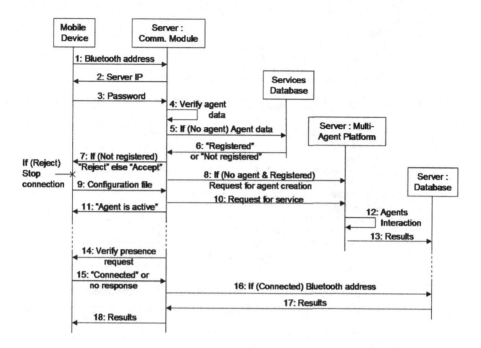

Fig. 9. Getting access to services

the user (steps 14–18) or left on the server, depending on the retrieval modality that the user has defined in the configuration file.

4.3   Results Retrieval

Whenever a new connection between a server and a mobile device is established, the communication module sends to the mobile device the IP-address of the server (step 2 on Figure 9). The mobile device stores the IP addresses of all the visited servers in an XML file, that is used later to retrieve all pending results. The format of the results produced by a personal agent is shown in Figure 10. It may contain the request identifier, contacts (e.g. phone number) of the user interested to buy or sell the book, the actual agreed price, etc.

As discussed in Section 3, a user has three different modalities to retrieve results: get the results immediately, get pending results using her mobile device, and get pending results using a PC. Each of these modalities has to be defined in advance by a user and can be changed at runtime by means of the mobile device application.

Choosing the first option, a user can receive the results immediately in her mobile device. Of course, she can receive the results if and only if she is still at a Bluetooth distance from a server. The communication module checks the availability of the mobile device and sends to it the results stored in the internal server database by the corresponding personal agent (see Figure 9, steps 14–18).

```
<responses>
  <response>
    <ip>         192.168.2.151                    </ip>
    <name>       UnitnServer                      </name>
    <description> Buy a book </description>
    <parameters>
      <param>
        <paramname> Book title           </paramname>
        <paramtype> String                </paramtype>
        <paramvalue> Lord of the Rings </paramvalue>
      </param>
      <param>
        <paramname> Price        </paramname>
        <paramtype> int          </paramtype>
        <paramvalue> 20          </paramvalue>
      </param>
      <param>
        <paramname> Buyer name           </paramname>
        <paramtype> String                </paramtype>
        <paramvalue> Stefano Fante    </paramvalue>
      </param>
      <param>
        <paramname> Buyer phone number    </paramname>
        <paramtype> String                </paramtype>
        <paramvalue> 555-321-555           </paramvalue>
      </param>
    </parameters>
  </response>
  ...
</responses>
```

Fig. 10. List of responses

Figure 11 shows the interaction protocol of retrieving pending results via mobile device. Consider for example a situation in which a user is near to the server of the central library. After the connection has been established, the mobile device sends the list of IP-addresses of all previously visited servers (e.g. faculty servers, departments servers, etc.) to the library server (step 2). The communication module of the server sends then the Bluetooth address of the mobile device to all listed servers (step 3). In turn, the communication module of each server extracts from the internal database all the stored results related to that user and sends them back to the requester server (steps 4–7). All the results are collected by the communication module and finally sent to the mobile device (steps 8–10). If the mobile device is no longer connected to the server (e.g. the user has left the library), the retrieval process will fail and the results will be cancelled (they are still available on the original servers).

Figure 12 shows the interaction protocol of retrieving pending results via a PC. A user connects her mobile device to a PC via Bluetooth and sends the list of all visited servers to the PC component (step 2). Now, the user can decide either to retrieve the results from all the servers or just to select some of them. An interface on the PC allows the user to connect to the servers and then to view or download the pending results (steps 3–7).

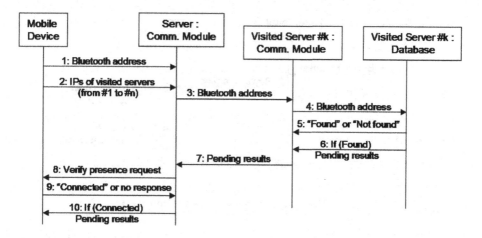

Fig. 11. Pending results from the mobile device

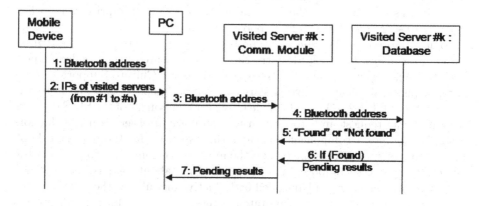

Fig. 12. Pending results from PC

4.4   Agents Interaction

As we said, in this first prototype we implemented just one kind of service, namely the "buy/sell books" service. The multi-agent system has been implemented in JADE (Java Agent DEvelopment framework) [6], FIPA-compliant [7] framework for multi-agent systems development. The agent interaction includes two phases: elaboration of user request and agent negotiation.

During the first phase the request of buying/selling a book is elaborated and detailed. For example, the request of "Buy a textbook on Java for the price from 10 to 20 euros" is incomplete as the exact title is not specified. The personal agent makes the request more clear exploiting the information about what textbooks on Java other users were recently interested in and what they have finally bought, at what prices, etc. Another example of request that needs to be elaborated could

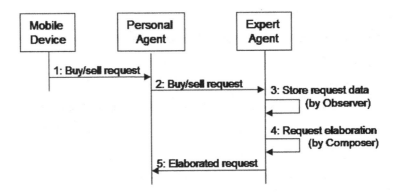

Fig. 13. User request elaboration

be "Buy *Thinking in Java* for the price less than 10 euros". It is unlikely that this request will be satisfied as all copies of *Thinking in Java* currently available, or sold so far, cost at least 20 euros. The user has clearly underestimated the price. In this case we want the personal agent to extend the price range when starting to search for a copy of the book.

Figure 13 presents the interaction protocol used by agents during the request elaboration phase. On each platform there is a dedicated agent, called Expert Agent (EA), which contains the System for Implicit Culture Support (SICS). After a personal agent receives its user's request (step 1), it sends it to the Expert Agent (step 2). On the EA side Observer component of the SICS extracts data from the request and stores it in the database of observed user behaviors (step 3). Composer component estimates the real price for the requested book and/or suggests the title of the book if the input was incomplete (step 4). For the elaboration process Composer uses the information about the past user actions, obtained from Observer and analyzed by Inductive module. At the end the user's personal agent gets back the elaborated request (step 5), which it will process during the second phase.

As it was explained in Section 3.5, SICS needs to gather information about user behavior. In the described prototype to observe the user behavior Expert Agent extracts data from the requests it gets from personal agents. Two other additional sources of observations could be added. The first one is the database where results of agent negotiations are stored. Each time two personal agents agree on buying/selling a book and send their proposals to the database, Expert Agents extracts necessary information (e.g. book title and the price) from the proposals and stores it in its internal database. The second source is the direct user feedback. When a user views the list of proposals on her mobile device, she can choose to make a phone call or to send an SMS to the other user whose contacts are in the proposal. When the proposals are viewed on the PC, the user can choose to write an e-mail to her potential partner. For the purpose of feed-back the system records the information about these phone calls/SMSs/e-mails

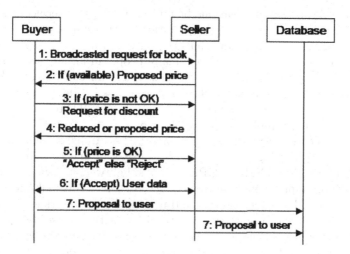

Fig. 14. Agent negotiation

assuming that if the other user of the proposal (the potential partner) was contacted then the feedback is positive, otherwise negative. The feedback information is sent to the Expert Agent as soon as a user establishes connection with the corresponding server via her mobile device or a PC.

On the second phase — agent negotiation — the interaction mechanism is very simple. Figure 14 presents the implemented agent interaction "from the point of view" of an agent which is buying a book. First, the buyer's personal agent broadcasts the request of looking for a specific book (step 1), information about title, desired price, etc. is specified in the message. If in the platform there is another agent that is selling the requested book, it responds to the buyer with the price it wants for the book (step 2). If the price is greater than the maximum price specified by the buyer, the interaction continues with the request for discount from the buyer agent (step 3). The seller responds either with the discounted price or with the initially proposed price (step 4) in case it does not want to give the discount. If this price is less than maximum price for the buyer, it accepts the deal (step 5). After that, the buyer and seller personal agents exchange their users' data (step 6), form the agreed proposals and send them to the server database (step 7). The proposals are then forwarded either to mobile device, or to the PC as described in Section 4.3.

4.5 Andiamo Project

The work presented at AOIS 2006 workshop, was a starting point for Andiamo project [8,9], which aims at providing users of lightweight devices a Rideshare, or Carpooling service. Rideshare is a method to reduce the use of cars in a specific town or area. The scenario is as follows: a car owner uses her car to move from one place to the other, while another person is interested in going to some point along the car owner's way to destination and is willing to share the ride cost with the car owner. The key motivations behind providing this service is saving the cost of transportation, reducing the pollution coming out of cars, and avoiding the formation of traffic jams (and thus, the waste of time). Rideshare constitutes a reliable means of transportation for many people in an increasing number of countries, with the matching of requests usually organized through a third party website. One of the essential drawbacks of web-based Rideshare applications is the necessity to be always connected to the Internet. Therefore, ease-of-use is only realized in using mobile based applications.

The architecture of the system developed within Andiamo is obtained by extending and customizing ToothAgent. It consists of one or more multi-agent platforms accessible via SMS or GPRS-enabled lightweight devices. On the platform there is an implemented multi-agent system where Personal Agents (PAs) of car owners and ride seekers interact and negotiate potential rides. When agents are started on the platform, there are several interaction phases taking place between them to reach a trip/ride agreement: the involved agents have to contract on many user's modifiable parameters, such as the exact departure time, the offered/requested money (contribution for the trip), the departure and the arrival meeting points, etc. As in ToothAgent, on each platform there is a dedicated Expert Agent, which contains the System for Implicit Culture Support. In Andiamo, the use of the IC framework allows the system to suggest the meeting points that are frequently used by other system users. An auction mechanism is used as a method of negotiation among car owners and ride seekers agents. Moreover, users have the possibility to apply both an autonomous or a semi-autonomous behavior to their PAs: this implies that the interaction between two agents can be either interrupted to prompt an inquiry to the user or self-organized. For the further details the reader is referred to [9].

The system was tested using Nokia 6630, N73, N70, 6600, Motorola v3 and Sony-Ericsson P910 mobile phones and PC/Server equipped with generic Bluetooth adapter. The tests were performed on different scenarios and involved a number of people, e.g. university students and workers. From these tests, it was noticed that the time to obtain an agreement between two agents is the same for every situation. In the cases in which there are more seekers than the seats offered by the offerers, the agents winning the auction are always the stronger agents (i.e. the agents that offer more money, that have a higher feedback, etc.). Currently, the deployment of the system is expected at the University of Trento, so its performance and usability will be tested on a real-life large scale basis.

5   Conclusions

In this paper we have presented an implemented prototype where multi-agent systems and Bluetooth wireless communication technology are combined together to support co-localized communities of users. We have discussed the general architecture of the system, and presented some implementation issues related to ToothAgent, the prototype we have built.

We are currently working with ArsLogica S.p.A. on the Andiamo project, in which the ToothAgent architecture was extended and customized for the Rideshare scenario. We expect the system developed within Andiamo to be deployed and tested on a real-life large scale basis in the nearest future. The preliminary tests have already shown the effectiveness of the system in supporting co-localized community of users.

Acknowledgements

We thank ArsLogica S.p.A. for the collaboration and the support to this project. This work has been partially funded by EU Commission, through the SENSORIA and SERENITY projects, and also by the Provincial Authority of Trentino, through the MOSTRO project. We also thank people working on Implicit Culture, in particular Aliaksandr Birukou and Enrico Blanzieri for their support in using the Implicit Culture framework. Finally, we thank the reviewers and participants of the AOIS 2006 workshop for the valuable comments and suggestions.

References

1. MIA project, http://www.uni-koblenz.de/~bthomas/MIA_HTML
2. The official Bluetooth website, http://www.bluetooth.com/
3. Implicit Culture website, http://dit.unitn.it/~implicit/
4. Blue Cove project, http://sourceforge.net/projects/bluecove/
5. JSR-82: Java APIs for Bluetooth, http://www.jcp.org/en/jsr/detail?id=82
6. JADE: Java Agent DEvelopment Framework website, http://jade.tilab.com/
7. FIPA: Foundation for Intelligent Physical Agents, http://www.fipa.org/
8. ANDIAMO project, http://dit.unitn.it/blueagents/andiamo/
9. Abdel-Naby, S., Fante, S., Giorgini, P.: Auctions negotiation for mobile rideshare service. In: ICPCA 2007. Proceeding of the IEEE Second International Conference on Pervasive Computing and Applications (2007)
10. Birukov, A., Blanzieri, E., Giorgini, P.: Implicit: An agent-based recommendation system for web search. In: Proceedings of the 4th International Conference on Autonomous Agents and Multi-Agent Systems, pp. 618–624. ACM Press, New York (2005)
11. Blanzieri, E., Giorgini, P., Massa, P., Recla, S.: Implicit culture for multi-agent interaction support. In: CoopIS 2001. Proceedings of the 9th International Conference on Cooperative Information Systems, pp. 27–39. Springer, Heidelberg (2001)
12. Bombara, M., Calì, D., Santoro, C.: Kore: A multi-agent system to assist museum visitors. In: WOA 2003. Proceedings of the Workshop on Objects and Agents, Cagliari, Italy, pp. 175–178 (2003)
13. Bucur, O., Beaune, P., Boissier, O.: Representing context in an agent architecture for context-based decision making. In: CRR 2005. Proceedings of the Workshop on Context Representation and Reasoning, Paris, France (2005)
14. Carabelea, C., Berger, M.: Agent negotiation in ad-hoc networks. In: AAMAS 2005. Proceedings of the Ambient Intelligence Workshop at Conference, Utrecht, The Netherlands, pp. 5–16 (2005)

Author Index

Lecture Notes in Artificial Intelligence (LNAI)

Vol. 4693: B. Apolloni, R.J. Howlett, L. Jain (Eds.), Knowledge-Based Intelligent Information and Engineering Systems, Part II. XXXII, 1380 pages. 2007.

Vol. 4692: B. Apolloni, R.J. Howlett, L. Jain (Eds.), Knowledge-Based Intelligent Information and Engineering Systems, Part I. LV, 882 pages. 2007.

Vol. 4687: P. Petta, J.P. Müller, M. Klusch, M. Georgeff (Eds.), Multiagent System Technologies. X, 207 pages. 2007.

Vol. 4682: D.-S. Huang, L. Heutte, M. Loog (Eds.), Advanced Intelligent Computing Theories and Applications. XXVII, 1373 pages. 2007.

Vol. 4676: M. Klusch, K.V. Hindriks, M.P. Papazoglou, L. Sterling (Eds.), Cooperative Information Agents XI. XI, 361 pages. 2007.

Vol. 4667: J. Hertzberg, M. Beetz, R. Englert (Eds.), KI 2007: Advances in Artificial Intelligence. IX, 516 pages. 2007.

Vol. 4660: S. Džeroski, L. Todorovski (Eds.), Computational Discovery of Scientific Knowledge. X, 327 pages. 2007.

Vol. 4659: V. Mařík, V. Vyatkin, A.W. Colombo (Eds.), Holonic and Multi-Agent Systems for Manufacturing. VIII, 456 pages. 2007.

Vol. 4651: F. Azevedo, P. Barahona, F. Fages, F. Rossi (Eds.), Recent Advances in Constraints. VIII, 185 pages. 2007.

Vol. 4648: F. Almeida e Costa, L.M. Rocha, E. Costa, I. Harvey, A. Coutinho (Eds.), Advances in Artificial Life. XVIII, 1215 pages. 2007.

Vol. 4635: B. Kokinov, D.C. Richardson, T.R. Roth-Berghofer, L. Vieu (Eds.), Modeling and Using Context. XIV, 574 pages. 2007.

Vol. 4632: R. Alhajj, H. Gao, X. Li, J. Li, O.R. Zaïane (Eds.), Advanced Data Mining and Applications. XV, 634 pages. 2007.

Vol. 4629: V. Matoušek, P. Mautner (Eds.), Text, Speech and Dialogue. XVII, 663 pages. 2007.

Vol. 4626: R.O. Weber, M.M. Richter (Eds.), Case-Based Reasoning Research and Development. XIII, 534 pages. 2007.

Vol. 4617: V. Torra, Y. Narukawa, Y. Yoshida (Eds.), Modeling Decisions for Artificial Intelligence. XII, 502 pages. 2007.

Vol. 4612: I. Miguel, W. Ruml (Eds.), Abstraction, Reformulation, and Approximation. XI, 418 pages. 2007.

Vol. 4604: U. Priss, S. Polovina, R. Hill (Eds.), Conceptual Structures: Knowledge Architectures for Smart Applications. XII, 514 pages. 2007.

Vol. 4603: F. Pfenning (Ed.), Automated Deduction – CADE-21. XII, 522 pages. 2007.

Vol. 4597: P. Perner (Ed.), Advances in Data Mining. XI, 353 pages. 2007.

Vol. 4594: R. Bellazzi, A. Abu-Hanna, J. Hunter (Eds.), Artificial Intelligence in Medicine. XVI, 509 pages. 2007.

Vol. 4585: M. Kryszkiewicz, J.F. Peters, H. Rybinski, A. Skowron (Eds.), Rough Sets and Intelligent Systems Paradigms. XIX, 836 pages. 2007.

Vol. 4578: F. Masulli, S. Mitra, G. Pasi (Eds.), Applications of Fuzzy Sets Theory. XVIII, 693 pages. 2007.

Vol. 4573: M. Kauers, M. Kerber, R. Miner, W. Windsteiger (Eds.), Towards Mechanized Mathematical Assistants. XIII, 407 pages. 2007.

Vol. 4571: P. Perner (Ed.), Machine Learning and Data Mining in Pattern Recognition. XIV, 913 pages. 2007.

Vol. 4570: H.G. Okuno, M. Ali (Eds.), New Trends in Applied Artificial Intelligence. XXI, 1194 pages. 2007.

Vol. 4565: D.D. Schmorrow, L.M. Reeves (Eds.), Foundations of Augmented Cognition. XIX, 450 pages. 2007.

Vol. 4562: D. Harris (Ed.), Engineering Psychology and Cognitive Ergonomics. XXIII, 879 pages. 2007.

Vol. 4548: N. Olivetti (Ed.), Automated Reasoning with Analytic Tableaux and Related Methods. X, 245 pages. 2007.

Vol. 4539: N.H. Bshouty, C. Gentile (Eds.), Learning Theory. XII, 634 pages. 2007.

Vol. 4529: P. Melin, O. Castillo, L.T. Aguilar, J. Kacprzyk, W. Pedrycz (Eds.), Foundations of Fuzzy Logic and Soft Computing. XIX, 830 pages. 2007.

Vol. 4520: M.V. Butz, O. Sigaud, G. Pezzulo, G. Baldassarre (Eds.), Anticipatory Behavior in Adaptive Learning Systems. X, 379 pages. 2007.

Vol. 4511: C. Conati, K. McCoy, G. Paliouras (Eds.), User Modeling 2007. XVI, 487 pages. 2007.

Vol. 4509: Z. Kobti, D. Wu (Eds.), Advances in Artificial Intelligence. XII, 552 pages. 2007.

Vol. 4496: N.T. Nguyen, A. Grzech, R.J. Howlett, L.C. Jain (Eds.), Agent and Multi-Agent Systems: Technologies and Applications. XXI, 1046 pages. 2007.

Vol. 4483: C. Baral, G. Brewka, J. Schlipf (Eds.), Logic Programming and Nonmonotonic Reasoning. IX, 327 pages. 2007.

Vol. 4482: A. An, J. Stefanowski, S. Ramanna, C.J. Butz, W. Pedrycz, G. Wang (Eds.), Rough Sets, Fuzzy Sets, Data Mining and Granular Computing. XIV, 585 pages. 2007.

Vol. 4481: J. Yao, P. Lingras, W.-Z. Wu, M.S. Szczuka, N.J. Cercone, D. Ślęzak (Eds.), Rough Sets and Knowledge Technology. XIV, 576 pages. 2007.

Vol. 4476: V. Gorodetsky, C. Zhang, V.A. Skormin, L. Cao (Eds.), Autonomous Intelligent Systems: Multi-Agents and Data Mining. XIII, 323 pages. 2007.

Vol. 4460: S. Aguzzoli, A. Ciabattoni, B. Gerla, C. Manara, V. Marra (Eds.), Algebraic and Proof-theoretic Aspects of Non-classical Logics. VIII, 309 pages. 2007.

Vol. 4457: G.M.P. O'Hare, A. Ricci, M.J. O'Grady, O. Dikenelli (Eds.), Engineering Societies in the Agents World VII. XI, 401 pages. 2007.

Vol. 4456: Y. Wang, Y.-m. Cheung, H. Liu (Eds.), Computational Intelligence and Security. XXIII, 1118 pages. 2007.

Vol. 4455: S. Muggleton, R. Otero, A. Tamaddoni-Nezhad (Eds.), Inductive Logic Programming. XII, 456 pages. 2007.

Vol. 4452: M. Fasli, O. Shehory (Eds.), Agent-Mediated Electronic Commerce. VIII, 249 pages. 2007.